Leadership
by
Design

Albert A. Vicere and Robert M. Fulmer

Harvard Business School Press / Boston, Massachusetts

First published in the United States by Harvard Business School Press, 1998. This edition published by arrangement with Capstone Publishing.

First published in the United Kingdom and outside North America by Capstone Publishing in 1996.
Oxford Centre for Innovation
Mill Street
Oxford OX2 0JX, UK

02 01 00 99 98   5 4 3 2 1

Library of Congress Cataloging-in-Publication Data
Vicere, Albert A., 1953–
  [Crafting competitiveness]
  Leadership by design / Albert A. Vicere, Robert M. Fulmer.
    p. cm.
  Originally published: Crafting competitiveness. Oxford : Capstone, 1996.
  Includes bibliographical references and index.
  ISBN 0-87584-831-1 (alk. paper)
  1. Executives—Training of. 2. Leadership. I. Fulmer, Robert M.
II. Title.
HD30.4.V53 1998
658.4'07124—dc21
                                                        97-36910
                                                        CIP

The paper used in this publication meets the requirements of the American National Standard for Permanence of Paper for Printed Library Materials Z39.49-1984.

*In recognition of their tremendous inspiration,
not to mention their incredible patience,
this book is dedicated to*

Nancy, Jana, and Marisa Vicere

and

Pat Fulmer and our children

Contents

v

Preface

IN TODAY'S CHANGING business environment, traditional processes for developing leadership talent are in such a state of flux that a new vocabulary is emerging. There is little interest in the old mainstay term *management development*. Managers today are often viewed as bureaucrats whose major function is to create complexity and preserve the status quo. *Executive education* is a more desirable term, but in today's flatter, more networked organizations, there is less demand for "executives," often viewed as aloof and removed from the realities of the competitive marketplace. And the word *education* connotes the esoteric contemplation of academic issues, a process at odds with today's fast-paced business environment. There does seem to be great interest in the term *leadership development*, which characterizes processes for identifying and developing exceptional people capable of moving an organization into the twenty-first century.

Although developing tomorrow's leaders is a critical concern for most organizations, equally important is the need to create new structures and processes that will enable the organization to effectively compete in a rapidly changing, global economy. Rather than viewing these two concerns as separate challenges, benchmark organizations from around the world have begun to combine them in an expanded developmental focus which we call "strategic leadership development." This focus blends traditional executive education activities with management, leadership, and organizational development techniques to create hands-on, real-time learning laboratories within organizations, which facilitate continuous learning, continuous knowledge creation, and organizational competitiveness. This book focuses on the challenge of strategic leadership development—what it is, how it arose and is evolving, and how it is being addressed today.

The ideas discussed in this book are based on our years of experience as professors, executive educators, consultants, and in Bob Fulmer's case, corporate human resources executive. Many of the examples reflect our firsthand experiences with consulting clients, but we have not relied on such experiences alone. Throughout our careers, we have conducted extensive research on executive education and leadership development. In addition, we recently completed a fifteen-year trend study of the field,[1] as well as a comprehensive study that included a thorough review of the literature and interview or survey data from 78 executives at 47 companies, 48 consultants, and 52 university leaders from 35 business schools throughout the world.[2] We have drawn from all of this information and experience to create the perspectives outlined in this book.

SETTING THE STAGE

We have observed that, for years, strategic leadership development was a "field of dreams"—if you built a program, participants would come.[3] During that time, university business schools seemed to have a lock on the leading-edge thinking in just about every field a businessperson needed to understand. Now corporate sponsors look at strategic leadership development initiatives as much as tools for strategic organization development as tools for individual development. This shift in perspectives has created a wave of change in the competitive dynamics of the field, change that has put university business schools on the defensive and opened the door to myriad alternative providers, including corporate "customers" themselves. All of these providers are in search of more effective ways to use leadership development as a tool to craft competitiveness in a changing world.

We have written this book to challenge both providers and users of strategic leadership development initiatives to rethink their approaches. Our intention was to blend practical theory with an abundance of relevant models and detailed examples to provide a thorough, ideally insightful, perspective on the field. That perspective is based on our observation of a number of general trends that we believe are changing the very nature of the field:

- Corporations today are increasingly interested in leadership development experiences that are linked to experience and the work environment. They are growing more convinced that the action learning model, described later in this book, is a powerful framework both for leveraging investment in strategic leadership development and for establishing methods for calculating a return on that investment. Yet there is danger that leadership development processes could become very limiting if focused only within a particular organization and only on its current business challenges.

- Corporations today seem to prefer leadership development programs that are customized to help them adapt to a changing marketplace, as opposed to traditional open-enrollment programs and seminars. However, they often are not sure what type of experience they need, and they often question their ability to develop and deliver those experiences internally in an effective, timely manner. The demand for consulting services from top providers of strategic leadership development is growing, creating new opportunities for providers willing to share both their content expertise and their *process* expertise with the corporate community.

- The operative word in today's strategic leadership development marketplace is *partnering*—partnering with corporate sponsors to develop process and content solutions, and partnering with providers to help meet aggressive delivery schedules and volumes. As in the business environment in general, partnerships and alliances seem to be a key to the future development of the field. Competitive advantage will go to those organizations that are willing and able to develop innovative partnerships among both providers and users.

- Universities can utilize their research capabilities to help organizations define and address future strategies for strategic leadership development. In fact, many corporations are actively requesting this kind of assistance. The dramatic growth of corporate/university research consortia in recent years suggests that universities may be slowly learning to blend academic interests in basic research with corporate needs for research-based solutions to real-world problems. These consortia are benchmark examples of educational partnerships in the new strategic leadership development marketplace. At the same time, consulting firms have learned that there is a huge market for applied research in the field and have begun to respond with their own research initiatives, consortia, and publications, challenging the traditional knowledge creation role of universities.

- As they explore new developmental techniques and new relationships with providers to address overwhelming demands for change and restructuring, corporations are more than ever focused on the need to build their pool of high-potential key managers. In the same vein, they are striving to make sure that leadership development initiatives are tightly linked to human resource management practices such as selection, appraisal, and compensation. And they are searching for ways to measure the personal and organizational impact of strategic leadership development initiatives.

- Finally, all of these changes seem to be occurring in an environment where the demand for strategic leadership development is expanding at a dramatic rate. We believe that demand will continue to grow. But it will be less for traditional programs and more for a new type of *process*. This process will be much more focused on the marketplace, driven by applied research, rooted in partnerships, and measured by contributions to the growth and success of corporate sponsors and individual participants. These new processes are the foundation for what we describe throughout this book as a new paradigm for strategic leadership development. This new paradigm presents significant challenges to organizations but offers enormous opportunity as well.

ORGANIZATION OF THIS BOOK

Our objective in writing this book was to prepare both a solid conceptual analysis of the field, as well as a handbook for operating effectively within it. We begin with an introduction to the context of strategic leadership development. There we discuss several critical ideas that are fundamental to our thinking, including the nature of strategic leadership and the concept of a learning organization. These two ideas are then combined to present a new paradigm for strategic leadership development—the way benchmark organizations are using leadership development techniques to facilitate both individual growth and organizational competitiveness. This introduction draws on our detailed investigation of the state of the practice of strategic leadership development, summarized in Appendix A. Our analysis, based on comprehensive research findings, portrays a field in the process of fundamental change.

The book is then divided into three parts. Assessing the challenge of strategic leadership development is the focus of the three chapters that make up Part 1. In Chapter 1, we expand our discussion of the new paradigm for strategic leadership development, tracing its evolution from the traditional process that is still in place in many organizations, to the more vibrant, flexible, learning-oriented process being used by benchmark organizations. In Chapter 2, we relate leadership development to organizational life cycles. In the process, we describe how strategic leadership development can contribute to the ongoing revitalization of a firm. The examination of a new strategic context for leadership development is the focus of Chapter 3. In that chapter, we discuss the nature of current restructuring efforts and the role of strategic leadership development in facilitating change and enhancing organizational performance.

Whereas the three chapters comprising Part 1 outline the *challenge* of strategic leadership development, the five chapters of Part 2 outline the *process* in some detail. A description of that process from a systems perspective is the focus of Chapter 4. In it, we create a systems model for strategic leadership development and present a framework for crafting strategic leadership development initiatives using a systems perspective. The methods and priorities for strategic leadership development are examined in Chapter 5. Several frameworks are introduced to help readers select from among the many options available to design and deliver the most powerful initiatives. Chapter 6 addresses the question of internal versus external strategic leadership development programs. Through case study analyses of university-based general management and company-specific programs, we attempt to define the strengths and weaknesses of each approach and guidelines for their use. Processes for selecting and managing providers of strategic leadership development are presented in Chapter 7, along with a discussion of the potential future role of universities in the field. The always challenging subject of evaluation is addressed in Chapter 8. Techniques are presented for ensuring the integrity of strategic leadership development initiatives, as well as the generation of adequate returns on corporate investments in those activities.

The third and final part of the book is devoted to the future. In Chapter 9, we present six examples of new paradigm approaches to strategic leadership development and an opportunity for organizations to benchmark against them. In Chapter 10, we summarize the book through a framework we call the "seven Ps," the seven core elements of strategic leadership development. We discuss their evolution over time and, based on the ideas described throughout the book, present our predictions of where they are heading in the future. We close with a checklist for ensuring the future effectiveness of strategic leadership development initiatives in your own organization. Two appendices follow. The first is a summary of our own research; the second, a summary of research commissioned by the Harvard Business School and facilitated by McKinsey & Company.

ACKNOWLEDGMENTS

There are many people who have helped make this book possible. First, we want to thank the many companies that have given us an opportunity to work with them and study their processes, especially AlliedSignal, Allstate Insurance, the American Red Cross, ARAMARK, AT&T, Bertelsmann Entertainment Group, British Airways, British Petroleum, Carpenter Technology Corporation, Conrail, Daimler-Benz, General Electric, Hoechst Celanese, IBM, Johnson & Johnson, Motorola, the World Bank, and Westinghouse.

We also wish to thank a number of other organizations for sharing their ideas and experiences with us, especially the Business Consortium (Miami University and the University of Cincinnati), the Center for Creative Leadership, the Center for Executive Development, the Columbia University Office of Executive Education, the Fuqua School of Business at Duke University, Harvard Business School, Indiana University, the International Consortium for Executive Development Research, UNICON—the International University Consortium for Executive Education, Kielty Goldsmith & Co., the MIT Center for Organizational Learning, the MIT Office of Executive Education, Penn State Executive Programs, the Penn State Institute for the Study of Organizational Effectiveness, and the Smeal College of Business at the Pennsylvania State University.

A number of individual colleagues also contributed greatly to our work. Although we could list dozens of names, we would like to acknowledge especially Gini Freeman Tucker, Maria Taylor, and Joe Cavinato at Penn State; Victoria Guthrie at the Center for Creative Leadership; Bernie Wetzel formerly of Westinghouse; Keizo Kawata at Fujitsu; Doug Ready at the International Consortium for Executive Development Research; Ken Graham at the University of Texas; Don Kuhn at UNICON; Roger Fine, Al Anderson, Jerry Kells, Myron Goff, and Inaki

Bastarrika at Johnson & Johnson; Garland Bolejack and Ron Meeks at Hoechst Celanese; Joe Isenstein at Bertelsmann Entertainment Group; Dan Burnham, Ron McGurn, and Don Redlinger at AlliedSignal; Roberto Artavis and Eduardo Montiel of INCAE; William E. Fulmer at George Mason University; Val Markos of BellSouth Corp.; Deepak Sethi of AT&T; Maurice Saias of Institut D'Administration des Enterprises Aix-En-Provence; Earl Sasser, Jay Lorsch, Leonard Schlesinger, Chris Argyris, and John Kotter at the Harvard Business School; Kirby Warren and Maryann Hedda at Columbia University; and Jack Goodwin at the University of Richmond.

Finally, we want to thank Debby Bennett and Brian Mihalic for coordinating the production of the manuscript and Beckie Pasipanski for keeping the process moving. We couldn't have done it without them.

Introduction
A New World for Strategic Leadership Development

JUST AS GREAT explorers like Magellan and Columbus set out on journeys through uncharted waters, leading-edge leadership development strategists are embarking on a challenging, uncharted journey into the future. The concept of a new world is a very appropriate analogy for our discussion of strategic leadership development. There are lessons we can learn from the great explorers. Columbus set out to find an alternative route to distant but familiar lands where untold opportunities awaited him. What he found, however, was something far more profound. He actually stumbled on a "New World," one that would reshape virtually every existing aspect of society, culture, and knowledge—an *unexpected* source of untold opportunity.

Interestingly, Columbus embarked on his voyage with dire warnings that his objective was unreasonable, perhaps even insane. The conventional wisdom of the day is summarized in a quote from the Talevera Commission in 1491: "The mission Columbus has proposed is folly. Among the many reasons that might be cited as to the folly of his enterprise is the well known fact that the Atlantic Ocean is infinite and therefore impossible to traverse."[1] Although some may wish that King Ferdinand and Queen Isabella had listened to their advisers, all would admit that the vision exhibited by Columbus literally changed the world!

What can we learn from Columbus's experiences? Perhaps most important, the objective of developing strategic leaders may be our goal, but our pathway to achieving that goal is taking us through the uncharted, currently stormy waters of the future. The traditional leader-

1

ship development objectives of identifying potential, appraising effectiveness, and developing competencies are still appropriate and achievable, but will most likely be met through the discovery of a "new world" of techniques and processes that are developing in response to changes on the business horizon. This chapter, and indeed this book, is intended to help you identify some of those changes and to guide you on your journey through the new world of strategic leadership development.

WHAT IS STRATEGIC LEADERSHIP?

Just about everyone agrees that strategic leadership is related to "vision." However, very few experts have provided a tangible definition of just what "vision" really means. Some time ago, one of us heard a terrific definition of vision from James Ross, formerly CEO of Cable and Wireless in the U.K.: "Seeing is auditing life. Vision is interpreting life so that others may see it." Given that definition, we can address the nature of strategic leadership.

Let's go back to our New World analogy. As the chief executive of the voyage, Columbus had a vision: that of finding a new, faster, and more economical course to familiar lands. He had a global perspective, one that said the world was round, the ocean navigable, and that opportunity awaited the adventurous person who sailed west. He made use of the leading technology of the day, primitive as it now seems, and he built alliances with governments, businesspeople, and crew members to stake his venture. Having made all the seemingly correct moves, Columbus set out. He didn't sail the ships—his crew did—but Columbus kept them focused and directed. He also kept watch on the horizon, searching for opportunities but staying his course. When the course seemed to be taking his crew nowhere, he kept them from jumping ship. And when the horizon finally became clear, he directed the ships to a landing.

Now, here is where vision came into play. We are sure it didn't take too terribly long for Columbus to figure out that he had landed in the wrong place. He had a great plan, and the plan took him somewhere, but it wasn't where he wanted to go. However, Columbus still saw opportunity, and he convinced his crew, his sponsors, and eventually even many of our ancestors that the New World had untold possibilities.

We believe that, above all else, strategic leaders must have a similar sense of vision—an ability to set broad, lofty goals and steer a course toward them, but with the insight and flexibility to adjust both the course and the goals as the horizon becomes clearer. They must be able to communicate the goals and the course to well-educated, technically skilled colleagues. And they must develop the internal and external alliances and supporting communication and reward structures that will ensure the appropriate resources are brought to bear on achieving the organization's strategic objective.

As companies struggle to maintain focus in today's tempestuous business environment, greater attention is being given to leadership development as a means of identifying and developing visionary leaders capable of promoting organizational transformation. The benchmark companies mentioned throughout this book have for some time realized the potential of strategic leadership development as a tool for crafting competitive advantage. These companies have helped establish a new, emerging perspective on leadership development which is focused not only on individual development but also on the overall competitiveness and strategic effectiveness of a firm. This new vision for strategic leadership development is rooted in the framework for creating what is being termed a "learning organization," an organization that is able to channel the energy of environmental change into a force for organizational growth and development.[2]

THE TOOL KIT OF A LEARNING ORGANIZATION

A central idea for a learning organization is the distinction between "single-loop" and "double-loop" learning, as defined by Chris Argyris and Donald Schon.[3] According to their thesis, when organizational learning involves detecting and correcting "errors" (performance gaps), so that an "organization [can] carry on its present policies or achieve its present policies or achieve its present objectives, then that error-detection-and-correction process is single-loop learning. . . . Double-loop learning occurs when error is detected and corrected in ways that involve the modification of an organization's underlying norms, policies, and objectives."[4]

In a manufacturing company, for example, changes in business conditions lead to adjustments in production rates, changes in material orders, and the hiring and firing of workers. This constant learning that occurs within an organization is what Argyris and Schon would call "single-loop learning." On the other hand, learning that leads to worthwhile changes in the organization of the manufacturing company and its ability to perceive its environment is double-loop learning. This approach to learning requires decision makers to challenge long-held assumptions and modes of operating. So the manufacturing company in our example could decide that to deal with constantly fluctuating demand, it might engage in strategic alliances, identify new geographic markets, or utilize new technology rather than simply react to customer orders. Not until companies adopt such new ways of looking at their environment are they likely to practice double-loop learning. We believe that effectively organized strategic leadership development efforts can help companies evolve toward this new way of thinking.

In addition to the single-loop/double-loop distinction, researchers have identified a number of theoretical categories of organizational learning. The following classifications can help readers analyze which type of learning scenario is the norm at a particular time in their organization.[5]

Maintenance Learning

Maintenance learning discovers better ways of doing what a business already knows how to do. It encourages doing things the best way without asking whether they are the right things to do. It is single-loop learning. Maintenance learning quite often misses important clues about a changing environment or emerging challenges. The search for "best practices" is at the heart of maintenance learning, in that it focuses on "catching up" with the best of contemporary practice. To the extent it is committed to preserving the status quo, maintenance learning offers little challenge to an organization's existing strategy and operations. It is therefore likely to miss emerging business opportunities—even those that could leverage existing strategy. The implications of emerging environmental change—or even news that should set alarm bells ringing, such as the appearance of new competitors or changes in customers' buying habits—are likely to be downplayed. The focus of maintenance learning is short term, so it is not surprising that crises eventually overtake organizations where it is the dominant learning focus.

When asked for examples of specific learning techniques used by their organizations, 200 executives from 12 countries provided us with the list in Table I.1. From this list it is clear that most organizational learning is maintenance in nature. You may wish to use this table as an audit of learning techniques used by your own organization.[6]

Shock Learning

In the event of a crisis, organizations undergo shock learning. At best, shock learning is reactive. At worst, shock responses aggravate the problems they are attempting to solve. Learning that takes place under the stress of a crisis is unlikely to adequately address the long-term consequences of present actions. Some managers have made careers out of managing turnaround operations. They are able to quickly perceive opportunity and adopt a creative strategy to seize it. However, although individual crisis managers may understand the likely impact of their decisions, research has shown that under intense levels of stress most individuals fail to exercise creativity. Rather, they fall back on ways of doing business that have always worked in the past.[7]

Anticipatory Learning

This type of learning addresses both the long-term consequences of present actions and the best ways to deal with a future environment. Effective anticipatory learning is:

- *Participatory.* Anticipatory learning is unlikely to take place when there is an assumption that one party or group has all the answers that it must then communicate to a less-informed constituency. Participatory learning demands that everyone in an organization be given an opportunity to analyze information, explore alternatives, and reach a true consensus on critical challenges.

- *Future-oriented.* As the term implies, anticipatory learning focuses on what is likely or possible in the future, rather than on what was or is.

TABLE I.1 How Organizations Learn: Techniques and Their Use

Technique	Type A/B/C/D	Extent of Use	Importance
Statistical process control	A/B	3.0	3.5
Task force	B/D	3.7	3.9
Best practices/benchmarking	C/D	2.7	3.4
Employee suggestion scheme	A/B	2.8	3.2
Outside management development programs	C/D	2.9	3.3
Joint ventures/alliances	C/D	3.0	3.5
Internal management development programs	B/D	3.4	3.9
Customer surveys or interviews	B/C	3.3	4.1
Total quality/Baldrige programs	B/D	2.6	2.9
"Work-out programs" (participative efforts to streamline work flow)	A/B	2.7	3.1
External advisory groups	A/C	2.7	3.1
Self-directed work teams	B	3.1	3.4
Process reengineering	B/D	3.1	3.6
Decentralized strategic planning process	D	3.0	3.3
Transferring successes within the company	A/B	2.9	3.5
Information technology (groupware, etc.)	A/C	3.5	3.8
Delphi technique	C	1.8	2.2
Scenarios	C/D	2.5	2.9
Content analysis	A/C	2.6	2.7
Impact analysis	C	2.7	3.3

Key: A = low participation, present-oriented; B = high participation, present-oriented; C = low participation, future-oriented; D = high participation, future-oriented
Rate each technique from 1 to 5: 1 = used little/not important; 5 = used widely/very important

Source: R.M. Fulmer and M. Saskin, "How Organizations Learn" (research in progress, sponsored by Presidents' Association of the American Management Association, 1996–1997).

It considers the possible future consequences of actions taken today. Future-oriented learning may also look backward from the anticipated future, exploring the actions required today and in the near term to reach an envisioned future.

HOW ORGANIZATIONS REALLY LEARN

The three classifications described above can be framed into four learning modes or operating styles that organizations adopt over time. Each mode is discussed below.

Because I Say So

In an organization that operates in the "Because I Say So" learning mode, an authority figure orders something to be done (or avoided), and all managers and employees then take their cues from that dictum. The essence of maintenance learning, this mode is in many instances highly appropriate. For example, when Ed Hennesey arrived to take over as CEO of AlliedSignal in 1980, his first impression was that the corporate staff was tremendously bloated. He told his subordinates that they had to cut $20 million from operating overhead within six months. It wasn't a debatable issue, and the organization accomplished the objective and learned from the process.

As You Like It

Another learning mode, "As You Like It," describes the type of learning that occurs when individuals and groups are left to their own devices to achieve preset targets or objectives. This type of learning can be observed in decentralized operations where performance is measured quarterly according to growth objectives, return on investment, or some other quantifiable measure. As long as operating executives meet their operating target, the way they get there is often left to the creativity of the executive team. Mike Dingman, who led the Signal companies into a merger with Allied and later coordinated the spinoff of more than 30 unrelated operating companies in the Henley Group, is viewed by Wall Street as a master of "As You Like It" leadership. He managed to let his operating managers have their own way, yet he effectively coordinated their efforts into overall corporate growth.

Change Masters

Some CEOs lead their organizations by setting goals and demanding that managers learn the new ways of thinking and doing business needed to accomplish them. When Jack Welch became CEO of General Electric, he insisted that every business be number 1 or number 2 in its market; if it wasn't, he expected the division to prepare a plan to either become the market leader or exit the business. Without asking for widespread participation, Welch established the goal of having all businesses be market leaders. However, his goal generated a wave of learning throughout GE. Such leaders—Rosabeth Moss Kanter calls them "change masters"— achieve organizational renewal by articulating their vision of what needs to happen and communicating it effectively to people who are willing to learn how to make it happen.[8] These leaders tend to capture the energy of this willingness to learn through strategically focused leadership and organizational development initiatives.

Inventing the Future

In the fourth mode, "Inventing the Future," anticipatory learning is practiced when a group of motivated individuals work together, not just to forecast, but to *create* a future to which they can commit themselves. In 1992 Ralph Larsen was planning a three-year executive learning effort for the top 700 executives at Johnson & Johnson, the world's largest diversified health care company. Such change initiatives are often given an innovative name, and their theme is usually proclaimed in advance. Contrary to expectations, Larsen declined to articulate an agenda for this conference. Instead, he outlined the importance of thinking about the future along with the dangers of trading on past successes. He refused to give more specific directions for this strategic initiative and asked a steering committee of key executives to work for several months to come up with a plan. Their experiences were supplemented with information from interviews involving almost 100 of their colleagues.

The theme they arrived at was "Creating Our Future." The program that evolved from their work included electronic meetings (exercises that use computer software to enable every individual to participate in large group discussions); discussion of a company case entitled "J&J 2002"; and a comprehensive strategic exercise for "creating a future," which included Delphi forecasting along with content analysis and impact analysis. This initiative is discussed in more detail in both Chapter 6 and Appendix A.

In talking with senior executives around the world, we were struck by how few of the strategic leadership development initiatives they mentioned were anticipatory in nature. Rather than the long-term focus we found at Johnson & Johnson, most companies targeted their leadership development initiatives at important, but short-term "maintenance learning" targets. The frameworks and techniques discussed in this book are intended to help organizations design strategic leadership development initiatives from an anticipatory perspective—as tools for building highly competitive learning organizations.

CHARTING A COURSE FOR THE FUTURE

Central to creating a learning organization is an enhanced ability on the part of members to learn from and through experiences—both their own and those of colleagues, customers, and competitors.[9] Although far from a revolutionary notion, the growing emphasis on learning as an element of corporate competitiveness has provided the impetus for revolutionary changes in how organizations are managing and utilizing strategic leadership development initiatives. The core elements of these changes are discussed below and elaborated on throughout this book.

Who?

Traditionally, leadership development efforts were reserved for an elite few individuals who had been identified as having high potential for advancement within the organization. This process helped companies create a small pool of executives from which senior managers could be drawn. In contrast, strategic leadership development in learning organizations is all-inclusive, involving managers at all levels in the process of continuous learning and team development. Through these processes, organizations are kept vital, flexible, and open to opportunities in the competitive environment.

What?

In the past, the leadership development process for most organizations consisted of a series of "checkmarks" in a manager's file indicating that he or she had completed a predetermined rite of passage into the next level of management. Today, strategic leadership development is managed as a process of lifelong learning through which managers at all levels of the organization are involved in ongoing experiences, including training, education, experiential assignments, team building, and enculturation. These processes are designed to facilitate not only individual development, but also the implementation of corporate strategies through the cultivation of the managerial talents and organizational values essential to long-term competitive effectiveness.

Where?

The main venue for traditional leadership development frequently was the classroom, where individual managers were exposed to issues and perspectives in general management. Today, the venues for strategic leadership development encompass not only the classroom, but also the workplace and even the world. The action learning model of executive development, in which managers learn by doing, is moving to the forefront of leadership development, as companies attempt to promote learning and personal growth through guided processes of real-world problem solving.

When?

For executives in most companies, traditional development opportunities were few and far between. Attending an external executive education program, for example, was often a once-in-a-lifetime event. Strategic leadership development is an ongoing process that fosters the ability to continuously learn, innovate, and improve.

How?

Formerly, leadership development was viewed as a series of relatively discrete programs, including classroom activities, rotational assignments, and perhaps some form of performance feedback. Individual managers frequently were left to their own devices to integrate these loosely coordinated activities into a personal developmental plan. For learning-oriented organizations, strategic leadership development is an ongoing process designed not only to influence individual talent but also to define and cultivate organizational values and culture. This systems view of leadership development enables an organization to tap into the energy and experience of all managers, to build a hard-to-replicate form of human resource–based competitive advantage.

Why?

Traditionally, leadership development activities were managed as rites of passage—"stripes" earned perhaps for achievement, but often simply for long-term organizational membership. The new learning-oriented perspective takes advantage of the real value of leadership development by utilizing it as a force for building organizational capability—the ability to maintain both flexibility and focus in a complex, changing environment. This type of organizational capability cannot be developed through management edicts, analytical techniques, or quick-fix programs. Rather, it requires a new perspective on leadership and organizational development which realizes the contribution of continuous learning to an organization's competitive advantage.

STRATEGIC LEADERSHIP DEVELOPMENT AS A FORCE FOR COMPETITIVENESS

In today's environment, the secret to long-term competitiveness is an organization's ability to continuously learn, evolve, and grow—to exhibit the kind of visionary leadership discussed at the beginning of this chapter. Strategic leadership development can be a key driving force for building and sustaining this essential capability. We believe that, to harness the potential of leadership development as a force for building organizational capability and influencing competitive advantage, organizations must adapt their leadership development efforts to the new learning-oriented paradigm outlined in this chapter. Making that shift in perspective requires commitment to the following basic assumptions, which are the foundation of the ideas discussed in this book:

1. *To compete in an era where speed, flexibility, and quality are essential to competitiveness, management processes must evolve from a focus on control to a focus on interpretation.*

Management by control is focused on techniques and analyses that extrapolate from the past into the future. Those processes do little to help leaders deal with rapid, unpredictable change. Leadership through interpretation helps leaders cultivate an ability not only to observe changes, but also to interpret and to respond proactively to those changes through a heightened awareness of the strategic directions and capabilities of the firm.

2. *Long-term corporate effectiveness is generated not by the develop-ment of a strategic plan but through commitment to strategic in-tent.*[10]

The learning organization is committed to the long term and develops an overarching objective that drives the learning orientation. Examples like GE's commitment to global market leadership and British Airways' commitment to becoming the "World's Favourite Airline" demonstrate how strategic intent can ingrain as a core organizational value the desire for continuous improvement, innovation, and learning. In a learning organization, strategic leadership development efforts become the vehi-cle for communicating those values, cultivating the talents, and build-ing the networks that translate them into action.

3. *The core purpose of strategic leadership development is not to build a small pool of successors to senior management, but to cultivate and refine the managerial talents needed to move the organization toward its strategic objectives.*

Through long-term vision and an enhanced ability to anticipate and interpret environmental change, the learning organization is better able to identify the core talents and capabilities necessary to gain competi-tive advantage. Strategic leadership development becomes the operative force that helps develop and refine these talents while continuously reinforcing the organization's strategic intent.

4. *Strategic leadership development is a process for cultivating both individual and collective talents of the organization.*

In today's business environment, competitiveness is most likely to be achieved by groups of talented individuals working together to address real organizational problems and issues. The learning organization focuses leadership development efforts on this type of teamwork. Leadership development is used not only to "round out and fill in" individual managers, but also to communicate and clarify strategic intent, promote teamwork and the development of internal networks, and solve real-world problems. In this mode, strategic leadership development becomes a core mechanism for communicating and implementing strategy, as well as a tool for promoting individual development.

We are living in a new world of opportunity for leadership development. That new world involves more than traditional, loosely coordinated efforts in executive selection, succession planning, job rotation, and training. It involves the charting of a course—a strategy to combine all of these elements into an integrated process designed to guide managers at all levels from the start of their careers toward a new world of competitive advantage. We hope this book will help you chart that course for yourself and your organization.

PART 1

The Challenge

1
Toward
a New
Paradigm

DECISION MAKERS HAVE traditionally learned from experience. Corporations tell us that they generally rely on experience to provide as much as 80 percent of the necessary learning for those whose careers will move to senior levels. Education and training provide about 10 percent of the preparation, and coaching and mentoring account for the remaining 10 percent. These percentages emphasize the importance of providing meaningful career development assignments for managers.

The purpose of leadership development, then, is not to create programs. At the very least, leadership development should broaden the horizons of participants so that they can see and understand different realities or alternative courses of action. At its best, leadership development should inspire and enable leaders to higher and higher levels of achievement. Like Plato's classic "allegory of the cave," one of the demands of leadership is to persuade individuals and organizations that have accepted limited approximations of reality, like flickering shadows on a cave wall, to see greater potential for themselves and their world. Instead of separate "roles and goals," corporations, higher education institutions, faculty members, and consultants involved in leadership development share a common objective: to develop (not train or teach) transformational leaders of learning organizations.[1] Yet the ability of a corporation and its leaders to learn is often hampered by the "traditional paradigm" for leadership development. This chapter describes the traditional paradigm and goes on to discuss today's challenges to this traditional way of thinking.

THE TRADITIONAL PARADIGM DEFINED

Over the years, we have conducted extensive research and worked with dozens of companies to assess leadership development needs and determine the most effective ways to address them.[2] During this time, we have noticed a remarkable consistency among the organizations in their perceptions of how the leadership development process should operate. This pattern of perceptions has been so widely used that it will be referred to in this chapter as the "traditional paradigm" for leadership development.

The traditional paradigm is based on several key assumptions:

- Age is a valid indicator of an individual's stage of development.
- An individual's formal education prior to employment is an adequate base for a 40-year career.
- Leadership development efforts should be focused primarily on candidates for senior management. However, once candidates reach senior management positions, further training and education are unnecessary.
- Senior officers are solely responsible for developing and communicating the corporation's missions, goals, and visions.
- Training and education programs should be developed course by course, based on specific current needs within the business.

This traditional outlook focuses on the leader as an individual. Organizations that subscribe to the traditional paradigm tend to support a somewhat regimented leadership development process in which high-potential managers are identified at an early age and move through a relatively standard progression of developmental experiences which includes job rotation, training, and further education. This cultivation of talent, skills, and experience is expected to lead to the achievement of senior management status by a select group of carefully nurtured individuals.

Typical of this traditional paradigm is a tendency to discuss leadership development in terms of candidates' ages or years of business experience. This led us to conclude that, for most companies, the leadership development process can be broken down into four distinct phases, as shown in Table 1.1. Each of these phases accounts for approximately one-quarter, or 10 years, of an individual's traditional 40-year career

TABLE 1.1   Executive Development: The Traditional Process

Developmental Phase	Age	Character- ization	Traditional Development Activities
1: "Learning the Ropes"	Mid-20s to early 30s	Individual contributor	• Selection • Initiation • Further technical education • Evaluation • Coaching • Project management • Rotation—functions/divisions • Supervisory experience • Identification of potential

2: "Rotational Assignments"	Early 30s to early 40s	Promotable midcareer	• Budget responsibility
			• Manage others in larger units
			• Rotational assignments across
			  —Business environments
			    (growth, mature, etc.)
			  —Line/staff units
			  —Divisions
			  —Functions
			  —Countries/cultures
			• Coaching
			• Evaluation
			• Limited external develop- mental experiences

3: "Becoming a General Manager"	Early 40s to early 50s	Experienced midcareer	• Move to senior functional positions • External executive education experiences • Leap to general management positions • Some rotation still appropriate • Manager of managers, devel- oping a CEO perspective • Executive education in depth if senior leadership potential
4: "Foundation for the Future"	Early 50s and beyond	Senior leader, statesman	• Occasional briefing sessions • External representative to society and other businesses (directorships, etc.)

Source: A. A. Vicere and K. Graham, "Crafting Competitiveness: Toward a New Paradigm for Executive Development," p. 284. Reprinted with permission from *Human Resource Planning*, Vol. 13, No. 4 (1990). Copyright 1990 by the Human Resource Planning Society, 317 Madison Avenue, Suite 1509, New York, NY 10017, Phone: (212) 490-6387, Fax: (212) 682-6851.

span. We also found that a consistent array of developmental techniques seems to be associated with each of the four phases. For the most part, those techniques are employed to help confirm an individual's executive potential and to refine individual capabilities during a career phase.

The leadership development process itself is frequently described as a pyramid with decreasing numbers of managers participating in the process at each phase. Movement from one phase to the next is based on the premise that an individual has already been identified and selected as one with high potential for increased managerial responsibilities.

The Traditional Process

Phase 1 of the traditional leadership development process begins when individuals are carefully selected from "good" colleges and hired into positions generally recognized as "breeding grounds" for future managers. At Procter & Gamble these positions were traditionally in brand management; at Johnson & Johnson and IBM they were typically in sales; at General Motors and Nissan they were usually in finance. Most often in their twenties, these individuals are exposed to leadership development activities that include initiation into or orientation to the company, technical or specialized training, evaluation and identification of their future potential, and some exposure to top management through focused project assignments and related developmental opportunities.

Those individuals identified as having "high potential" during this first stage are then advanced to phase 2. Now in their thirties, these managers are traditionally exposed to rotational assignments, increased levels of management responsibility, and further attempts to confirm their potential.

Those who emerge successfully from this stage move on to phase 3. Having advanced to their early forties or fifties, these managers are typically viewed as prime prospects for general management positions. They are likely to be given increased levels of management responsibility and very likely to be involved in both internal and external executive education programs. During this stage, they are carefully groomed for general management responsibilities.

Those who eventually become general managers are observed for their effectiveness and perhaps exposed to additional executive education programs. If successful, they advance to phase 4 of the process and move into senior leadership positions at some point in their fifties. At this stage of a leader's career, he or she is traditionally viewed as having "arrived" at full executive potential with little need for further leadership development attention other than occasional briefings on topical issues or perhaps participation as a director of an external organization.

We submit that, in a very general sense, this model portrays what was, until recently, the standard pattern of leadership development across most of the organizations we observed.

Training versus Education

Within the traditional model, there appeared to be some confusion with regard to the differences between training and education. Therefore, it might be useful at this point to draw a distinction between these concepts. The goal of training is to develop specific skill sets where performance can be measured. For example, a new employee is trained to work the cash register, then serves customers by ringing up sales. Performance can be tested, monitored, and verified. Training in particular skill sets is also essential for middle and senior managers. Corporate officers take training courses that build skills in effective oral presentations, in dealing with hostile securities analysts or reporters, or in "coaching" so that employees can be empowered rather than ordered about. Again, in some manner, their learning can be monitored and their progress verified.

Education, on the other hand, tends to focus on conceptual thinking: the ability to think in terms of relative emphases and priorities among conflicting objectives and criteria; relative tendencies and probabilities, rather than certainties; and rough correlations and patterns among elements rather than clear-cut cause-and-effect relationships.[3] Educational programs tend to be designed, not to teach specific skills, but rather to promote a higher level of leadership thinking. By encouraging a greater openness to and awareness of differing perspectives, education can build greater flexibility into an organization's decision-making processes.

From the end of World War II through the mid-1970s, most corporations were engaged in training. The focus was on addressing gaps in job-related skills as perceived by key managers within the organization. These needs were met one course at a time. The vast array of course titles still to be found in a course catalog from the American Management Association (AMA) would serve as an example of management training in the larger traditional context.

During this era, education was limited to a select handful of preidentified future senior leaders and was delivered primarily by business schools. According to a 1988 report issued by the American Assembly of Collegiate Schools of Business (AACSB—now the International Association for Management Education), Harvard and Stanford controlled one-third of the total general management education market.[4] This type of executive education typically stressed the use of cases and might be described as "a tour of the significant functional areas of a corporation." Other observers have labeled the traditional general management program as a "mini-MBA."

Traditionally, an exposure to executive education would occur once in a lifetime for a given corporate executive. With fewer than 15 percent of all corporate executives then holding business administration degrees, leadership development relied more heavily on experience than on the study of business. But that has changed. A global survey of 1,508 executives predicted that 78 percent of all CEOs would have a graduate degree in business by the year 2000.[5] The value of traditional general management executive education programs becomes less significant as a larger percentage of managers already hold business degrees.

AN EMERGING NEW PERSPECTIVE

The exclusive, individualistic focus of the traditional era was acceptable in a stable business environment. Today, due to profound environmental changes, many of the assumptions underlying this traditional viewpoint have become obsolete.[6] As a result, a new paradigm for leadership development is being framed. Four critical drivers of this emerging perspective are discussed below. They include changing views on the role of age and career longevity in the leadership development process, as well as new perspectives on who should be involved in leadership development efforts and what perspective those efforts should take.

Age

In an era of decreasing numbers and layers of managers, age can no longer be considered a valid indicator of an individual's stage of development. Today the determining factors must be an individual's expertise and experience base. This is largely the result of downsizing and reorganization efforts that have pushed significant amounts of decision-making responsibility down in organizations. As a result, authority and autonomy often are delegated to individuals at much earlier career stages. These individuals tend to be bright, well-educated, ambitious specialists who bring high levels of technical, financial, marketing, or other types of functional expertise to their organizations as members of various project teams.[7] As noted by Jon R. Katzenbach and Douglas K. Smith in their book *The Wisdom of Teams*,

> teams—real teams, not just groups that management calls "teams"—should be the basic unit of performance for most organizations. . . . In any situation requiring the real-time combination of multiple skills, experiences, and judgements, a team inevitably gets better results than a collection of individuals operating within confined roles and responsibilities. . . . The record of team performance speaks for itself.[8]

The authors go on to cite example after example of organizations like GE, Motorola, Kodak, Ford, Hewlett-Packard, and others that have begun to use teams as the basic building blocks of their organizational structure. These companies' ability to move faster, more efficiently, and more aggressively in the marketplace is undisputed. But teams require new skill sets for both team leaders and team members, all of whom must have a much deeper understanding of the workings of the organization and the marketplace than in the past. To fulfill their responsibilities, these individuals must receive earlier and broader orientations to strategic management issues than would have been necessary under the traditional approach to leadership development.

For example, in the mid-1980s Allstate Insurance Company eliminated the zone offices that separated each region from corporate headquarters. As a result, regional vice presidents suddenly found themselves with multifunctional responsibilities and a direct reporting relationship to the home office far earlier in their careers than traditional Allstate executives. Many had been prepared for careers as functional specialists and had little exposure to the generalist perspective required in their new roles.

This situation caused Allstate to rethink its corporate approach to leadership development. The firm decided to give greater attention to promoting an organizationwide cross-functional management orientation among managers at all levels of the company. These efforts focused on building depth across the entire management team—not the kind of technical depth for which a specialist is originally hired, but business depth: a working knowledge of the insurance business and a vision of the entire organization as an operating entity comprised of interconnected, often interdependent, parts. Allstate's objective was not simply to use leadership development to facilitate business depth within individual managers. Rather, it was to evolve a distinct form of competitive advantage in its industry by creating well-prepared, well-informed teams of managers at all levels who were committed to growing and to developing an aggressive, strategically focused company.

In organizations with fewer management levels and greater demands for specialized knowledge, some leaders may never achieve what we have traditionally labeled "management status."[9] This is especially true in industries that rely heavily on research, scientific, or technical expertise. In this era of specialized talent, multifunctional project teams, and networked organizations, it is crucial that team members, whether managers or not, are helped to develop an early appreciation of the business as a whole in addition to a network of contacts throughout the firm. Without this exposure, the broad-based, team-oriented perspective required in today's organizations is difficult, if not impossible, to cultivate.[10] For example, 3M Corporation is widely recognized for its ability to sustain an innovative culture through the use of shared information, cross-pollination of ideas, and tolerance for risk taking. Similarly, General Electric (GE) encourages its research and technical experts to develop ideas and then market them throughout the company. As a result, the *Wall Street Journal* reported, "GE is turning around the equation of U.S. business. Instead of pushing marketers to come up with ideas and then asking scientists to make them work, the company gives researchers wide berth to imagine and invent—and then shop the invention around GE's divisions."[11] This form of cross-pollination helps GE blend the expertise of its managers and technologists to more effectively manage the transfer of technology from laboratory to market—a critical success factor for competitiveness in the nineties.

Longevity

Traditional approaches to leadership development were based on the notion that an individual's formal education prior to employment would provide him or her with an adequate base for a 40-year career. Today, however, restructuring efforts, coupled with continuous environmental and technological change, contribute to rapid job obsolescence at all organizational levels. As a result, John Kotter listed as one of his "new rules" for success: "Never stop trying to grow; lifelong learning is increasingly necessary for success."[12] Thomas Stewart, in a recent *Fortune* article, footnoted Kotter's rule: "In biblical times, a talent was a unit of money. These days . . . learning is the coin of the realm. Treat your wealth of knowledge as the wise servants did in the parable of the talents: Invest it and make it grow. If you bury it, as the fearful servant did, you'll lose it."[13]

"Intellectual capital" is becoming one of the few real sources of competitive advantage today—for both individuals and organizations. Stan Davis and Jim Botkin described tomorrow's successful business as

> one that leverages the economic value of knowledge. It is always figuring out how to define, acquire, develop, apply, measure, grow, use, multiply, protect, transfer, sell, profit by, and celebrate the company's know-how. And it may be know-how about developing new products, about serving customers, about any number of things.[14]

This emerging focus on knowledge creation requires that leadership development efforts begin to focus as much on continuous learning and networking across the entire organization as they do on the identification and development of high-potential management talent. For example, General Electric has long understood the importance of leadership development to both individual and organizational effectiveness. GE's expansive commitment to leadership development processes such as "Work-Out" (discussed in Chapter 10 and Appendix A) is testimony to the strategic importance the organization attaches to the function. The mission statement for GE's Crotonville education and development center underscores the critical role leadership development plays in the company:

> [Crotonville's] mission is to leverage GE's global competitiveness as an instrument of cultural change, by improving business acumen, leadership abilities and organization effectiveness of General Electric professionals.

Noel Tichy, a former director at Crotonville, refers to the operation as "a staging ground for corporate revolution."[15] He credits GE's leadership development efforts with being a major force for positive evolution and change throughout the company. He also emphasizes the critical importance of GE Chairman Jack Welch's commitment to making the process a force for competitiveness. Dave Ulrich adds that, to fully utilize leadership development as a tool to facilitate competitiveness, "top managers, particularly the CEO, are involved. . . . [It requires] top management ownership, visibility and commitment."[16] When top management assumes ownership for building the organization's talent base, leadership development often becomes a major catalyst for knowledge creation and organizational development. We will discuss several examples of this idea in Chapter 3.

Focus

One of the major problems in today's competitive business environment is that organizations are facing a lack of "bench strength." Due to reorganization and rightsizing (downsizing) efforts, they simply do not have ready replacements available to fill vacated management positions. At the same time, with fewer management positions available, the notion of a promotion every two years is a thing of the past for incumbent talent. These perplexing developments have challenged the traditional belief that leadership development efforts should focus primarily on candidates for senior management. Finding and developing tomorrow's CEO is clearly important, but that person will need a team of well-educated, competent, dedicated managers in middle-level positions to bring strategic visions to reality.

Kenneth Labich stated in a *Fortune* article, "It is the worst of times for middle managers . . . either jobs are vanishing in mergers, takeovers, and restructuring, or management vogues are radically altering their traditional roles."[17] Without the luxury of excess organizational layers and the resulting stockpiles of management and professional talent, today's organizations must work to keep all their sources of knowledge and intellectual capital committed and involved. They also must learn to cultivate the abilities of these individuals to function in teams, make decisions, and convey the lessons learned from their experience to newly developing talent within the company. GE Chairman Jack Welch noted, "As for middle managers, they can be the stronghold of the organization. But their jobs have to be redefined. They have to see their roles as a combination of teacher, cheer leader, and liberator, not controller."[18]

Leadership development planners today must acknowledge that middle managers have options:

- They can play a key role in the organization's future development.
- They can be part of a flexible, project-oriented talent pool which enables the organization to move in a swift, agile manner.
- They can improve and enhance the job they currently hold.
- They can act as intellectual resources for senior managers who develop and implement policies and strategies.
- They can serve as instructors, coaches, mentors, and role models for technical specialists and newer managers.
- They can function as external scanners for environmental trends, opportunities, and challenges that are identified more easily by seasoned managers than by novices.

However, these benefits can accrue only if middle managers are encouraged to maintain their vigor and intensity. Horizontal moves, rotational assignments, knowledge updates, and other developmental experiences must be coordinated for these individuals. The value and importance of their efforts must become an acknowledged part of the corporate culture. Without these experiences, their potential for individual boredom, withdrawal, and disaffection could spell disaster for the organization.

This focus on the continuous, ongoing development of talent at all levels is a core element of a learning organization.[19] As we noted in the Introduction, a learning organization is a company that engenders within itself the capacity to change—the ability to anticipate, embrace, and capitalize on events and opportunities in the business environment. I. Nonaka has called this built-in capacity "middle-up-down management."[20] He noted that middle managers working in multifunctional teams are best positioned to integrate information from top managers and line workers in the development of new products, processes, and perspectives. As such, he charged that it is "middle management's role to create and realize verifiable business concepts for the creative solution of contradictions and gaps between the ideal and the actual." In a case discussion of the highly successful Honda Motor Company (a company with a distinct middle-up-down culture), Nonaka showed the kind of competitive leverage that can be gained when organizational development efforts adopt this middle-focused perspective on developing strategic and competitive effectiveness. In that example, through the use of a focused, committed team of top-notch managers, designers, and engineers, Honda was able to create a revolutionary new product, the Honda City, that helped the company set a new standard for small car design in Japan.

Perspective

One of the most dramatic shifts taking place in leadership development is based on the need for today's organizations to change their view of what leadership really is. Traditionally, leadership was seen as the province of senior officers. For the most part, only the top women and men in the organization were expected to deal with the public, interface with the political environment, facilitate joint ventures, plan globally, or explain corporate policies and directions to subordinates. That is no longer the case. In streamlined, more flexible, "shadow pyramid" organizations (see Chapter 3), these skills and abilities must be shared at all levels of the firm. Failure to cultivate an understanding of that role early in an individual's career can leave a company dangerously vulnerable to external influences. As Raymond Miles notes, "In the newer, flatter, and leaner firms, management jobs are fewer, more demanding and, for the most part, more satisfying . . . instead of being in charge of a division or department, the top executive of production, design or supply components is a general manager running a complete business itself. His or her staff must also share a broader vision."[21]

Traditional approaches to leadership development left the tasks of developing and communicating corporate missions, goals, and visions to senior officers. In a highly competitive environment characterized by growing reliance on the network or project organization form, these capabilities must be developed throughout the organization. Driving this strategic focus down to lower levels of the organization requires greater emphasis on communication and team-building efforts during leadership development. As a result, the skills-oriented training programs that were the backbone of internal management education and development efforts at phases 1 and 2 of the traditional model are now being supplemented by leadership development efforts geared to a deeper understanding of corporate strategic issues. These company-specific leadership development programs, formerly reserved for managers at phases 3 and 4 of the traditional model, are fast becoming a core element of organizational efforts to facilitate change and development.[22] This shift is a key factor in the dramatic growth of "customized" leadership development programs.

For example, Allstate determined that, in order to quickly and effectively implement its reorganization and facilitate competitiveness, managers at all levels must be actively involved in policy-level discussions of corporate objectives and directions. Through an ongoing series of internal leadership development programs, Allstate managers, directors, and officers discuss not only their firm's current policies but also the strategic "why's" behind the policies. These programs help open channels of communication within Allstate, thereby facilitating management's understanding of and commitment to key policy decisions and organizational changes.

Similarly, in 1976 the U.S. Congress enacted legislation to form the Consolidated Rail Corporation (Conrail), a company comprised of a number of bankrupt railroads serving the Northeast and Midwest. Early on, Conrail senior management realized that the key to the company's viability was to move away from a traditional railroad culture toward a new strategic vision of a market-driven transportation company.

One effort to enact this vision involved establishing a leadership development program targeted to the company's middle managers. The purpose of this two-week general management program, developed in conjunction with the Smeal College of Business at the Pennsylvania State University, was to enhance the management capabilities of participants by strengthening their abilities to work *as a team* to understand, communicate, and implement this new marketing-oriented strategy. The positive contribution of this effort to Conrail's impressive record of performance improvement is reflected in the following comment from a past program participant: "Now I can more knowledgeably talk about why our corporate structure has changed with time. . . . I can build into my conversations an 'advertisement' for the importance of a market orientation for Conrail."

THE NEW PARADIGM CONTEXT

As a result of our analyses, we concluded that, although many organizations had within their grasp the elements for a successful, forward-looking leadership development effort, most companies made little effort to focus these elements to build overall organizational competitiveness. For a few notable companies, however, leadership development had become more than just a vehicle for individual development. For them it had become a mechanism for cultivating the collective managerial talents, perspectives, and capabilities that would help propel the organization into the future. The exceptional companies that shared this strategic, organization-oriented approach to leadership development were also remarkably consistent in how the process should work. Consequently, we will refer to their views as the "new paradigm" for leadership development.

As mentioned in the Introduction, this new paradigm has as its fundamental purpose the utilization of leadership development as a force for overall organization development—as a tool to develop knowledge and intellectual capital, shape organizational culture, create commitment to strategic directions, promote teamwork, facilitate a broader understanding of the organization, and cultivate an environment for continuous improvement and innovation. One of the greatest challenges facing organizations today is how to retool and reinvigorate organizational cultures after sustained periods of retrenchment, reorganization, and turmoil. New paradigm companies are turning to leadership development processes to help refocus the organization and enhance competitive effectiveness.[23]

Instilling a Learning Orientation

To harness the potential of leadership development as a force for building competitive advantage, organizations are adapting leadership development efforts to the new, learning-oriented paradigm discussed throughout this book. The basic operational requirements of this new approach to leadership development seem to be a commitment to a strategy that includes

- Early and ongoing cross-functional, project, and action learning assignments designed to build business depth

- Early and ongoing education and training in interpersonal skills and strategic management, coupled with opportunities for coaching and mentoring that help cultivate and hone leadership capabilities

- Early and ongoing opportunities for external executive education designed to refresh perspectives and challenge basic operating assumptions

- Early, ongoing, and regular performance appraisals and feedback, coupled with regular briefings on the organization and its culture and strategy designed to facilitate communications, commitment, and organizational development

- Opportunities to serve as a coach or mentor to teach others about the organization and its business

Individually, each element is far from a new idea. Together, however, they form the major elements of a leadership development process that can help foster overall organizational development and a renewed sense of competitiveness. All of these activities help maintain the open, broad-based management perspective necessary for competitiveness. Throughout this book, we endeavor to present frameworks that bring these elements together.

Adapting to the New Paradigm

The experiences of organizations like GE, Conrail, Allstate, and the many others we will discuss are helping us learn how to harness the potential of leadership development as a force for change. Their experiences suggest that, to be effective, a company's leadership development process must flow logically from its strategic agenda. The focus of the process should be on identifying and developing the talents and perspectives that the company needs to achieve its long-term strategic objectives. Specific initiatives should be built around this market-oriented focus, coupled with a strong element of competitive analysis, to help managers at *all* levels understand the strengths and weaknesses of the firm and what it will take to build competitive advantage. This understanding must then be related to the organization itself—the systems, structures, processes, goals, and relationships necessary for success in a highly competitive world. Armed with this strategy/culture/consistency focus, an organization engaged in strategic leadership development is positioned to build both competitive advantage and management depth in pursuit of organizational excellence.[24]

As leadership development practitioners step back from the traditional process and analyze their function, many are concluding that there must be a better way to cultivate leadership talent. By overcoming preoccupations with individual development, age, and tenure as driving forces in the process; by refining views on middle managers and teamwork; and by viewing leadership development as a key tool for influencing organizational change and development, strategic leadership development can move beyond a process that benefits only a few individual managers toward a process that helps drive the flexibility, commitment, and competitiveness of the entire organization.

2

The Cycles
of Leadership

IN TODAY'S ERA of reorganization, revolution, and change, strategic leadership is essential to an organization's competitiveness. We described in Chapter 1 how organizations are refocusing their leadership development efforts to better develop their pool of strategic leadership talent. This chapter discusses how strategically focused leadership development processes can help build sustainable organizational competitiveness.

A MODEL OF THE STRATEGIC LEADERSHIP DEVELOPMENT PROCESS

One very useful way to examine strategic leadership development is to discuss typical patterns of leadership through an organization's lifetime.[1] A number of authors have made significant contributions to understanding this crucial process.[2] The model portrayed in Figure 2.1 is a synthesis of the work of these authors, coupled with new insights on the role of strategic leadership in building organizational competitiveness.

The model is a simple presentation of the stages of an organization's development over time, from its inception through its *potential* demise. The dimension of time is charted on the vertical axis. In this instance, time is signified by five developmental stages from emergence—when an organization comes into existence—through growth, maturity, decline, and decay—when an organization ultimately ceases to exist. *It is important to note that demise is not inevitable, that effective strategic leadership can enable an organization to avoid the consequences of the final two stages.*

The horizontal axis is a measure of orientation to change based on the

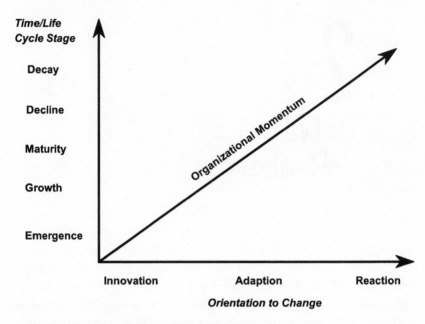

Figure 2.1 The Organizational Development Model

Source: A. A. Vicere, "The Strategic Leadership Imperative for Executive Education," p. 17. Reprinted with permission from *Human Resource Planning*, Vol. 15, No. 1 (1992). Copyright 1992 by The Human Resource Planning Society, 317 Madison Avenue, Suite 1509, New York, NY 10017, Phone: (212) 490-6387, Fax: (212) 682-6851.

concept of adaption/innovation theory.[3] This theory holds that creative style and orientation to change can be gauged on a continuum ranging from a very strong focus on adaptive creativity, or a preference to work with what exists in an effort to do what is currently being done *better*, to a very strong focus on innovative creativity, or a preference to give little credence to what currently exists, leading to a tendency to do things *differently*.

To survive and prosper in an industry, an organization must be able to adjust its strategic behavior to the changing demands of the marketplace. Adaption/innovation theory asserts that both adaptive creativity and innovative creativity are effective styles of dealing with such changes. But, whereas innovators are focused on creating new and different organizational elements, adapters are focused on creating effective ways to implement and perfect those elements.[4] As such, the most effective organization is one that can blend the strengths of each approach in a culture that avoids the tendency to favor one preference to the exclusion of the other.

We submit that, as organizations develop, their cultures tend to evolve from being more innovative and open to change, to being more adaptive and focused on improving what currently exists in the organization's competitive domain.[5] To a degree, this *momentum* is essential and necessary in order to deal with growth and success. Over time, however, an organization can become so inwardly focused that it eventually ceases to be creative at all. It no longer does things differently. It no longer improves what exists. It simply reacts to the pressures of the outside environment.

When an organization reaches this reactive stage, it is left with only three options. First, it can continue in its reactive mode and eventually cease to exist. Second, it can be acquired (or conquered) and somehow refocused through external influence. Third, it can attempt a massive restructuring of the status quo (a "revolution") in an effort to revitalize its culture—a very difficult and painful process. Again, it is important to note that this evolutionary process can be managed. An organization need not evolve to a stage of decline or decay.[6] Rather, strategic leadership development processes can be used to manage the cycles of change in an organization, enabling it to better balance the need for innovation and adaption in an effort to build organizational capability and competitiveness.[7]

THE STAGES OF STRATEGIC LEADERSHIP

The implications of the strategic leadership model can be clarified through a discussion of the expanded model depicted in Figure 2.2. The style of strategic leadership typical at each stage is indicated in this model. Each of those styles is detailed below.[8]

Prophet

In the emergence stage, the style of strategic leadership necessary for organizational growth and development is typified by the notion of a *prophet*. A prophet is a visionary, a zealot driven by an ideal, typically embodying a new and different way to deal with the world and some of its opportunities. Prophets lead organizations that are intense but unstable, often surviving on a day-to-day basis. Commitment to the visionary

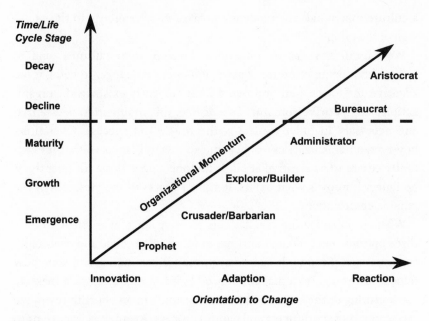

Figure 2.2 The Strategic Leadership Model

Source: A. A. Vicere, "The Strategic Leadership Imperative for Executive Education," p. 18. Reprinted with permission from *Human Resource Planning*, Vol. 15, No. 1 (1992). Copyright 1992 by The Human Resource Planning Society, 317 Madison Avenue, Suite 1509, New York, NY 10017, Phone: (212) 490-6387, Fax: (212) 682-6851.

ideal is the prime reason for membership in the organization and the primary driver of motivation. Throughout history, there have been many prophets. And throughout history, many of those prophets have been ostracized, exiled, and sometimes even killed. But those that survived often were responsible for revolution and change—because prophets challenge the system, break with the status quo, and discount conventional wisdom. Real change and development are unlikely to occur without them.

The history of business is populated with prophets—people like Ray Kroc of McDonald's, Thomas Edison of GE, and Stephen Jobs of Apple Computer. These individuals envisioned new worlds, created new products, and established new industries. They and their fellow prophets have been the lifeblood of technological and social change and development.

Clara Barton was the prophet who founded the American Red Cross in

1881. Through her energy and unflagging commitment to that ideal, she helped create one of the world's foremost humanitarian organizations. In doing so, she established a growing concern, one that demanded an expanded form of strategic leadership exemplified in the next stage of the model.

Crusader/Barbarian

If the prophet survives and is persistent, as was Clara Barton, the ideal he or she champions and the loosely structured organization that supports the ideal begin to take root. At that point, the strategic leadership focus required by the growing organization must shift from the prophet's zealous pursuit of an ideal to the development of an organization capable of making that ideal a reality, the *crusader/barbarian* stage. To some, strategic leaders at this stage are crusaders, spreading the word and enhancing the survival of the ideal. For others, these leaders are barbarians who are ruthlessly transforming the ideal into a structured, regimented process. Control is the essence of strategic leadership at this stage, as leaders seek to put structure to the often-chaotic zeal of the emerging organization. It is also at this stage that many would-be entrepreneurs fail as the unbridled intensity of innovative creativity and the structured control of adaptive creativity collide in the formation of a viable organization.

Some prophets are able to recognize the need for different leadership skills and develop successors with the appropriate talent to take their organizations to the next level. However, many prophets falter at this stage, falling victim to the need to run their organization more like a business and less like an informal network. Stephen Jobs met such a fate at Apple, as did Clara Barton. Barton is held in the highest esteem in the history of the American Red Cross, but she was so successful in building support for the organization in its early days that the organization outgrew her ability to lead it. With the ideal firmly in place, the growing organization needed structure and controls. Clara Barton was proficient at neither. So in 1904 Mabel Boardman forced founder Clara Barton out of office. Was Boardman a crusader or a barbarian? To supporters of Barton, she may have been the latter. But to supporters of the ideal of the American Red Cross, Boardman was a crusader, taking the organization to new heights of growth and achievement by adding a necessary element of structure and control to chaotic growth.

Explorer/Builder

If crusader/barbarian leaders are successful in bringing structure to the emerging organization and positioning it in the marketplace, the strategic leadership style must again shift. At this stage, organizations enter a period of "textbook management," having taken a prophet's ideal at the emergence stage and turned it into a viable organization during the crusader/barbarian stage. The term *textbook management* is used to describe the *explorer/builder* stage because it tends to be a period of opportunity and growth. The organization is past the startup, entrepreneurial stage. It has met the need to secure investment capital, and it has established a position in the marketplace. It is now at the point of development most frequently assumed by business management textbooks. Analytical management techniques are much more applicable at this stage, as demand for products and services often exceeds the organization's capacity to produce them, and external competition has yet to become a factor.

Growth is the watchword of the explorer/builder stage, and strategic leaders seek to capitalize on growth by investing in business development, "perfecting" the organizational structure, hiring new people, expanding into new markets, and developing new management systems to meet the demands of growth and success. Gradually, however, those systems can begin to dominate the strategic thinking of the organization, driving it to the next stage of the model.

Administrator

Growth and success bring about several crucial consequences for the organization. First, they invite competition. As outsiders see the possibilities for success in the organization's domain, they attempt to enter the arena. Then, as competition heats up, the inevitable inefficiencies created by growth but hidden by seemingly boundless opportunity become apparent. Organizations that reach this stage are often described as "mature" businesses or in "mature" (slow-growing) markets. The need for greater efficiency and control in a mature market signals a movement toward further adaption—major efforts to improve and enhance the efficiency and effectiveness of existing products, services, structures, and systems.

This call for greater control and adaption leads to the *administrator* stage. Generally, there is a tendency toward centralization in planning, budgeting, and controls during this stage. In fact, control systems and processes seem to dominate the managerial agenda as the organization seeks to gain consistency and stability. Simultaneously, leadership tends to become more impersonal as administrative systems become the driver of organizational decision making.

Administration is a two-edged sword. When asked if *administrator* is a positive or a negative term, most people hesitate to answer. That is because there is a fine line separating the positive contribution of effective controls through administration from the negative consequences of overorganization caused by overemphasized administration.[9] This type of overorganization can propel the organization into a bureaucratic morass. As a result, some form of corporate reinvention is called for.

The "succession by clone" syndrome that often typifies organizations at this stage can be disastrous—as IBM, General Motors, and Westinghouse discovered in the early 1990s. Some companies are able to navigate these treacherous waters through recognition of the constant need to reassess strategic leadership capabilities. At Johnson & Johnson, Jim Burke balanced his external orientation, vision for global growth, and commitment to traditional corporate values with a down-to-earth, pragmatic administrator, Dave Clare, who served as his chief operating officer. Clare was less widely known than the visionary Burke, but he was a vital part of the J&J management team. Similarly, former General Electric CEO Reginald Jones recognized, as he neared retirement in 1979, that the management skills and practices that had caused him to be named the most admired executive in America for three successive years would not be enough to lead GE into the new era of challenges it faced. Consequently, Jones launched a search for his successor which resulted in the selection of a younger, more flamboyant leader in the person of Jack Welch, a leader not in the traditional GE mold who consciously began a process to reshape the corporation.

Bureaucrat

If the organization fails to follow the path to reinvention typified by Johnson & Johnson or GE, the efficiency focus that dominates the administrative era tends to become the strategic leadership focus of the organization. At this point, the organization crosses into the stifling *bureaucrat* stage. The ideals of the emergence stage have been left behind and all but forgotten. The market orientation of the explorer/builder stage has been lost to efficiency measures and controls. Strategic leaders have become bureaucrats, no longer innovatively creative, no longer adaptively creative, but reactive to the pressures of the outside environment.

A bureaucracy is easy prey to new crusaders and explorers (competitors) in the marketplace. Some leaders at this stage see these new competitors as prophets/barbarians to be "shot" for challenging the status quo, changing the rules of the game, and swaying marketplace commitment away from traditional ideals. This reactive posture propels organizations dominated by a bureaucratic perspective into the next stage of the model. For other leaders, however, the appearance of new competitors on the horizon is a sign that a new social order is called for within the organization, and revival efforts are put into place in an effort to restore competitiveness and "bust" the emerging bureaucracy.

Revivals are often painful and difficult undertakings for organizations that have reached the bureaucracy stage. Typically, it has been quite some time since attention has been given to the ideals on which the organization was founded. Consequently, the organization is often adrift and devoid of its core competencies.[10] Furthermore, many current leaders have risen from the ranks of "successful" administrators and therefore lack either the vision of prophets or the market knowledge of explorer/builders. For that reason, revivals often require crusader/barbarian leaders who are able to mount a revolution to restore focus on the ideal and reposition the organization in the marketplace.

L. Stanley Crane, former CEO of Conrail, is an example of such a revolutionary. Crane took over the top spot at Conrail in 1981. At that time, Conrail was a quasi-government-owned railroad with over 70,000 employees. During the period between 1976 and 1980, Conrail had posted losses in excess of $1.5 billion. When Crane assumed his CEO position, Conrail was losing over $1 million a day.

Formerly the president of Southern Railway, Crane was an experienced manager and a capable leader. He presided over a massive reorganization effort that included substantial divestment of unproductive assets and headcount reductions of nearly 60 percent. Crane worked with managers, union leaders, and employees to build understanding and support for these changes—changes that resulted in an operating profit of $431 million in 1986, marking six straight years of profitability for Conrail.

Crane ultimately helped transform Conrail from a hemorrhaging appendage of the government to a highly profitable transportation services company. When Elizabeth Dole, then U.S. secretary of transportation, recommended that the government sell the now profitable Conrail to Norfolk Southern in 1986, Crane was able to lobby Congress and the financial community to secure a public offering of Conrail and ensure its independence and viability.[11]

It is important to reiterate that evolution into bureaucracy is not inevitable. Some corporations are able to recognize the need for significant cultural and strategic change and select leaders who have the appropriate vision and strength of character to carry out this task. Stanley Crane had the vision to reinvent Conrail. Jack Welch saw that GE could not succeed with such a wide array of diverse businesses without the competitive advantages associated with market leadership.

To explore the connection between corporate culture and performance, John Kotter and Jim Heskett of the Harvard Business School collected data on a number of firms that had successfully made the transition from bureaucracy to renewed growth.[12] The common characteristics of those firms were

- An effective leader on top
- An outsider's openness to new ideas
- An insider's power base
- A perceived need for change
- Communication of a new vision
- Motivation of a growing group of "believers"
- Adaptation to environmental change and opportunity, typified by movement into new products and new markets, and possibly by the establishment of partnerships and alliances that promote growth

History is written by firms that exhibit these characteristics. Organizations with long lifespans inevitably have been able to predict the need to change and have had the courage to make change happen. Those organizations have always had a strong pool of leaders from which to draw intensity and inspiration.

Aristocrat

Sometimes revolutionary turnaround efforts, like those we have discussed above, do not occur. If a bureaucracy is strong enough, and if it has become too entrenched in the organization, senior leaders can become *aristocrats*, removed from the realities of the organization and sheltered from the storms of change. In many ways, aristocrats are engaged in a struggle for survival similar to that of the organization's founding prophets. But, whereas prophets press for the survival of the ideal, aristocrats press for their personal survival, often at the expense of the organization itself. Strategic leaders at these organizations tend to suffer a sad but inevitable fate. Typically, they are purged from the organization, sometimes at the cost of the organization's very existence. Recent senior executive turnover at companies like IBM, General Motors, Digital Equipment Corporation, Westinghouse, and Morrison Knudsen are blatant examples of what can happen to an organization at this stage.

THE STRATEGIC LEADERSHIP MODEL IN ACTION

Ichak Adizes[13] noted that the life cycle stage of an organization can be gauged by observing the degree to which control systems and administrative procedures dominate an organization's decision-making process. He further suggested that overreliance on administrative systems is a major factor in the demise of many organizations. As such, the strategic leadership model depicts one of the most significant challenges facing organizations. That challenge is how to deal with the aftermath of growth and success in a turbulent environment. To meet that challenge, an organization must have the appropriate leadership capabilities in place to initiate and implement competitive change.[14]

This idea is clearly depicted in the rise and fall of the Soviet Union. Although Lenin was clearly a prophet to the Soviet Union, it was Stalin who crusaded for the ideal and created the "empire." Stalin was followed by a progression of leaders who became more and more removed from the people, until the society itself was on the verge of collapse. Enter a new prophet, Mikhail Gorbachev, who presented the people with new ideals and visions of a new social order. Gorbachev was unable to lead the crusade for his new ideals and was "exiled" in favor of Boris Yeltsin, who is struggling to forcefully take control of the "new" Russia.

The Soviet example illustrates the difficulty faced by an organization attempting to revitalize from the stages of decline and decay. The challenge is immense. It is imperative, therefore, to prevent the natural momentum of organizational evolution from leading the organization into bureaucracy and decay. Meeting the challenge of this imperative is the essence of strategic leadership development.

This imperative is evident in the organizational development efforts implemented at General Electric. GE was far from a declining company when CEO Jack Welch took over in 1981, but Welch believed that the seeds of bureaucracy and aristocracy were taking root throughout the organization. His focus on making GE a "boundaryless" company, his commitment to making each of GE's businesses number one or number two in world markets, and his support for employee involvement efforts such as "Work-Out" reflect his strategic leadership role as a prophet/crusader for a new social order at GE—one focused on an ideal and rooted in the marketplace.[15]

But the real lesson of the GE example is not the contribution made by Welch as a strategic leader. Rather, it is the company's overall management of its leadership talent pool. When former CEO Reginald Jones and the GE board of directors selected Jack Welch, they knowingly unleashed a prophet/crusader whose management perspective was a far cry from the analytical, administrative focus that dominated GE at that point in time. Welch brought a renewed sense of purpose to the company, one that helped GE regain its balance between the forces for innovative creativity and the forces for adaptive control.

Under Welch, leadership development processes have continued to play a key role in the company. GE's ongoing management development and employee involvement efforts have helped instill the new ideals of boundarylessness and competitiveness across all levels of the organization. These processes have enabled the company to identify executive talent and observe potential through action learning projects and task force assignments.[16] In short, GE has used executive education and leadership development to build a strategic leadership talent pool and to use that pool to create dynamic tension in the organization—tension that stymies the organization's natural drift toward bureaucracy.

British Petroleum's reorganization efforts in the early 1990s provide another example of the strategic leadership model in action. When former CEO Robert Horton took office in 1990, he saw the need to rekindle the ideals of the organization, in order to prevent stagnation and bureaucracy from stifling competitiveness. He initiated BP's "Project 1990," an effort to survey the company's employees, review current operations, and generate recommendations for enhancing the firm's effectiveness.[17] Horton was influential in selecting the project head, a middle-level "high flier" with a proven track record, thanks in part to BP's highly regarded high-potential management development program.

Horton gave the project head the freedom to select six other "high fliers" from throughout the organization to serve on the team. Horton maintained weekly contact with the project head but empowered the team to do its own analysis and make independent recommendations. As a result, the Project 1990 team painted a candid portrait of BP as an overcontrolled organization in need of radical transformation.

The team's final report led to a massive reorganization effort designed to make the company more responsive to the marketplace. This reorganization included the development of BP's "egg" organization, an oval organization chart that depicted the breaking down of organizational "chimneys" in the new organization and the establishment of BP's OPEN culture, a set of behavioral ideals based on *O*pen thinking, *P*ersonal impact, *E*mpowerment, and *N*etworking.[18] For BP, OPEN was an ideal designed to focus all members of the organization on the marketplace. Ultimately, Horton hoped that OPEN would enable the company to reach its objective of being the world's most successful oil company in the 1990s and beyond.

BP has made major progress toward these goals, but without Mr. Horton. It seems that, despite the early success he achieved with the Project 1990 initiatives, Horton was unable to avoid the fate of a leader raised on the principles of traditional management. In a *Forbes* magazine interview on the changes he instituted within BP,[19] Horton stated, "Because I am blessed with a good brain, I tend to get to the right answer rather quicker and more often than most people. That will sound frightfully arrogant, but it's true." The aristocratic perspective reflected in this quote cost the once-prophetic Horton his job later that year.

A final and more positive example of the model in action is once again offered by the progress of Conrail. The U.S. government established Conrail in 1976 in an effort to maintain essential rail service in the northeast manufacturing corridor of the United States. At its inception, Conrail was a conglomeration of seven bankrupt railroads, each with a long history and a distinctive culture. As such, Conrail uniquely began its organizational life as a bureaucracy. Its first CEO, Ed Jordan, worked to establish the controls, systems, and infrastructure necessary to make Conrail a viable railroad. In short, he succeeded in making Conrail a well-administered entity. Jordan was followed by L. Stanley Crane, mentioned earlier, who crusaded for the survival of Conrail as an independent company by relentlessly pursuing a drive for efficiency and effectiveness in the company's operations. Crane's tenure was capped by the public sale of Conrail in 1987, in what was the largest public offering in U.S. history to that date.

Crane was succeeded in 1989 by Richard Sanborn, who brought a new market-focused, employee-oriented ideal to Conrail. Following Sanborn's untimely death that same year, James Hagen took over the top job. Hagen has added his own version of market-focused, employee-oriented ideals to the company, enabling Conrail to continue to evolve toward progressively higher levels of performance in a highly competitive industry. Recently David M. LeVan was named CEO. LeVan brings financial and operating experience back to the top of the company, along with a strong market orientation gained when he served as head of strategic planning under Stanley Crane, Dick Sanborn, and Jim Hagen. These experiences have proven to be essential as Conrail has been forced to deal with pressures for consolidation within its industry by merging with Norfolk Southern and CSX—at an enormous gain for the company's shareholders.

Conrail is clearly a story of the right strategic leader being selected at the right time in the organization's development.[20] But it is more than that. Like GE and BP, Conrail made a massive effort to use leadership development to drive its remarkable turnaround and transformation. Conrail senior and upper-middle managers operated in a well-oiled network that engaged influential managers in the active analysis and implementation of key organizational decisions.[21] Conrail middle managers were brought into the loop in an intensive leadership development program that involved Conrail senior managers, including Hagen, LeVan, and other key leaders, as instructors.[22] Finally, Conrail brought this strategic leadership thrust to the supervisory level through additional development efforts.

Since 1983, Conrail has used leadership development to communicate and to build commitment to a strategic leadership focus that helped fuel one of the business world's most stunning turnarounds. In so doing, Conrail created a strategic talent pool from which it could draw effective, proven leaders capable of meeting the challenge of change and competition.

Lessons Learned

The lessons learned from the above examples can be drawn as the strategic leadership model depicted in Figure 2.3. In this version of the model, the organizational momentum of strategic leadership development is portrayed as a cycling process in which an organization is engaged in the

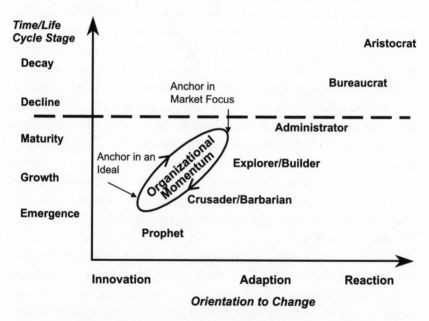

Figure 2.3 The Strategic Leadership Model: Anchors for Effectiveness

Source: A. A. Vicere, "The Strategic Leadership Imperative for Executive Education," p. 26. Reprinted with permission from *Human Resource Planning*, Vol. 15, No. 1 (1992). Copyright 1992 by The Human Resource Planning Society, 317 Madison Avenue, Suite 1509, New York, NY 10017, Phone: (212) 490-6387, Fax: (212) 682-6851.

continuous effort to identify, develop, and harmonize a cadre of leaders capable of performing the roles of prophet, crusader/barbarian, explorer/builder, and administrator. By building this type of strategic leadership talent pool, an organization is better positioned to exploit the opportunities of a changing competitive environment.

This is not to suggest that an organization must actually change leaders at different stages. But it does suggest that an organization needs leaders who are able to recognize the developmental stage of the organization, the competitive demands of the marketplace, and the style of strategic leadership needed to maintain competitiveness in that environment. Leadership development processes should be in place to ensure that the organization maintains a pool of leadership talent adequate to match the strategic leadership perspective of managers and the demands of the competitive environment. This requires the development of a consistent strategy for the recruitment, selection, and development of leadership talent.

In order to do that, leadership development strategies must focus on the evolutionary nature of strategic leadership as implied by this model. The first component of that evolution can be found in the prophet stage, in the zealous pursuit of an ideal. In studying defunct organizations, there is one striking commonality. As those organizations developed over time, they seemed to lose sight of their ideal, their reason for existence, their competitive essence. In short, they lost their ability to learn, change, and develop in order to achieve continually higher levels of success.

We learn from the demise of the Soviet Union that, when people no longer hold their founding ideal, the country or organization lives on borrowed time. We learn from GE that an ideal (boundarylessness) can be used to drive the development, transformation, and effectiveness of an entire organization. We learn from Conrail that instilling the ideal is a time-consuming process that requires relentless commitment but can yield enormous results. Thus the first anchor point necessary for the establishment of a strategic leadership talent pool is commitment to an ideal—a reason for being that serves as motivation and a guide for decision making. Gary Hamel and C. K. Prahalad have labeled this anchor point a "strategic intent."[23]

Commitment to an ideal or a strategic intent is not sufficient, however. The organization also must have the ability to implement that ideal, to bring the ideal as close to reality as possible despite the enormity of the challenge. As the organization develops from emergence through the explorer/builder stage, it is building a base of competitiveness by providing value for its customers in a unique manner. In studying defunct organizations, a second striking feature stands out. As these organizations moved through the explorer/builder stage and into the administrator stage, they tended to take market growth and acceptance for granted. Because growth had been the norm for a time, and because the market had been continually expanding, they tended to develop a sense of invincibility. This overconfidence was magnified by the adaptive focus inherent in an organization's culture at the administrator stage. As a result, these organizations became rapidly and dangerously reactive, ultimately falling victim to their inability to adapt to a changing environment.

Once again, we learn from the demise of the Soviet Union that the market (in this case, the people) will ultimately determine the value of the product and will eventually make the ultimate purchase decision. We learn from GE that a strong market focus (the target of being number one or two in world markets), coupled with commitment to an ideal (boundarylessness), can be an immensely powerful force for organizational development and competitiveness. We learn from Conrail that a market focus coupled with strong commitment to an ideal can lead to stunning turnarounds and exceptional corporate performance.

So the second anchor point in the establishment of a strategic leadership talent pool must be a strong focus on the marketplace, on the value added by the organization, on the unique capabilities that make the organization competitive, and on the core competencies that are the heart and soul of the organization.[24]

Implications for Strategic Leadership Development

The model depicted in Figure 2.3 suggests that a leadership development strategy anchored in an ideal/strategic intent as well as a strong market/customer focus is more likely to create a pool of strategic leadership talent capable of dealing with the challenge of organizational change and development.[25]

Commitment to the ideal anchors the organization in innovation and encourages prophets to be creative and to pursue new ways to bring the ideal to reality. The market focus anchors the organization in the external world, encouraging explorer/builders to expand the boundaries of the organization through market development and to exploit the organization's core competencies through product and service development.

Prophets and explorer/builders are complemented by crusader/barbarians who are called upon to lead revolutions and capture new territories in this dynamic, growing organization. Administrators are called upon to enhance organizational effectiveness by designing ways to learn from experience and thereby enhance performance. The tension created by the interplay of these four perspectives serves to keep the organization vital and in a state of dynamic equilibrium between the forces for innovation (continuous undirected change) and adaption (continuous stability and constant analysis).

Can an individual leader operate across all four strategic leadership perspectives? Miller suggested they seldom can, although the ability to bridge two perspectives is not uncommon.[26] Nevertheless, through leadership development processes, individual leaders can be schooled in the art of building management teams and networks that embrace all four perspectives and are therefore more effective in dealing with the challenge of change.[27] The creation of this kind of talent pool is the essence of strategic leadership development as a force for competitiveness.

The Challenge of Strategic Leadership Development

Analysis of the strategic leadership model presents several challenges to organizations attempting to create a strategic leadership talent pool—the kind of talent pool that enables the organization to maintain dynamic equilibrium in a changing environment. These challenges are directly related to some of the core recommendations presented in the Introduction of this book.

1. *The organization must view management as a process of interpretation, not a process of control.*

To prevent the natural progression into bureaucracy, leadership development strategies must view management as much more than a series of analytical techniques and planning processes. Rather, management must be viewed as a process of interpretation which requires a heightened sense of leadership judgment in order to focus the strategic directions of the organization and exploit its capabilities.

GE's utilization of action learning and "Work-Out" exemplifies the application of this idea.[28] This type of orchestrated interaction helps to focus management attention on the ideals of the organization, promote network building, and enhance market orientation. Most important, it helps to develop an open leadership perspective among managers through the challenge of interaction and group problem solving. Such a perspective enhances awareness of the need for dynamic tension between innovation and adaption in leadership style.

2. *Organizations must view leadership development as a tool for building commitment to strategic intent and engendering a market focus.*

GE's and Conrail's management development programs are good examples of this concept in action. These efforts help both to indoctrinate leaders in the ideals of the organization and to empower them to work together to bring those ideals to reality by exploiting marketplace opportunity. In so doing, these exemplar companies are utilizing leadership development as a focal point for building organizational focus and competitiveness.

3. *Organizations must design leadership development strategies to create a talent pool of strategic leaders at all levels of the organization.*

A leadership development strategy that focuses only on the creation of a small pool of successors to top management can actually add momentum to the progression toward bureaucracy. Instead, development strategies should focus on cultivating, across managerial ranks, the core talents, perspectives, and capabilities necessary to build long-term competitive advantage.

The former Soviet Union focused on developing a small pool of successors to senior management. The result was a succession of clones, each farther removed from the realities of society and each more of an aristocrat than his predecessor. Effective leadership development strategies take a broad approach to talent development, and they build into development efforts the opportunity to observe performance and identify potential.

4. *Organizations must focus leadership development efforts on building both the individual and collective talents of leaders.*

Every individual leader has developmental needs that must be addressed in order to reach full potential. These may include skill building through training, organizational knowledge building through internal educational programs, background development through experiential assignments, or perspective broadening through external executive education. All of these efforts are valid *tactical* interventions necessary to build a strategic leadership talent pool.

But effective leadership development strategies need to go beyond tactical interventions in order to chart a course toward organizational competitiveness in a dynamic environment. This means that the organization's ideal and strategic intent always remain the focus of the development agenda and that the marketplace always remains the context. Strategic leadership development, then, is an effort to promote individual development through the creation of internal and external networks focused on building organizational effectiveness and competitiveness.

Once again, the networks, interactions, and project teams that have been described within GE and Conrail serve as examples of this concept in action. These processes show that leadership development can and should be more than narrowly focused training and development programs. Rather, leadership development, when viewed in a strategic context, can be a core lever for organizational change and development, fostering organizational development while promoting individual development.

5. *Organizations must recognize leadership development as a competitive capability that assists in the development, implementation, and revitalization of organizational strategy.*

Strategic leaders use executive development as a tool to help focus the organization, build competitive capabilities, and cultivate a leadership talent pool. Welch's involvement with GE's leadership development programs and Hagen's involvement with Conrail's management network and development program both serve as testimony to this principle. Strategic leaders use leadership development as a focal point to pull an organization together and move it through the cycles of growth, revitalization, and competitiveness (see Chapter 3).

6. *Organizations must view leadership development as an element of strategic business development.*

Strategic leadership development is a tool to prevent the natural bureaucratization of an organization. As such, it is a driver of both strategic ideals and intent *and* of market awareness and development. In short, it is an arm of the strategic business development process. Managers of leadership development, then, must be strategic leaders themselves. They must understand the business and the competitive environment. They must develop a perspective that views executive development as a competitive weapon.

7. *Organizations must make leadership development part of a consistent human resource strategy that blends the processes of recruitment, selection, development, appraisal, and reward into an integrated system for talent pool management, rooted in the ideals of the organization and focused on the marketplace.*

Creating such a talent pool is the driving imperative for leadership development efforts.

CONCLUSION

In a time of reorganization, revolution, and change, strategic leadership is essential to the competitiveness and development of an organization. The strategic leadership model can provide insight into meeting this challenge. At the core of this challenge is a new strategic context for leadership development, as well as an emerging systems approach to the process. Those issues are discussed in Chapters 3 and 4.

3

The Changing Strategic Context

IT GOES BY MANY names—among them, the virtual organization, the horizontal organization, the network organization, the modular corporation, the boundaryless company.[1] Whatever its name, it represents a fundamental challenge to conventional wisdom. It is today's "new" organizational form, the business world's response to the postindustrial society. And it is taking its toll on traditional approaches to strategic leadership development.

The purpose of this chapter is to discuss the nature of this new paradigm for effective organizations, how it operates, and how it relates to the evolving approaches to leadership development discussed in the two previous chapters. It is not meant to be an academic treatise on organizational theory, nor is it an endorsement of current trends in organizational structure. Rather, it is a practical look at a phenomenon that is reshaping the world of work, the nature of careers, and the essence of both organizational effectiveness and leadership development.

THE ROOTS OF THE CHALLENGE

The history of modern organizational forms can be traced back over two centuries, to the work of Adam Smith, then Frederick Taylor, Max Weber, and other organizational theorists.[2] Responding to the needs and demands of the industrial revolution, these theorists created elegant frameworks for managing increasingly large and complex firms in what was, in comparison to today, a relatively stable business environment. The models they created held that the key to managing the large "machine bureaucracies" created by the industrial revolution was *control*—clear lines of authority, narrow spans of control, and vertical and horizontal integration.[3] The way to establish control was to create what might be called the traditional organizational form, the hierarchical pyramid.

In the early stages of the industrial revolution, the hierarchical form of organization worked remarkably well. And it helped companies like General Motors, Sears, IBM, US Steel, and others grow into large, profitable entities.[4] There is no denying that the bureaucratic form of management that these companies perfected added great value to their operations; their past successes are part of business history.

As we moved through the 1970s and 1980s, however, the business environment changed. The bureaucratic, control-oriented form of organization no longer seemed to work. The economic environment had gone global, and traditional management practices, once viable and value-adding, grew surely but steadily obsolete. To complicate the situation further, the world was experiencing the onset of the information age, and the very nature of management practices, at once slow, controlling, impersonal, and directive in the bureaucratic model, had to adjust to the needs of knowledge workers who demanded more open, empowering management processes.[5] These compounding influences gave rise to a rash of restructuring efforts resulting in a frantic search for new approaches to organizational design.[6]

THE NEW ORGANIZATIONAL FRAMEWORK

The establishment of a new framework for organizational design did not come about in a single wave. Rather, it emerged through fits and starts that together reflect a fundamental shift in management thinking.

As noted previously, throughout the 1970s and early 1980s, global competition and enhanced information technology gave rise to the dramatic restructuring of markets around the world. Established organizations were challenged to rethink their competitive strategies and operational processes. Many once-dominant competitors seemed nearly powerless to fend off the onslaught of new competitors that did not follow traditional rules.[7] As a result of this intensified competitive environment, many established organizations lost market share and saw dramatic declines in profit margins. To deal with these competitive pressures, numerous actions were taken, perhaps the most significant of which involved extensive downsizing efforts that continue even today.

Downsizing in itself was a reasonable response to the competitive pressures of the emerging global economy. Many "new" competitors were much younger, much leaner, and through increased utilization of information technology and related capabilities, significantly more streamlined in their organizational processes. These "new" competitors were often faster moving, more efficient, and more in touch with the marketplace than their "traditional" competitors. So first-wave responses to this new competitive environment tended to involve attempts to "do more with less" by flattening organizational pyramids and incorporating new technologies, thereby gaining efficiency and improving cycle times.[8]

In order to make these leaner, flatter, faster structures work, and in order to further enhance competitiveness, many organizations simultaneously embarked on efforts to engrain total quality management (TQM) into their "new" management structures. TQM was seen as a way to revitalize organizational processes, thereby rekindling the competitiveness of a firm.[9]

Yet, despite the apparent logic of these first-wave downsizing efforts, despite the unrefuted importance of total quality management to global competitiveness, and despite wave after wave of continued restructuring, many organizations still were unable to reestablish their competitive position. It appeared that, although fewer layers and fewer people could make a short-term contribution to an organization's bottom line, although new technologies could streamline and speed up certain processes, and although total quality management could create a short-term fervor for reinventing a culture, these efforts frequently did little to help revitalize an organization's long-term competitive position in the now established global economy.[10] That realization has triggered a second wave of restructuring efforts and the emergence of a new organizational form—a form that is fundamentally changing the nature of work, of organizations, and of the practice of management.

The Emergence of a New Form

One way to trace the evolution of the new organizational form is through the simple set of symbols depicted in Figure 3.1. In Figure 3.1(a),

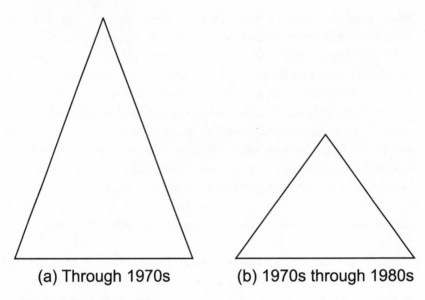

(a) Through 1970s   (b) 1970s through 1980s

Figure 3.1 Evolution of Organizational Forms

Source: A. A. Vicere, "The Changing Context for Leadership and Organizational Development," working paper 95-01, Institute for the Study of Organizational Effectiveness, University Park, PA, 1995. Reprinted by permission.

the traditional organizational model is symbolized as a tall pyramid. With the onset of the global competitive environment and its dynamic, unpredictable change, the traditional model became dysfunctional. The tall-pyramid organizational form fell prey to first-wave downsizing and delayering efforts, resulting in the flatter organizational pyramid portrayed in Figure 3.1(b).

At least theoretically, the flat pyramid held great promise. Its supporters proclaimed that, in addition to being more cost-effective due to the need for fewer people, it brought the customer closer to the firm's decision-making mechanisms; it eliminated unnecessary layers of bureaucracy; it gave workers broader scope and scale of responsibilities; and it sped up decision making and cycle times—all potentially positive benefits. Yet, although these benefits often would accrue to a recently "downsized" organization for a short while, many organizations never really regained the competitive position they sought through their restructuring efforts. This tended to result in another wave of flattening (downsizing), then another, and so on. This vicious cycle of activity left many organizations in search of a better way to address the competitive challenges of the global economy.[11]

A key explanation for the inability of the flat pyramid to deliver on renewed competitiveness is revealed in Figure 3.2's "oval of activity." At the risk of oversimplification, this symbol depicts all of the activities and processes in which an organization engages to accomplish its work. In the traditional tall pyramid, the oval of activity is shown standing on its end. In first-wave downsizing efforts, organizations tend simply to push the oval of activity onto its side; that is, they often continue to do all the things they always have done, but with fewer people. Consequently, even if the organization generates some short-term benefit from its "restructuring" effort, the resulting chaos and stress often trigger a different set of performance problems, leading to another round of downsizing, and so on.[12]

Until recently, most companies seemed to be caught up in this restructuring nightmare. Rather than restructuring with a purpose, they seemed to be moving through this vicious cycle of continuous shrinking, with no focus on creating unique value in the marketplace, no focus on growing and developing the organization as a competitive entity.

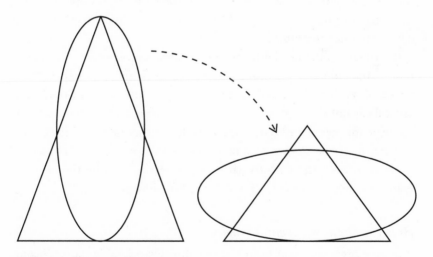

Figure 3.2 The Oval of Activity

Source: A. A. Vicere, "The Changing Context for Leadership and Organizational Development," working paper 95-01, Institute for the Study of Organizational Effectiveness, University Park, PA, 1995. Reprinted by permission.

Rather than finding new ways to craft competitiveness for a changing world, they seemed committed to doing what they always had done—but with fewer people.

The Impetus for Evolution

Two of today's most provocative and influential management theorists are Gary Hamel and C. K. Prahalad. Through a compelling series of articles and a best-selling book, they have described how competitive effectiveness is related to a focused sense of purpose—a "strategic intent," coupled with a unique set of "core competencies" that together drive the development of the organization.[13] Similarly, in *The Discipline of Market Leaders*, Michael Treacy and Fred Wiersema discuss an organization's need to focus on "value disciplines" to build real competitive advantage within their industry.[14] Again, the authors suggest that an unyielding sense of purpose coupled with unique sets of capabilities are the keys to organizational competitiveness. In their recent *Harvard Business Review* article, Tracy Goss, Richard Tanner Pascale, and Anthony G. Athos noted that a clear and distinct declaration of purpose was essential if an organization was to successfully ride what they termed the "reinvention roller coaster," the path of continuous change that organizations must follow if they are to remain competitive in today's dynamic marketplace.[15]

Regardless of the label attached to the process—whether strategic intent, core competencies, value disciplines, declarations, or some other terminology—the need to define the strategic purpose of a firm and its critical capabilities is of paramount importance in current approaches to strategic management.[16] Organizations that subscribe to this logic seem to pare themselves down to a core of activities resulting in a new and evolving organizational form that can be symbolized by the shape in Figure 3.3, perhaps best described as the "shadow pyramid."[17]

How the Shadow Pyramid Works

The new organizational form portrayed in Figure 3.3 is flatter, leaner, more focused, and very directed. The organization itself has been pared down to its essence. It represents only that mix of competencies, capabilities, functions, and processes that enable the organization to com-

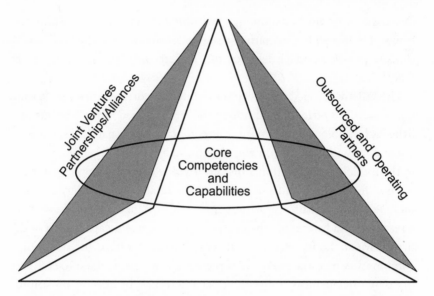

Figure 3.3 Shadow Pyramid Organization

Source: A. A. Vicere, "The Changing Context for Leadership and Organizational Development," working paper 95-01, Institute for the Study of Organizational Effectiveness, University Park, PA, 1995. Reprinted by permission.

pete on a truly unique basis as an industry or world leader. All nonessential activities and functions have been removed from the core.

Some of the removed activities have been deemed by the organization to be unnecessary, to add no value to the work of the firm, and therefore have been eliminated entirely. Many organizations have created enormous efficiencies through such efforts. Other activities, although not unique in themselves and therefore not defined as part of the core, still are necessary for the effective operation of the business. For the organization to compete, it must find alternative ways to economically and effectively engage in these essential noncore activities.

It is quite common today to talk of "outsourcing" as a means of dealing with this challenge.[18] This establishment of a network of supplier/partners of goods and services in noncore areas is often viewed as a key to building efficiency and flexibility into an organizational structure. At the same time, it can help ensure that corporate investment is being appropriately directed toward those core competencies and capabilities that enable the organization to compete on a truly global level.

Discussions of the outsourcing phenomenon with a Penn State colleague, Dr. Joseph L. Cavinato, led to the development of the "full-scale" shadow pyramid model depicted on the left and right sides shaded in Figure 3.3.

The fully developed shadow pyramid model portrays the organization not as a fully vertically and horizontally integrated monolith, but as a lithe and nimble core of unique competencies and capabilities, competing and growing not by control, but through relationships. As reflected in the model, these relationships can involve contract suppliers or temporary workers in traditional outsourcing relationships. They also can include joint ventures, partnerships, and alliances—"new" ways of stretching and leveraging the core competencies and capabilities of the firm.[19] Most likely, an organization's shadow pyramid includes some combination or variation of all of these, as it positions itself to compete in a dynamic business environment characterized by new organizational principles and leadership roles. Those principles and roles are symbolized by a new oval of activity in Figure 3.3, an oval that does not encompass the entire organization, but rather links part of the core to a dynamic network of partners that enable the organization to leverage its core competencies in the marketplace.[20]

THREE CASES IN POINT

The following three examples, although brief, help to characterize the nature of the shift toward the shadow pyramid framework and its impact on organizational strategies and processes. All three examples will be discussed in greater detail throughout the remainder of this chapter.

Carpenter Technology Corporation

Carpenter Technology Corporation (Cartech), a U.S.-based producer of specialty steel and other advanced materials, has embarked on an ambitious plan to nearly double its business over the next few years. Building on its core expertise in steel production, metallurgy, and advanced materials development, and customer service based on advanced electronic data interchange capabilities, Cartech is positioning itself as a global player in the advanced materials business. Its recent acquisition of Aceros Fortuna, a steel distributor in Mexico, and the establishment of a joint venture with Walsin Liwah in Taiwan have given the company a solid foothold in growing markets outside its traditional market in

North America. In addition, joint ventures and acquisitions in structural ceramics development and production, as well as expansion of its European distribution network, have helped to better position Cartech as not just another American specialty steel company, but as a serious global producer and distributor of advanced materials used in the automotive, aerospace, and chemical industries. In effect, Cartech is attempting to build a network around its core capabilities in advanced materials production and distribution, to enable itself to evolve, grow, and prosper in the global economy.

ARAMARK

ARAMARK (formerly ARA Services), is a world leader in contract/managed services, including food service, facilities services, uniform rentals, and health care management. Purchased by its employees in a leveraged buyout ten years ago, ARAMARK is a highly successful company that is benefiting greatly from the development of the shadow pyramid. As other businesses seek to pare down to their core and gain efficiencies in their organizational structure, ARAMARK finds itself in a rapidly growing market for contract/managed services, a market in which it is a dominant player. But ARAMARK itself faced a dilemma—how to move from a collection of independently operating service provider businesses to a flexible provider of multiple services capable of assisting customers to both gain efficiency and enhance internal operations through partnerships with ARAMARK across multiple fronts. Today ARAMARK is working to build its own internal network to help position itself as the world's premier managed services provider with a permanent position in the shadow pyramid "wings" of its customer base.

Daimler-Benz

As one of the largest conglomerates in Europe and the largest industrial company in Germany, Daimler-Benz is among Europe's "crown jewel" corporations. Yet Daimler-Benz, too, is adjusting to the shadow pyramid challenge. Reeling from economic pressures in Europe and throughout the world, and anticipating a dramatically different and more intensely competitive environment, Daimler-Benz has begun a corporate restructuring of its own with a core focus—to be the world's premier transportation systems technologies company.[21] Daimler-Benz hopes to use this focus to stretch and leverage its resources by gaining greater focus and therefore greater synergies across its vast global network of operating partners, including subsidiaries like Mercedes-Benz, Freightliner, and Mercedes-Benz Credit Corporation; venture partners like Ssang Yong, SMH Corporation, and Detroit Diesel; and other relationships. In effect, Daimler-Benz is attempting to carve out a niche as a world-class competitor in transportation and mobility-related technologies and is building its internal and external networks to leverage those capabilities.

IMPLICATIONS OF A SHADOW PYRAMID

As these and other organizations evolve toward the shadow pyramid form, they are redefining the essence of leadership and organizational effectiveness, and reconfiguring processes for developing organizational, leadership, and individual effectiveness.[22]

Leadership and Organizational Effectiveness

The formation of a shadow pyramid is a process that requires a great deal of time, effort, and leadership. Senior leaders must lead the charge to define and clarify the organization's strategic intent and its core competencies and capabilities. They also must enable and empower the organization to build the internal and external networks that must be in place for the organization to function effectively in a relationship-based environment. Similarly, business unit leaders within corporations must work to define the core of their business unit and facilitate the network development necessary for business unit success, including appropriate interfacing with the corporate center and other internal business units. Operating managers within business units must create the same type of focus within their own area of responsibility. Even individual managers and professionals, if they hope to build a successful career, must continually ask themselves what their personal core competencies are, and what they must do to build the internal and external network connections that will enable them to maximize their contributions to the organization.

This fundamental shift in thinking changes many of the rules of leadership and organizational effectiveness. Leaders no longer manage by control; they manage by relationships, trust, and communication.[23] As a result, effective leaders in a shadow pyramid must combine exceptional technical knowledge with superior influence skills to develop a unique blend of relationship-focused leadership capability. With such relationships in place, organizations no longer grow by controlling their entire supply chain. Rather, they grow by performing some portion of that supply chain very well, and by linking up with partners and providers to complete the process.[24] The most successful organizations, and the most successful leaders within them, are those that are best able to manage the "interfaces" that must be established between their "core" and their partner/provider network (see the oval of activity in Figure 3.3).

As a result, this new organizational form brings two business functions to the forefront of management thinking: logistics (supply chain management)[25] and information technology.[26] In earlier times, business schools emphasized marketing and financial capability as the essence of competitive advantage. Today, world-class capabilities in finance and marketing are simply the ante to the business game. Similarly, quality and productivity recently have been championed as the essence of competitive effectiveness. These capabilities have run their course as differentiators as well. Excellence in quality and productivity is essential and expected.

In a shadow pyramid, however, logistics management and information technology become key differentiating capabilities which enable an organization to effectively manage the critical interfaces within their operating network. These two functions, long viewed as peripheral areas within a business, move to the forefront of strategic thinking in an organization where internal and external relationships must be woven together in an efficient operating system.[27] The examples of ARAMARK, Daimler-Benz, and Carpenter Technology provide testimony to the nature of this shift.

Organizational Development

Implemented effectively, a shadow pyramid can enable an organization to focus its activities and build momentum toward a strategic intent, a core sense of purpose that drives the organization's development. In effect, it can enable the organization to stretch its aspirations, leverage its resources, and grow toward the future. This not only requires an organization to define its strategic intent and core competencies, but also demands an operational focus that drives investment in those core activities that can lead to world-class competitiveness in particular technologies, functions, and processes. This helps the organization to develop and leverage its core competencies and capabilities through the relationships it establishes with its shadow pyramid partners.[28]

Although there is an intuitive logic to this process, it presents a host of challenges to organizations. One is the mistaken notion that mission and vision statements are surrogates for core competency identification. Defining a company's essence is not something that can or should be done superficially. Rather, defining the "core" is a process that requires careful consideration, as suggested by IBM Chief Executive Lou Gerstner's 1993 statement, "the last thing IBM needs now is a vision."[29] IBM's recent level of success is testimony to the fact that Gerstner was onto something.

In the early stages of restructuring and transformation, what IBM or any other company needs is a thorough understanding of external opportunities, internal capabilities, and possibilities for developing competitive advantage. Wordsmithed vision statements not rooted in this level of strategic analysis can direct a company's focus away from the marketplace, a surefire way to lose position in today's competitive environment. But an organization that takes careful stock of its essence may be in a better position to create a form of values-based "glue" that can enable it to better stretch and leverage its resources[30]—a challenge IBM seems to be slowly but steadily meeting.

This may lead to a conclusion that developing a core focus is likely to be a time-consuming process—and it is, to a degree. To create such a focus, senior management must be intimately involved in an effort to define strategic intent and core competencies. They must get input, agreement, and commitment from organizational members on the definition of the core and what it means to business practices and processes. And they must help establish the internal and external networks necessary to leverage that core into a thriving, growing business. Paul Evans of INSEAD referred to this senior management responsibility as "applying glue technology."[31] The model in Figure 3.4, adapted from Evans's work, suggests how organizational glue technology can be used to craft competitive effectiveness within a shadow pyramid organization.

Establishing Face-to-Face Relationships. For most companies, developing organizational glue technology requires significant rethinking of hu-

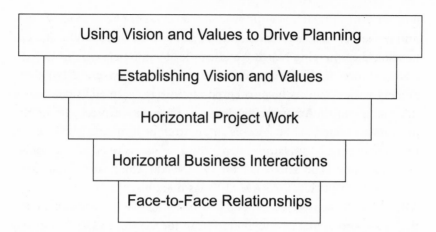

Figure 3.4 Organizational Glue Technology

Adapted from: P. Evans, "Management Development as Glue Technology," pp. 85–106. Reprinted with permission from *Human Resource Planning*, Vol. 15, No. 1 (1992). Copyright 1992 by The Human Resource Planning Society, 317 Madison Avenue, Suite 1509, New York, NY 10017, Phone: (212) 490-6387, Fax: (212) 682-6851.

man resource management, organizational development, and business development practices. The first step in this process involves the establishment of face-to-face relationships among the leaders of the organization. However, this relationship-building process goes well beyond the socializing commonly associated with face-to-face contact. Rather, it involves a more in-depth process of helping managers across the organization get to know each other's businesses and personal capabilities as a basis for internal network building.

For example, for Daimler-Benz to truly leverage its core competencies and capabilities in mobility systems technologies, it must make significant progress in building bridges across business units that heretofore have been fully independent operations. To establish preliminary linkages, Daimler-Benz is conducting a series of seminars in various world regions, in which groups of senior managers from each region gather to discuss issues, share experiences, and learn about one another's operations. Because of where the company is in its repositioning effort, these sessions are designed to build face-to-face contacts among leaders across the organization, as well as greater understanding of the entire Daimler-Benz family of companies.

As the North American region has gone through the first round of this process, part of which is built around a discussion of the shadow pyramid model, considerable momentum has built for maintaining and enhancing the emerging North American leadership network. In this instance, however, the senior managers in the region are driving the process rather than its being a corporate initiative. In addition, two of the major North American business units have adapted part of the program to their own businesses in an attempt to define and leverage their own "core." For Daimler-Benz, the glue seems to be taking hold—and spreading. The challenge for the North American region is to move to the next level. ARAMARK has done just that by creating the ARAMARK Executive Leadership Institute (ELI), an intensive organizational and individual development forum for the top 150 leaders in the company. From CEO Joe Neubauer down, this budding leadership network has worked to redefine the future of the company and revitalize its already-successful organization, putting it on a track for even greater growth and profitability in the years ahead.

As part of ELI, ARAMARK leaders participate in two educational seminars totaling eight days of classroom involvement. At the outset, participants share a brief outdoor leadership development experience to help break the ice. This exercise is followed with a core curriculum of classroom sessions designed to create a common vocabulary and develop frameworks for business analysis. Through the use of company-specific case studies and carefully focused discussion sessions, participants share insights on each others' business units to promote better awareness of the overall core competencies and capabilities of the firm. The out-of-classroom social interaction that takes place serves to cement the establishment of the network further. This type of activity lays the foundation for the second phase of the process.

Horizontal Business Interactions. Once face-to-face relationships have been established and a common language developed, then the organization must provide opportunities for cross-business interaction to further advance the development process. In other words, the organization must promote cross-organization learning through business-focused interaction of leaders from all parts of the organization. For example, the Daimler-Benz North America Leadership Program includes a session in which participants from the same business group analyze a particular business within their group, prepare a report on that business, and share that report with their fellow program participants. In this manner, working relationships are developed among program participants while knowledge of business capabilities is shared across the emerging network of leaders.

Going a step farther, ARAMARK ELI participants engage in an action learning experience they call "Action Projects," in which they work in cross-organization teams to tackle real business issues submitted by the heads of ARAMARK business units. They do this work under one constraint: no individual can work on a project within his or her own business unit. In this manner, ELI gives ARAMARK firsthand experience with other parts of the company. This type of interaction promotes cross-organizational awareness of capabilities and cross-business assessment of opportunities, laying the foundation for phase three of the process.

Horizontal Project Work. With growing interaction and broader understanding of the competencies and capabilities of the organization, leaders are prepared to explore on a real-time, hands-on basis opportunities to grow and expand the organization across multiple fronts. ARAMARK uses its Action Projects to facilitate this process. ELI participants work on their Action Projects, over and above their regular job responsibilities, for approximately six months. At the end of that time, they present their findings to both senior management and their business unit project sponsors. This horizontal project work ensures that "glue" is taking hold within the organization while it reinforces the networks, vocabulary, and business processes established in the early stages of ELI. With their "glue technology" now firmly in place, the organization is prepared to move on to the next phase of the process.

Clarification of Vision and Values. Once the internal operating network has been initiated, the organization is in a position both to define its core competencies and capabilities and to create a process to leverage these capabilities in the marketplace. As ELI evolved, ARAMARK senior management used their budding leadership network to help restate, clarify, and begin the process of communicating the company's vision, values, and competencies across its 130,000 employees. Taking advantage of the anniversary marking ten years of employee ownership, linking that occasion to the creation of a new name and corporate identity, and leveraging both those activities through the ELI internal network, ARAMARK positioned itself to enter the final phase of the process with remarkable momentum.

Use Vision and Values to Drive Business Planning. Once the strategic intent and core competencies have been defined, the organization can use them as the focal point for organizational development initiatives. For ARAMARK, the challenge is to continue its positive momentum by aligning human resource management systems with the strategic imperatives and organizational values created through ELI. Most of the Action Projects were focused on analyzing ways to better manage interfaces with customers, partners, and providers, both internal and external. However, others focused on creating both organizational structures and human resource management systems (compensation, appraisal, and so on) to enable the organization to grow and prosper. ARAMARK is using the input generated by these ELI teams to develop a new leadership competency model, design a related performance appraisal process, rethink compensation systems, and refocus business metrics. In that manner, they are positioning the organization for continued growth and success.

Leadership Development

Organizational development is not the only thing impacted by the shadow pyramid. Leadership development is impacted as well, including career planning processes. Note the different form the oval of activity took in Figure 3.3. This oval does not encompass the entire organization as in previous organizational models. Rather, it spans a segment of the core of the organization and segments of the wings. This drawing symbolizes the personal challenge of leadership and career development within a shadow pyramid—shifting from a focus on control to a focus on networks and relationships.

A leader in this new form is, in effect, a node within the core—a node from which relationships are established, developed, and nurtured. As such, the battered and bruised middle managers of today's corporations, as well as aspiring managers and professionals of tomorrow, find themselves in a unique position. As organizations have pared to their core, middle-level positions slowly but surely have been whittled away. As that has happened, however, those few individuals left in the middle of a shadow pyramid must take on new and critically important roles that are radically different from their former roles in the traditional model.

To succeed in this type of environment, an individual leader must be able to think and operate beyond the confines of his or her organization and job responsibilities. In short, he or she must be willing and able to facilitate opportunities for relationships both within the organization and with external partners.[32] To do this with any degree of success, the leader must be a true expert in his or her area of responsibility—both because there is so little depth in the middle of the organization and because the establishment of business relationships often is related to the leader's ability to link the organization's unique capabilities with the unique needs and capabilities of a partner. This means that leaders not only must be technical experts, they also must truly understand the business of their organization and the potential benefit of various relationships. They must have a detailed understanding of the marketplace in which the organization operates in order to identify opportunities for stretching and leveraging organizational resources through relationship building. They also must be masters of influence processes, capable of leading and directing people and partners over whom they have no direct authority.[33] The scale and scope of these jobs are, by comparison to the traditional model, enormous. In the shadow pyramid, midlevel managers and professionals are the true backbone of the organization. Without their commitment and involvement, the organizational network will simply fall apart. Developing these leadership capabilities, however, is a challenging task.

The establishment of the Daimler-Benz North America (DBNA) leadership network is an example of an initiative designed to challenge leaders to better understand and adjust to their new competitive environment. The company designed the Daimler-Benz North America Leadership Program, with the help of partner Penn State Executive Programs, to bring together the top 150 leaders from DBNA companies, in groups of 25 to 30 at a time, both to build an internal network and to address the leadership development challenge described above. Each group is hosted by one of the DBNA business groups for a four-day session. The first day is spent learning about the host business. The next two days are spent discussing key leadership issues for the future development of the organization. The final day is spent interacting with a board member from parent company Daimler-Benz, AG, who discusses key strategic issues from a worldwide perspective. This gives North American executives an opportunity to further the development of their "glue technology" while at the same time promoting the development of the individual leadership skills of the participants.

Similarly, Carpenter Technology Corporation realized the critical nature of this challenge when it began to establish its own internal network. After having defined a set of strategic imperatives for business development, Cartech partnered with Penn State Executive Programs to create the Strategic Leadership Development Program. This program has been ongoing since January 1994 and has involved the top 120 managers in the company. The program includes a series of five two-and-a-half-day seminars geared to both internal network building and leadership competency development. Action Projects also are being used, with a focus on building the internal and external networks essential to the company's growth and creating a "practice lab" for putting newly developed leadership competencies to work. Cartech managers have visited other countries, analyzed potential partners, and reconfigured systems and processes as part of the effort. Cartech CEO Bob Cardy is intimately involved in the initiative, as are the senior officers of the company. In this manner, the new leadership capabilities being discussed within Cartech are not just topics on a syllabus, they are key strategic issues being discussed, debated, and modeled throughout the company.

Individual Development

A shadow pyramid not only demands a different kind of leader, it creates one as well. To better understand this challenge, think of a leader in the middle of a shadow pyramid. These individuals are less likely to be looking for the type of long-term employment security sought by previous generations of managers; they realize that there is much less of that in this new form. They are more likely to be concerned with finding positions that enhance their overall "employability," with how a given position or assignment contributes to their personal portfolio of skills and experiences, and how their experience with an organization will contribute to their advancement within or apart from their current employer.[34]

Because of this shift in worker values, the issues of employee loyalty and motivation are critical within the shadow pyramid. The form requires a radically new definition of the employer-employee compact, one more focused on open communication, personal involvement, and personal development.[35] For some senior managers, this appears to be a welcome change. It can enable an organization to have a continuous flow of new ideas and "fresh eyes." It can lead to employees becoming more intense, more interested in making their mark on the organization.[36] Yet, left unchecked, this individualistic focus also can lead to the emergence of an army of "mercenaries" in the middle of the organization, mercenaries more concerned with advancing themselves than with advancing the organization.

As companies become more aware of this potential problem, the need for creating some form of glue technology becomes critical, bringing new approaches to human resource management and organizational development to the forefront of the organization's strategic agenda. A shadow pyramid's demand for defined core competencies and a clear strategic intent enables an organization to channel the energy of high-achieving managers and professionals in pursuit of the organization's long-term goals. In addition, the focus on network interactions and project work gives organizations enormous opportunities to truly enrich jobs and challenge capable people. Yet few of these opportunities will be capitalized on unless the organization actively creates strategic leadership development processes.

Aligning Human Resource Management Systems with the New Model

A full-scale discussion of the human resource management implications of a shadow pyramid are beyond the scope of this chapter. However, a look at a few broad implications are in order. First, the sheer scope of the manager's job in this new form demands an individual focus on continuous learning and an organizational focus on continuous development. The logistics of these developmental processes may need to change, however. The idea that leadership development should be focused on identifying and cultivating individual potential of only a select group of high-potential managers must give way to the idea of combining individual development with organizational development to create competitive effectiveness.[37] In addition, the idea of removing a high-potential employee from the business core in order to enable that individual to participate in a longer-term, off-line, formal education experience is likely to be a thing of the past. Instead, companies will endeavor to blend ongoing education with ongoing experience through the more effective use of new educational technologies and action learning experiences similar to those described within ARAMARK and Cartech.[38]

Second, the world of employee education and development, including traditional university degree programs, will be under incredible pressure to adjust to new demands for real-world, on-line, just-in-time training, education, and development practices.[39] Perhaps the most visible example of this challenge is the training, education, and development initiative being mounted by Motorola. The company spends over $100 million annually on these activities and claims to have proof that, when implemented properly, these investments pay off at a rate of 30:1. Motorola is so convinced of the value of the process and its superiority over traditional providers, that they are working to establish their own fully accredited Motorola University.[40]

Finally, employee benefits and reward systems will need to change, adjusting to the demands of the more fluid organizational structures and processes created by a shadow pyramid. Retirement programs and health care benefits will need to be "portable" and more the responsibility of the individual. Reward systems must be more individualized and linked to the accomplishments of networks, project teams, and other types of horizontal business groups.[41] All of these elements of the human resource management infrastructure will need to be reconsidered and redesigned to accommodate the demands of this new organizational form.

BEYOND THE SHADOW PYRAMID

If the shadow pyramid model describes the nature of organizational structure in today's environment, then what's next? Will the pendulum swing back to the traditional pyramid, or will a new model emerge? We believe that, like all good ideas in the field of management, the shadow pyramid idea will be overdone. It will be taken too far, implemented without careful consideration of its ramifications, used as a temporary fix for a much more significant problem. But, when the dust settles, we believe the lessons learned from the shadow pyramid will forever change the nature of effective organizations. As we learn to work in networks and through relationships in a global economy, and as we learn to use technology and information backbones to a fuller extent, the potential benefits of a shadow pyramid will be in even greater demand. Organizations will continue to evolve toward more "virtual" designs, involving dynamic networks of partners operating across many aspects of business operations (see Figure 3.5). As this new structure evolves, the skill sets deemed necessary to operate in today's shadow pyramid will become even more critical to an organization's ability to forge competitive advantage.

The core leadership challenge is framed by an apparent paradox: by defining a set of boundaries around a strategic intent and a set of core competencies, an organization is in a position to become "bound-

Figure 3.5 What's Next? The "Virtual" Corporation

aryless," to grow faster and more profitably than before by leveraging its shadow pyramid partnerships. If the profits from that growth are reinvested to keep the organization's core competencies at the leading edge, the organization creates for itself a powerful cycle of continuous growth, innovation, and development around those unique capabilities that enable it to add value for its customers.

Competing in a knowledge-oriented, information-driven, global economy requires that leaders give serious consideration to the shadow pyramid organizational form as they develop their companies' competitive strategies. The model, in all its simplicity, can help in the visualization of this challenge. The task at hand is to further investigate how to avoid the pitfalls and reap the benefits of the opportunities this new model presents. That task is addressed throughout the remainder of this book.

PART 2

The Process

4

Developing a Roadmap

COMPLEX ORGANIZATIONS HAVE grown increasingly aware that they must take a broader perspective, become more open to external opportunities, and maintain a constant learning orientation to be competitive in today's environment. These demands have created an expanding market for leadership development as traditional programs have been replaced by strategic initiatives. With the substantial increase in resources devoted to this activity, more sophisticated approaches are required to assure an adequate return on the investment. We believe that systems thinking can be a powerful tool for mapping and creating strategic leadership development processes.

It is our hypothesis that powerful forces within the field of leadership development drive both provider and consumer behaviors.[1] Without an understanding of these forces and their origins, companies investing in leadership development will be unable to exert maximum leverage in controlling their future. Armed with an understanding of the systems dynamics, consumers of leadership development and their provider partners should be able to manage the explosive growth in this industry and achieve a satisfactory return on their allocated resources.

In this chapter, a systemic model of leadership development is presented to illustrate the major forces shaping the behaviors and outcomes within the field. By understanding these forces, we can compare our mental models with what is actually occurring. We hope that this insight will lead to specific ways that consumers of leadership development can manage their efforts to achieve, in addition to adequate return on their dollar investment, greater alignment with strategic objectives and achievements.

SYSTEMS THINKING

The concept of systems thinking is not new. Its roots are found in general systems theory, developed by researchers in the 1920s.[2] These researchers began to look at ways in which systems[3] from many different fields of science functioned and discovered that they were all governed by the same general rules of organization. This led to an understanding of how systems in various fields were related to each other and how the behavior of complex processes was driven. Jay Forrester of the Massachusetts Institute of Technology (MIT) has been a leader in applying systems theory to the fields of business and economics. He pioneered its application in economic and organizational systems and established an ongoing stream of research that has been sustained by the Systems Dynamics Group at MIT. In recent years, Peter Senge has popularized many of the concepts of systems thinking through his popular book *The Fifth Discipline*.[4] In the following discussion, we apply some of the concepts of systems thinking to leadership development processes.

Patterns of Behavior

One basic concept within systems thinking is the identification of archetypes. An archetype is simply a pattern of behavior that repeats itself over time. For example, one such archetype is called "escalation," illustrated in Figure 4.1 as the escalation of new product introductions, or product proliferation, which the telecommunications industry is now experiencing. For example, MCI introduces a new product, Friends and Family, which attracts many new customers. This represents a threat to AT&T, so it in turn introduces a new product. When AT&T brings out its product, MCI perceives this as a threat and feels compelled to introduce another new product. As the process continues, it becomes reinforcing (indicated by the symbol ♨ in the middle of the diagram), and the proliferation of products continues. As customers of the telecommunications industry, we have all been bombarded by the numerous offerings of competitors that result from the escalation process. For most of us, the number of options offered has clearly surpassed our ability to evaluate their utility; hence, additional products offer little or no benefit.

Numerous examples of this archetype can be found in a broad range of organizations and activities. The nuclear arms race was a classic geopo-

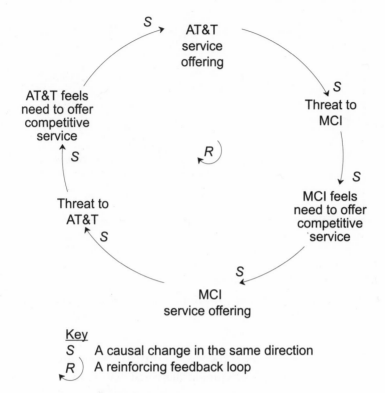

Figure 4.1 The Escalation Archetype

Source: Jack Goodwin and Robert M. Fulmer, "The Systems Dynamics of Executive Education," *Executive Development*, 8, no. 4 (1995). Reprinted by permission.

litical example of this archetype's resulting in behaviors that, in retrospect, made little sense. Many organizations find themselves in severe price competition, another form of this behavior. The important point is that the pattern repeats itself again and again. Organizations and individuals caught in the pattern become victims of the forces driving it, and they often verbalize this feeling openly rather than managing the process to achieve the results they desire. We believe several archetypes have major implications for the field of leadership development.

Factors Driving Leadership Development. The growth pattern for leadership development is similar in nature to that for most other services and can be described, very simply, with a "generic" growth curve, as shown in Figure 4.2. Growth rates increase when the perceived need for

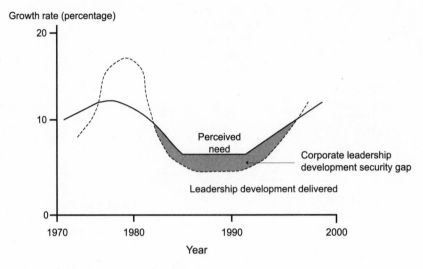

Figure 4.2 Leadership Development Growth Pattern

Source: Jack Goodwin and Robert M. Fulmer, "The Systems Dynamics of Executive Education," *Executive Development*, 8, no. 4 (1995). Reprinted by permission.

leadership development exceeds the level of initiatives that are actually provided (the "Leadership development delivered" curve in the graph). These rates tend to decline when initiatives delivered exceed the perceived need for development. Exceeding the perceived need may occur when consumers (corporate clients) begin to feel they have mastered the current need for increased knowledge or when the quality of the initiatives is perceived as not meeting their needs or expectations. This problem is particularly acute when there is no overarching strategic reason for participation in various leadership development initiatives. Employees at well-managed companies like Johnson & Johnson or General Electric are much less likely to complain of having "attended too many courses" than those at less successful or strategically oriented firms. In other words, they have a greater learning orientation or capacity than many other organizations. This fundamental analysis leads us to hypothesize that the principal factor driving demand for leadership development could be called the "corporate leadership development security gap."

This gap is a function of the two factors presented in Figure 4.2: the perceived need for leadership development, which we will call the leadership development security goal, and the perceived value of programs delivered, or the current leadership development security level. This gap represents the principal force driving the growth of the field.

A Growth Model for Leadership Development. Eventually some limiting factor will be encountered which slows or reverses the growth pattern. The limiting factor may be any of a number of possibilities, including providers' inability to deliver the leadership development demanded (a lack of capacity), an excess of providers saturating the market, or declining economic conditions which reduce investment capital available for leadership development.

As leadership development is delivered, the current "security level" is increased until it exceeds the perceived need; in other words, the security gap is negative (see Figure 4.2). At this time, less leadership development activity takes place. For example, during the early 1980s, expenditures for management development at AlliedSignal increased at a compound rate of almost 40 percent per year. By the mid-1980s, a corporate directive mandated that these expenses be capped or reduced. An outsourcing effort enabled the firm to improve quality and maintain the same level of activity with a 20 percent reduction in cost. After three years of this arrangement, however, management development became a casualty of a corporate cost-cutting initiative.

As we know from systems theory, this balancing process will work in concert with the reinforcing process in an attempt to keep the leadership development security gap in equilibrium. Of course, the world is an imperfect system, and there are significant delays in the development and delivery cycle for this service. Hence, it is unlikely that the goal and the current level will ever remain in equilibrium except for very short periods of time.

Several side effects are likely to occur which complicate the situation. These side effects can be characterized as "organizational arrogance." Assuming that leadership development is delivered properly, organizational learning improves and leads to greater organizational success. An increasing level of organizational success then reinforces organizational learning. However, this can negatively impact the leadership development security goal. After widespread recognition as head of one of the best-managed companies in the world, Johnson & Johnson chairman

Ralph Larsen expressed considerable concern in 1992 that the firm might be caught "in the comfort zone." He insisted that a leadership development initiative be designed specifically to address this issue.

Exerting Leverage on the System. Although the side effect of arrogance has a negative impact, this is not an inevitable development. Rather than allow organizational arrogance to lower the leadership development security goal, practitioners must deliver leadership development that creates increasing capacity and appreciation for greater learning challenges. The elements of organizational success that result from the learning process should include a culture and set of values that promote learning, experimentation and risk taking, a flexible structure with permeable boundaries, reward systems that recognize and reinforce learning, and information that is accurate, timely, and widely shared. In essence, the organizational learning must lead to an organization that recognizes learning as the only source of sustainable strategic success and embraces learning as a core competence of the organization.

Implications of Systems Dynamics

As we review the systems analysis of leadership development, several implications seem to stand out. It appears that corporate investment in leadership development is doomed to repeat a cyclical pattern of expansion followed by contraction unless companies do the following things: (1) focus leadership development initiatives on the strategic agenda of the firm; (2) partner with providers to help their organizations become learning organizations rather than merely increasing their knowledge base through leadership development initiatives; and (3) measure the impact of leadership development efforts on organizational success. These challenges, if met, can help HRD executives to influence their firms' leadership development security goal and will create the leverage to sustain a positive growth pattern.

Based on these observations, we believe that a major shift in the market is currently under way, being driven to a significant degree by the forces outlined in our model. As we note in Appendix A, many traditional leadership development providers are struggling, and a number of new providers have entered the market with considerable success. As the field's participants change and its boundaries shift, rare opportunities to assume leadership in the industry and to shape its future are open to providers that understand the pressures at work. We are convinced that systematic forces will continue to exert powerful influence on the future of the field, and that the most successful practitioners will be those that not only understand these forces, but also are able to gain leverage by managing the factors that create them.

A ROADMAP FOR LEADERSHIP DEVELOPMENT PLANNING

There is a growing awareness among major corporations that executive and organizational development activities must be employed in concert with firm strategy and other human resource programs. This concept of aligning corporate activities also reflects systems thinking. In the following pages, we outline an emerging role for leadership development in the strategic management process, develop a preliminary model for integrating executive development into an organization's strategic planning system, and present a case study of a firm that is committed to developing a systems approach to strategic leadership development.

A recent research report published by the International Consortium for Executive Development Research noted the following observations, which comprise the fundamental redefinition of purpose taking place within the field of leadership development:[5]

1. Executive education and leadership development activities are being highlighted as vital components of the strategic development of a firm, especially with regard to the recognized need for continuous improvement and learning.
2. Organizations are focusing more on organizational development efforts than on individual development as they seek to enhance their ability to adapt to the global competitive environment.
3. In order to leverage their investment in learning, organizations are using fewer external development opportunities and are focusing instead on development activities specific to the organization and more tightly linked to the realities of the workplace.
4. Organizations are planning to increase their level of activity in leadership and organizational development efforts, to help facilitate change and revitalization.

These observations suggest that, as strategic leadership development has matured over the past decade, it has assumed a much more crucial role in the organization. Once an activity offered only to a select few individuals identified as having high potential for future senior leadership positions, leadership development has become a major tool for revitalizing corporations and building learning-oriented competitiveness.

As a result of this change in stature and purpose, the field is undergoing a number of dramatic changes, not the least of which is a growing level of attention by researchers and academics seeking to help redefine the process. For example, in response to a dramatically changing business environment, much attention has been given to identifying the competencies and characteristics of the "twenty-first-century leader." This search for the leader of the future has been a dominant theme in the redefinition of leadership development practices and techniques. At the same time, some critics of contemporary leadership development practices have argued that placing too strong an emphasis on specific leadership competencies is insufficient for preparing managers and executives for enacting complex strategies in the future. By concentrating too heavily on specific competencies, organizations may find they have done a very effective job of developing *yesterday's* leaders for *tomorrow's* business environment.

This debate has led to a careful reappraisal of leadership development activities and a greater push for the development of a systems approach to the function. In this systems approach, all involved parties are actively engaged in the development process. The organization uses development activities to build commitment to a corporate direction and to promote a learning orientation. Individuals are encouraged to take responsibility for their own learning and to encourage the same among their subordinates and colleagues. Leadership development specialists are actively engaged in the development of the core strategic objectives of their organization as well as the development of their individual "clients." All of this activity is focused on enhancing the ability of all parties to engage in continuous learning.

To develop a systems perspective, organizations must endeavor to understand which developmental processes will be most effective under a variety of changing circumstances, for different levels or target groups of participants, and at different stages of individual development, in order to maximize the ability to promote both individual and organizational learning.

Crafting an Integrated Systems Framework

Executive education and training is but one small component of a much more complicated set of choices that companies must make as they strive to identify and develop the critical human resources that will create their firm's superior ability to learn.

One of the major challenges faced by HRD professionals is aligning leadership development objectives more closely with strategic and organizational objectives, something that sounds logical and easy but is very difficult to do. This challenge is made all the more difficult as leadership development has become more of a professional field, with its own language, specialties, and specialists. Clear danger exists that, as subspecialties grow within the field, the prospects for strategic integration could become even more remote.

The model depicted in Figure 4.3 is an attempt to illustrate the necessary linkages among those elements that can leverage leadership development as a force of organizational learning and competitiveness. The model depicts a view of an integrated systems framework for leadership development.

The catalyst for this systems perspective is a focus on the organiza-

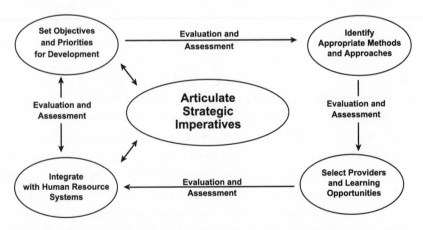

Figure 4.3 Leadership Development Planning: An Integrated Approach

Source: Adapted from D. Ready, A. Vicere, and A. White, "Towards a Systems Approach to Executive Development," *Journal of Management Development* 13, no. 5 (1994): 67.

tion's strategic imperatives, the core drivers of its competitive thrusts. The importance of this core focus has been emphasized throughout this book. Based on these imperatives, the firm must define priority objectives for leadership development as well as target clients for developmental activities. Once these second-level objectives and priorities have been identified, the organization must then determine the appropriate methods for achieving the target objectives and select potential providers of those opportunities. Throughout the entire process, evaluation and assessment are conducted at critical points to ensure that focus and integrity are maintained and expected results generated. The evolving leadership development process is thus fully integrated into the strategic and human resource management systems of the firm. This last step helps maintain a consistent focus on strategic imperatives and priority objectives for development. In this systems framework, all elements of the leadership development system are linked together to focus on the most essential outcome of the process—the development of a sustainable focus on organizational learning and, ultimately, competitiveness.

A Case in Point: Leadership Development at AT&T

One of the best examples we have found to illustrate the power of this model involves the approach to strategic leadership development being taken at AT&T.[6] AT&T is known for its commitment to all forms of management, executive, and leadership development. The company is currently in the process of developing a new Leadership Framework as part of its strategy to reexamine and revitalize *every* aspect of its business. The nature of that framework is summarized in Figure 4.4 and discussed below.

1. Define Strategic Imperatives. At AT&T, former CEO Bob Allen recognized that dramatic shifts had occurred in the global business environment which required changes in the company's strategy, operations, and skills. Allen articulated a set of strategic imperatives for the company which included improvements in customer focus, globalization, diversity, total quality, and innovation. He further suggested that, if AT&T was to compete in this fast-paced, changing environment, an across-the-board transformation of leadership style was required. This became one of the top challenges for HRD at AT&T.

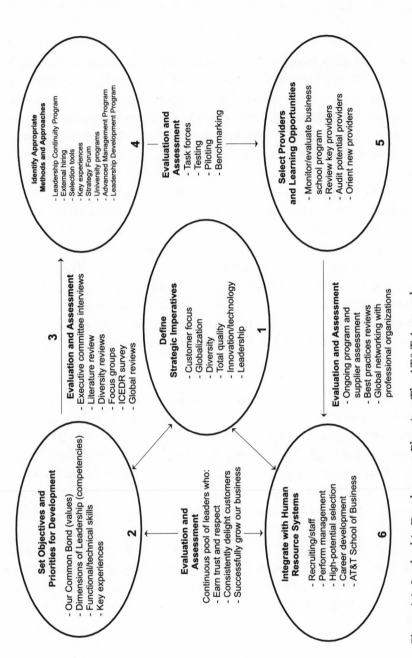

Figure 4.4 Leadership Development Planning: The AT&T Approach

Building depth and breadth of expertise, as well as an understanding of how to integrate both business and technical perspectives and capabilities, was deemed essential for leadership development. For current and aspiring leaders that meant moving beyond a traditional role of one who "knows all and decides," to one who has a knack for awakening knowledge and competence in others. It involved inspiring a *shared* purpose and being responsible for creating the climate necessary to pursue that purpose. It meant developing a process for helping leaders learn how to act with urgency, and how to decisively seize upon opportunities by building partnerships with other people, business units, corporations, communities, industries, cultures, and countries. And it meant finding ways to ensure that leaders embraced and embodied what AT&T called "Our Common Bond," a statement of five major corporate values including "Respect for Individuals, High Standards of Integrity, Dedication to Helping Customers, Innovation, and Teamwork." Enabling AT&T leaders to deliver on these values became a key strategic initiative for human resources in 1993, entitled "Leadership Talent Transformation."

2. Set Objectives and Priorities for Development. The "Common Bond Values" and the strategic imperative for "Leadership Talent Transformation" became the foundation for a process for setting objectives and priorities for leadership development. The Common Bond Values were developed in more detail, with specific illustrations of the kinds of behaviors that could be associated with each. This set of leadership behaviors or competencies became a starting point for discussion of what would become the AT&T "Transformational Leadership Framework." The framework outlined categories of specific functional and technical skills and behaviors associated with the new leadership focus. Each business unit then articulated specific expectations within its area, as well as key experiences for helping managers master the new leadership skill set.

3. Evaluation and Assessment. Between each step in the model, evaluation and assessment are essential. For AT&T, the first step in the evaluation process consisted of becoming familiar with current wisdom and practice in leadership development. Books, articles, and leadership competency frameworks from within AT&T and from other organizations were reviewed and discussed. Based on this information, the team fashioned a straw Transformational Leadership Framework incorporating the best ideas from the diverse sources.

Next, the team tested the straw framework with focus groups of managers from multiple business unit/divisions (BU/Ds) and business functions. These groups validated much of the straw framework but noted some missing and underemphasized concepts. They identified ambiguous phrases and generated written examples of effective and ineffective leadership behaviors for use in developing measurement tools to accompany the framework. Concurrently, interviews with Management Executive Committee (MEC) members and other executives were conducted to gain an understanding of the driving forces affecting their business, and to ensure that the framework addressed the most critical issues faced by the company.

A refined version of the framework was then shared with the cross-BU/D Diversity team and line managers from 18 countries. These sources provided invaluable new perspectives that were incorporated into the framework to make it more inclusive and universally applicable. To further validate the concepts that were being developed, AT&T also participated in a global study of emerging leadership characteristics which was being sponsored by the International Consortium for Executive Development Research. Additionally, the framework was enhanced by the work of a separate Technical Leadership Task Team.

In summary, the Leadership Framework was the result of a broad-based research effort which melded together input from many perspectives. The outcome was a customized set of competencies that reflected what AT&T expected of its leaders to support the successful execution of its new strategic imperatives.

4. Identify Appropriate Methods and Approaches. AT&T has a rich tradition of utilizing varied approaches to leadership and organizational development (see Chapter 7). To ensure alignment, these approaches were carefully coordinated to reinforce the new strategic imperatives being pursued in the Transformational Leadership initiative. Among the many coordinated approaches were new or revised efforts in the following areas:

- Leadership continuity programs
- External hiring strategies

- Key experiences definition

- Internal development programs, including, among others, the Strategy Forum, the Internal Advanced Management Program (senior management), and the Leadership Development Program (middle management)

- Active use of external (university-based) executive programs

- Extensive use of 360-degree feedback

While these methods and approaches were being refined, there was a regular ongoing effort to validate their appropriateness in terms of "best practices," as well as their internal consistency or fit with the firm's new framework and firm's strategic imperatives.

5. Select Providers and Learning Opportunities. AT&T is known for its comprehensive approach to evaluating existing leadership development programs and staying abreast of current developments in the field. This is related to their ongoing, detailed assessment of programs based on feedback from previous AT&T participants. We will provide more details on this process in Chapter 7.

On a regular basis, members of the HRD staff review existing providers as well as key providers being utilized by other leading corporations. AT&T is active in such organizations as Executive Development Network, the International University Consortium for Executive Education (UNICON), the International Consortium for Executive Development Research (ICEDR), and many other networks. Staff members are expected to audit programs offered by potential providers, including individuals and groups that may be potential contributors to internal programs offered by the company. When a provider has been selected to work with the company, effort is made to orient that provider to the company. Each provider is expected to be familiar with both the existing culture and the extent of significant changes being sought. All of these mechanisms have enabled AT&T to develop a comprehensive list of potential providers, all prescreened, that can partner with the company in its strategic leadership development efforts.

6. Integrate with Human Resource Systems. As the new leadership system began to take shape, the Transformational Leadership Framework was incorporated into recruiting and staffing efforts. Job assignments were made in a manner consistent with integrating the new values and competencies with the selection process. The company's performance management system was revised in order to incorporate the new framework. High-potential individuals were identified who seemed to possess the qualities embodied by the new framework. Career development opportunities began to shift toward the new model. The AT&T School of Business, the company's broad-based internal management education arm, incorporated the framework into its extensive catalog of offerings. Alignment was and is a key attribute of the integrated approach at AT&T.

For AT&T, the final and ultimate level of evaluation and assessment is the presence of a continuous pool of leaders who are able to earn trust and respect within the AT&T community, consistently delight customers, and successfully grow the businesses for which they are responsible. Each of these attributes is measured through a customized internal evaluation process that gauges the perceived effectiveness of the company's leadership development process. The ultimate goal is the complete transformation of AT&T's talent pool to provide leadership in the global marketplace.

IMPLEMENTING A SYSTEMS PERSPECTIVE

A systems perspective is essential for corporations to leverage their investment in leadership development. Firms interested in building an integrated leadership development system like that of AT&T need to engage in an orchestrated effort to:[7]

- *Define and articulate their strategic imperatives.* These are the priorities, competencies, and capabilities considered by top management to be the basis of the firm's future competitive advantage and target areas for leadership development.

- *Clarify core objectives for development based on the strategic imperatives.* This should include efforts to define critical competencies and capabilities; engender a market focus throughout the company; build networks to leverage competencies and capabilities; enhance communication and teamwork; change organizational culture; and implement competitive strategies. In addition, the company must prioritize "clients" for development by defining which levels, functions, regions, and competency areas are the most important targets for development initiatives.

- *Select methods and approaches to be used for development,* ensuring consistency with the strategic imperatives and overall learning/development objectives. This could include team or task force assignments, action learning projects, rotational assignments, classroom education, and competency identification and development.

- *Build strategic partnerships* with a select group of leadership development providers to help gain leverage and round out internal resources; reassess those relationships periodically to ensure that they are achieving the objectives initially outlined.

- *Link development processes with human resource practices.* To leverage the impact of leadership development efforts, they must be tightly linked to the organization's human resource management infrastructure, including performance management and reward systems, recruitment and selection procedures, and succession and executive resource planning processes. This final step ensures that a learning orientation becomes ingrained within the organization's culture and operating philosophy.

SUMMARY

A major shift in the field of leadership development is currently under way. This shift is being driven to a significant degree by the forces outlined in this chapter. Those forces suggest a move away from quick-fix education and training initiatives toward a more integrative, systems-oriented approach. As the players in leadership development change and redefine their roles and boundaries, rare opportunities to shape the future are emerging for those who understand the forces at work. We are convinced that the move toward a systems perspective will continue to exert powerful influence on the future of the field. Successful participants will understand this approach and gain leverage by managing leadership development in an aligned, anticipatory manner.

In subsequent chapters, we will present a more detailed analysis of the core elements of this systems process along with recommendations for crafting integrated leadership development planning systems that truly promote and enhance organizational learning and competitive effectiveness.

5

Methods and Priorities

STRATEGIC LEADERSHIP DEVELOPMENT initiatives can and should be a major force for facilitating organizational change and crafting competitiveness. A white paper published by the International Consortium for Executive Development Research noted:

> Executive and [leadership] development must be focused strategically on both the target population and the issues that enable companies to create and sustain superior organizational capabilities. The cultivation of those capabilities is the strongest contribution that executive development professionals can make to improve firm performance and competitiveness.[1]

Three issues must be addressed if leadership development initiatives are to contribute effectively to the creation of such superior organizational capabilities.

1. The initiatives must be linked to the strategic imperatives of the firm.
2. Individual and organizational development must be addressed in parallel through innovative approaches to the leadership development process.
3. A comprehensive, systems-oriented approach must be developed to create and maintain positive organizational momentum.

This systems approach includes establishing priorities for leadership development based on the strategic imperatives of the firm, as well as matching appropriate methodologies with those priorities. This chapter discusses the nature of various techniques and methodologies for leadership development and presents a framework for selecting among them.

Recently, a series of studies was completed by researchers at the Smeal College of Business Administration at the Pennsylvania State University. These studies profiled the evolution of corporate executive education and leadership development initiatives over a 15-year span.[2] A representative sampling of major companies from around the world was surveyed in 1982, 1987, 1992, and 1997 to determine the most-favored leadership development techniques (see Table 5.1).

Responding companies reported that task force/special project assignments, job rotation, and on-the-job training were the most frequently used methods for development within their firms. In-company educational programs, coaching/mentoring, performance feedback, and external educational programs comprised the second tier of methods. Teaching or consulting with fellow employees appeared at the bottom of the list. This reflects a pattern in the research. Experiential methodologies have increasingly gained in emphasis, while traditional programs, especially external programs, have dropped in prominence. Interestingly, performance feedback, highly regarded in 1982, fell out of favor in 1987 and 1992 when it was mentioned by less than 10 percent of the respondents of both surveys as a core developmental technique. We believe performance feedback's impressive return to prominence in 1997 reflects the trend toward increased use of 360-degree feedback as a developmental tool.

The results of these studies reflect a shift in user perspective toward

---

TABLE 5.1 Most-Favored Leadership Development Techniques (percentages)

	1982	1987	1992	1997
Job rotation	20	72	58	64
In-company executive development programs	34	47	56	39
Task forces/special projects	28	32	39	68
External executive development programs	37	48	33	30
On-the-job training	20	28	28	45
Coaching/mentoring	37	26	22	32
Performance feedback	48	6	9	30
Teaching/consulting with other employees	19	1	5	9

Percentages indicate the frequency with which each leadership development technique fell among a company's top three choices.

executive education and leadership development. Work experience and company-specific educational programs have emerged as the core focus of leadership development efforts. These findings support the evolution of the "new paradigm" for leadership development introduced earlier in this book. Companies that subscribe to this new paradigm are more likely to create coordinated leadership development strategies that blend job experience, educational initiatives, guided practical experiences, and targeted performance feedback into a systemic process for ongoing leadership development at all levels of the organization. This type of process is focused not only on individual development, but also on the ongoing development of the organization as a whole.

Although we find tremendous enthusiasm among companies for this new approach to leadership development, most organizations still struggle with the challenge of how best to match individual and organizational development needs with the most appropriate developmental experiences, techniques, and methodologies. The knowledge creation cycle depicted in Figure 5.1 provides a framework for dealing with this challenge.

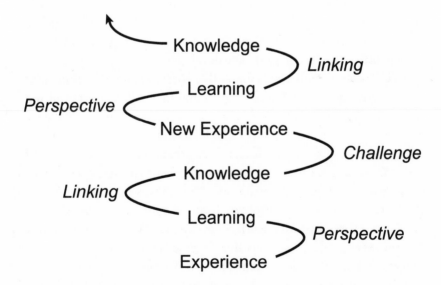

Figure 5.1 Leadership Development: The Knowledge Creation Cycle

Source: A. A. Vicere, "The Knowledge Creation Cycle: A Framework for Assessing Executive Development Techniques," working paper 96-001, Institute for the Study of Organizational Effectiveness, University Park, PA, 1996. Reprinted by permission.

A FRAMEWORK FOR ESTABLISHING OBJECTIVES

The knowledge creation cycle is a model for mapping leadership development processes. It portrays leadership development as a constantly escalating process that builds on the experience base of the leader to create an ongoing cycle of both individual learning and organizational knowledge creation.[3] An understanding of the knowledge creation cycle can enable an organization to dramatically enhance both its ability to learn and its awareness of the appropriate use of various techniques for leadership development. A brief discussion of each stage of the cycle and its implications for leadership development appears below.

Experience

There is an old saying: "Experience is the best teacher." This appears to be especially true when it comes to leadership. In a landmark study on the lessons of experience, Morgan McCall, Michael Lombardo, and Anne Morrison of the Center for Creative Leadership (CCL) found that leaders attributed most of their current success to past work experiences.[4] It is quite reasonable, then, for companies to give a great deal of attention to providing high-potential leaders with challenging and varied work experiences. It is through such experiences that leaders have the opportunity to learn, grow, and develop.

McCall and his colleagues found that there was no such thing as generic work experience. Rather, they found that different types of work experiences provide different opportunities for development. For example, there are different lessons to be learned by a leader operating in a startup situation than for a leader in a turnaround situation. Similarly, shifts from staff to line assignments, or vice-versa, trigger even different sets of developmental opportunities. The authors noted that the most well-rounded leaders were often those who had experienced assignments in several dissimilar work environments. Because of their broader base of experiences, these individuals seemed to be more aware of themselves and more flexible in their approach to leadership challenges.

A brief summary here cannot do justice to the richness of the CCL studies on the lessons of experience. It is clear, however, that the research strongly supports the belief that experience is the key to leadership development. Yet, even if they are involved in diverse, learning-rich work assignments, how many leaders are actually prepared to learn from their experiences? In today's environment of constant change and ongoing time pressures, how many of them actually take time—or even have time—to step back from their experiences to consider lessons learned? Chances are that the answer to both questions is "Very few." That is why a fundamental objective for leadership development is to provide developing leaders both the tools and the opportunities to gather the lessons of their experiences—to gain *perspective.*

Perspective

The most commonly used techniques for helping leaders gain perspective, or learn from their experiences, are

- Classroom education (external, internal, and consortium)
- Feedback approaches
- Personal growth approaches
- New learning technologies
- Coaching/mentoring

This list reflects the longstanding stated goals of classroom-based leadership development programs. The classroom is a valuable and readily accessible forum for giving leaders an opportunity to prepare for and learn from their experiences. Classroom-based programs generally can take the form of externally delivered open-enrollment seminars; internally delivered, customized programs; or consortium-based programs, discussed later in this chapter.

In addition to classroom-based programs, feedback approaches to leadership development, relying primarily on 360-degree assessment, have been rapidly gaining in popularity. These initiatives, often delivered in a classroom format, are designed to help leaders gain a better understanding of their leadership styles and their ability to influence the people around them. Personal growth approaches, such as outdoor adventure experiences, also have gained some degree of notoriety. These initiatives focus primarily on helping leaders gain a better understanding of themselves and their aspirations. New teaching and learning technologies, such as groupware and internet/CD-Rom methodologies, are gaining popularity as techniques for enhancing and expanding traditional classroom-based programs. Finally, mentoring can make a major contribution to leaders' ability to learn from their work experiences.

It may seem obvious to many reading through the above list that the most effective leadership development initiatives would draw from all of the techniques. We agree. Yet, to blend them in the most effective manner, it is important to consider the nature of each one independently. For that reason, a brief discussion of each technique and its potential contribution to leadership development appears below.

Classroom-Based Approaches. Jay Conger recently conducted a "hands-on" study of a number of leadership development programs.[5] Conger or one of his associates actually participated in several programs in order to ascertain their potential contribution to leadership development. In addition to participation, Conger and his colleagues conducted interviews and surveys of program participants to develop a framework for assessing the potential value and contributions of each approach. He categorized these programs into four approaches. Two of those approaches were classroom-based: skill-building approaches, in which complex leader behaviors are broken down into skill sets that can then be taught to leaders, and conceptual approaches focused on the presentation of ideas and concepts for leaders to consider. Two additional categories—feedback approaches and personal growth approaches—will be discussed shortly.

Skill-Building Approaches. As noted previously, skill-building approaches to leadership development assume that leadership is comprised of practical, teachable skill sets that can be taught and developed through a well-designed training experience. These types of programs have traditionally been the backbone of corporate internal leadership training initiatives. Conger noted that certain leadership skill sets did appear to be teachable, particularly in areas like communication and motivation. This was particularly true when the skill sets to be taught could be framed by simple, straightforward models, and when the program process included plenty of practice and opportunities for feedback. However, skill-building approaches did not seem to help with more complex skill sets like "visioning." Furthermore, skill-based programs were often targeted at lower-level managers. Senior leaders frequently, and often erroneously, were assumed already to have mastered the skills in question. Conger noted:

> Skill-building approaches should be the most effective of all because they are under the highest expectations to produce tangible results. And with some leadership skills, this can be the case. The difficulty is that many of the skills currently associated with leadership are quite complex, and a three- or five-day program offers little time to truly develop these in lasting ways. Back on the job, the workings of the organization and the manager's daily life-style may further erode his or her initial efforts to implement skills. Awareness development may be a more realistic expectation for program outcome than actual in-depth skill development.[6]

To maximize the value of skill-building approaches, then, organizations must ensure that the skills being taught and the message being delivered are well known and accepted throughout the organization. Moreover, skill-building approaches are most likely to be effective when the training cascades down from the top of the organization, as discussed in later chapters.

Conceptual Approaches. Conger noted that programs based on conceptual approaches to leadership development assume that leadership is a complex, poorly understood art. Therefore, development programs should focus on creating awareness among developing leaders of the complexities of the leadership challenge. Programs such as university-based executive programs have long been designed around this model.

According to Conger, programs based on the conceptual approach were essential to creating understanding of something as complex as leadership. He reported that such programs could create greater awareness and understanding of the leadership challenge if the conceptual models presented were simple and straightforward; if they were supported by films, case studies, or exercises that illustrated concepts; and if some form of practice in applying the models was provided through simulation or other forms of hands-on exercise. The weakness of the approach was that its effectiveness was almost entirely related to the motivation of the individual participants and their willingness or ability to apply the lessons learned to their personal situations.

Organizations making use of such experiences must, therefore, be sure to establish objectives and expectations with participants prior to their participation. And they must create some mechanism for bridging learning from the program back to the job. Even so, Conger noted,

> ideas and concepts were critically important in framing the notion of leadership in participants' minds—especially when distinctions were being made between leadership and managership. This awareness-building provided the important first step in behavior development and change. Alone, however, it is not sufficient.[7]

Conger's analysis of these two forms of classroom-based programs outlines one of the biggest challenges facing leadership development practitioners; that is, how to take advantage of the strengths and overcome the weaknesses of both approaches when designing leadership development initiatives. In an attempt to deal with this challenge, much attention has been focused on program delivery modes. The three primary delivery modes for classroom approaches are external, open-enrollment programs; company-specific, customized programs; and consortium programs. The strengths and weaknesses of these modes are discussed below.

External Executive Education Programs. External, open-enrollment leadership development programs are among the most commonly utilized leadership development techniques. Perhaps the best known of these experiences are university-based executive education programs. These highly regarded, longer-term (frequently several weeks long), residential programs offered by major business schools around the world have long been recognized as a key element of corporate executive and leadership development strategies.[8]

Because of their longer duration, university-based programs seem to address many of the key challenges posed by Conger: they tend to be built around solid conceptual models, and they tend to involve plenty of case study applications, simulations, and other opportunities for practice. The perceived benefits of university-based executive programs, as indicated by respondents of a study conducted by researchers at Penn State, are that they:

- Provide outside perspective, exposure to other viewpoints, and networking.
- Generalize specialists and broaden their vision.
- Allow executives to reflect on and gain insight into career, work role, personal style, and effectiveness; encourage renewal; and insulate from work.
- Expose executives to faculty experts and latest management information in a high-quality academic setting.
- Expose executives to a variety of programs that cannot be delivered as economically or effectively within the company.
- Complement in-company programs.
- Provide rewards and contribute to self-esteem.[9]

These programs were profiled by survey participants as opportunities to provide leaders with exposure to outside viewpoints, thus enabling them to build external networks, broaden individual perspectives, and promote personal revitalization. All of these benefits seemed to be related to the *individual* development of leaders.

Company-Specific Programs. Corporations increasingly are turning to internal, customized executive education/leadership development programs to address the critical demands of a changing corporate environment. Formerly, these programs tended to focus on skill building. Increasingly, however, customized executive education programs such as the GE, ARAMARK, Johnson & Johnson, and Cartech programs described earlier in this book, are being developed to help companies transition to the global competitive environment, and to help promote a broader conceptual understanding of the strategic directions of the sponsoring organization. Looking again at the Penn State surveys, the perceived benefits of internal programs are shown below.[10]

- Programs are more specific to the organization and its needs
- Help develop an organizational culture, build teams, and implement change
- Provide a discussion forum or idea exchange; internal networking

- Savings in both time and money
- Better control of content, faculty, and participants
- Complementary to external programs
- Provide interaction with top management
- Better availability of resources; scheduling efficiency

From the above discussion, it appears that external, open-enrollment programs serve a different purpose and generate different outcomes than do internal, company-specific programs. External programs seem to be viewed more in the context of individual development. Internal programs seem to be viewed more in the context of organizational development. As such, both types of experience can contribute significantly to the leadership development process when used appropriately. Because the current debate over internal versus external classroom initiatives is so intense, we will devote the entire next chapter to special case study analyses of the impact of each type of program on leadership and organizational development.

Consortium Programs. A relatively new form of classroom-based leadership development is the consortium model. This type of classroom-based experience attempts to blend the perspective-broadening benefits of traditional open-enrollment programs like university-based programs with the specificity of company-specific programs. A group of several companies is brought together by the program sponsor, and a focused curriculum is designed around the specific needs of the member companies. Typically, representatives from member companies participate on a committee that oversees program design and delivery. In addition, teams of participants from member companies attend the program, enabling the discussion to be both specific to each individual organization, yet enriched by the perspectives of other teams.

Rapidly gaining in recognition and respect, the consortium format provides unique opportunities for perspective building. According to Ron Thomas and Cam Danielson, directors of the Indiana University Consortium, "We see the consortium model of executive education as the best of both worlds. It is a unique combination of open enrollment and custom programs that stands alone."[11] In a very unique arrangement that involves multiple business schools as well as multiple companies, the business schools at Miami University (Ohio) and the University of Cincinnati have combined to form the Business Consortium®, a partnership among the two schools and nearly a dozen Cincinnati-area companies. Judy Cornett of corporate member Cinergy Corporation noted:

> Historically, our emerging leaders have participated in development programs throughout the United States designed primarily for the utility industry. The Business Consortium® is providing us a unique learning and partnering opportunity with a diverse business community right here at home.
>
> Collaboration among the membership has resulted in a learning model that allows participants to regulate and apply their own learnings back in the work environment. They learn how to learn the lessons their particular job offers up each day.
>
> This cooperative effort is a win-win for both the business and academic communities. The initial added value of our participation has been the direct access to the bounty of expertise and experience right here in Cincinnati.[12]

It is clear that the consortium model holds a great deal of promise for both users and providers of executive education and leadership development. It is an emerging format that could address a major need for blending individual and organizational development in a focused manner (see the World Bank EDP description in Chapter 9).

In addition to classroom-based approaches to leadership development, there are several other approaches that can contribute significantly to perspective building.

Feedback Approaches. Conger described feedback approaches as initiatives that operate under the assumption

> that many who aspire to be an effective leader already possess in varying degrees and strengths the skills they need. The aim of the program, then, is to point out to participants their own key strengths and weaknesses so they can work to strengthen their weaker skills and can act with confidence when relying on their strengths.[13]

Feedback-based programs tend to rely heavily on 360-degree feedback, also known as circular feedback, a process in which an individual rates him- or herself on a set of leadership dimensions, then is subsequently rated on the same dimensions by his or her boss, several peers, and several subordinates. In some instances, the ratings of customers also are obtained. The consistencies or inconsistencies across the various ratings are then used as the basis for discussions with the individual about performance, potential, and development.[14] For many organizations, 360-degree feedback is linked to competency modeling, a technique discussed later in this chapter.

Conger himself attended the Center for Creative Leadership's Leadership Development Program, one of the most highly regarded and popular leadership development programs in the world. This one-week program makes heavy use of 360-degree assessment, other forms of testing, peer and staff feedback, and goal setting to help individual leaders learn about their strengths as a leader, confront their weaknesses, and develop a plan of action for improvement. Although he found the program to be both stimulating and a worthwhile personal experience, he noted:

> Our results . . . indicated that feedback often had less impact than we had expected. Only in a few cases did managers describe feedback as significantly enhancing their leadership skills. Factors within the individual and outside the program played major roles in mitigating the contributions of feedback.[15]

To maximize the potential contribution of the feedback approach, then, it is essential that the company manage the development context, making sure the feedback has meaning for the participant, and that resulting development plans are linked to appropriate elements of the company's human resource management infrastructure—specifically, development, appraisal, and reward systems, as noted in Chapter 3. The Westinghouse example discussed later in this chapter will further illustrate this point, as will the research on the impact of followup and action planning activities conducted by Keilty, Goldsmith & Co. discussed in Chapter 8.

Personal Growth Approaches. According to Conger, personal growth approaches assume that

> leaders are individuals who are deeply in touch with their gifts and passions. Therefore, only by tapping into and realizing one's passions can a person become a leader. Thus, if training can help managers get in touch

with their talents and sense of purpose, they will presumably have the motivation and enthusiasm to formulate inspiring visions and to motivate those who work for them.[16]

Conger noted that the goal of personal growth approaches was to help participants understand the extent to which they have given up their personal sense of power and efficacy in their personal and professional lives. This is accomplished through outdoor adventures that involve some degree of risk taking, such as high-ropes courses,[17] or indoor experiences that force participants to reflect on the discrepancy between their personal aspirations and their current state of affairs. Administered appropriately, these experiences can be both eye opening and empowering.

Conger participated in an outdoor adventure experience at the Pecos River Learning Center in New Mexico, where he engaged in trust walks, ropes courses, and other forms of personal challenge. His indoor experience was in ARC International's VisionQuest program, in a highly interactive process for developing a personal vision for the future. Overall, he noted that the elements of action, experience, and risk taking in these approaches tended to magnify the learning experience. Yet he also noted that the learning seemed to be focused on areas most salient to participants at the particular time of their program experience. Still, he reported,

> the power of personal growth approaches is that they directly challenge us to examine our most deeply felt emotions and most entrenched values. And if leadership is in part the emotional manifestation of one's passionate interests and aspirations, then this is where a significant portion of training must take place.[18]

The question becomes, however, whether face-to-face developmental interventions like those discussed thus far are the only medium that can promote leadership development.

Technology-Based Learning. In addition to the above approaches, there is increased interest in the use of electronic media and telecommunications to develop leaders. In a recent article, it was noted that most organizations currently are using new technologies to supplement traditional programs and methodologies.[19] For example, participants are often kept in touch during a multiphase leadership development program through email, voice mail, or videoconferencing.

Many programs and networks based on various forms of groupware are also appearing. A recent *Forbes ASAP* article defined groupware as a tool "designed to enhance productivity by allowing users to share information . . . it also allows individuals to easily customize the view of this information to suite their needs."[20] The term *groupware* can include technologies such as group decision support systems, teleconferencing systems, videoconferencing systems, and desktop conferencing systems. Through the use of groupware, groups or "classes" of people from various locations can be electronically linked to discuss issues, solve problems, analyze data, or simply network.[21] All of these tools enable the creation of the "virtual classroom."

Taking advantage of this development, Carrollton, Texas–based Westcott Communications has launched EXEN—the Executive Education Network. A number of major business schools, including Penn State, Wharton, the University of Southern California, the University of North Carolina, Southern Methodist University, Carnegie-Mellon, and Harvard have signed on with the network to conduct executive education programs via telemedia in a format often labeled "distance learning." Companies subscribing to the service will have programs beamed to their remote sites, where "classes" of students will interact while attending broadcast seminars by noted faculty. All students will have direct access to each other and electronic access to the faculty for questions and discussion during the program. EXEN is the tip of the iceberg in the movement toward delivering classroom-based "conceptual" programs via electronic media. In this distributed format, organizations have the potential to maximize the audience for programs while maintaining some degree of classroom interaction and intimacy.

The Fuqua School of Business recently launched its Global Executive MBA Program, an ambitious attempt at conducting virtual classes worldwide. Duke initially attracted 45 executives, managers, and entrepreneurs from 14 nations, who paid $75,000 apiece to take part in the program. Equipped with laptop computers, the students participate in class debates, complete team projects, take tests, and interrogate visiting experts in cyberspace. For face-to-face contact, they meet every three months in two-week sessions held on four continents.[22]

On a slightly different note, LOMA, the Atlanta-based association of life insurance companies, is offering courses for member companies on topics such as "The ABCs of Multimedia Training" and "Management Development and Multimedia Training." These types of courses offered by growing numbers of providers establish the foundation for an organization to engage in interactive distance learning—training programs distributed to multiple sites through the use of multimedia technology. Federal Express has spent almost $70 million to develop an automated interactive video disk (IVD) training system at over 700 company locations. The system includes self-administered tests for skill upgrades.[23] IBM has distance learning projects in multimedia interactive learning with Cal Tech, Rensselaer Polytechnic Institute, and the state of Alabama.[24] Similarly, the Institute for Management Studies (IMS), a highly successful provider of quality executive education seminars, has launched Athena Interactive Corporation, an award-winning producer of CD-ROM–based programs. Even the Harvard Business School Press, the venerated publisher of cases, books, and journals, has ventured into electronic media through the production of CD-ROM and other electronic media–based materials.

Despite all of this activity, technology-based learning is still "finding itself" as a tool for leadership development. Although it has enormous potential, the role technology will play in future leadership development efforts is still to be determined.

Coaching/Mentoring. A frequently mentioned, but often misunderstood technique for promoting perspective involves coaching and mentoring by bosses or more experienced colleagues.[25] Mentoring can be defined as a relationship in which a person of greater experience or expertise teaches, guides, or develops a person with less experience, helping him or her to perform more effectively or to advance in the organization.

In investigating the potential role of coaching/mentoring in the leadership development process, McCall and colleagues noted that:

> Mentoring, in the sense of long-term apprentice/teacher relationships, was rare or nonexistent among these successful senior executives. Between their own rapid advancement and the movement of their bosses, they were seldom with the same person for as long as three years. What seemed to matter most was almost the opposite anyway: exposure to a variety of bosses, good and bad, who possessed exceptional qualities of various kinds.[26]

The researchers found that bosses frequently were mentioned as sources of significant learning for developing leaders from several perspectives. Through their observations and advice, bosses could round out and fill in the gaps in an individual's experience base. For example, bosses could teach some lessons that assignments alone could not, particularly in the area of values and ethics. In addition, a boss's personal approach to the job could serve as a counterbalance to the lessons of a particular individual's experience, again impacting values and perspectives on leadership roles by providing a "standard," either good or bad, against which individuals could measure themselves.

The researchers noted that few bosses actually were good teachers. Yet, as with experiences, exposure to a variety of bosses could have a powerful, positive impact on an individual leader's development. Perhaps most important, bosses could add perspective to experience by helping developing leaders crystallize values—both organizational and personal. This could help them develop a broad-based view of what leaders do, form opinions on how good and bad leaders behave, and understand and cope with organizational politics.

Some organizations, such as AT&T, Bell Labs, Johnson & Johnson, Federal Express, Merrill Lynch, and others, have inaugurated formal mentoring programs. The Hoechst Celanese Specialty Chemicals Group has launched a program staffed by volunteers who express a willingness and have demonstrated the ability to mentor colleagues. Participants in the program report that they have received useful guidance and advice with regard to performance, career advancement, visibility, and other critical developmental issues.

It also is quite common for organizations to use external mentors, often consultants or well-known university professors, to provide advice and support for senior leaders facing critical issues or challenges. Organizations like the Levinson Institute in Cambridge, Massachusetts, specialize in this activity, as do certain staff at think tanks like the Center for Creative Leadership.[27]

Summary. As noted earlier, a review of perspective-building techniques readily suggests that the most effective leadership development process is likely be a blend of all of the above approaches and delivery modes. Classroom programs can be used to promote conceptual awareness of critical issues and enhance essential skill sets. Within that mode, external programs can be used to provide leaders with an awareness of broad-based challenges and opportunities. Internal programs can be used to develop necessary skill sets and facilitate understanding of the strategic directions and expectations of the company. Consortium programs might be designed to bring the best of both worlds to the leadership development process, focusing on specific developmental issues within the multiple contexts of a diverse group of sponsoring organizations. Feedback and personal growth programs can help leaders better understand themselves and empower them to create a better future. New technologies can be employed to expand and enhance traditional approaches to training and development. Mentoring might be relied on to round out and fill in gaps in an individual's experience base. Blended together, all of these techniques help to facilitate *learning*, the next step of the knowledge creation cycle.

Learning

Shaw and Perkins noted that learning is "the capacity to gain insight from one's own experience and the experience of others and to modify the way one functions according to such insight."[28] When leaders are given the opportunity to step back and see how their experiences have contributed to their growth and development, they are far more likely to learn. This type of learning is the cornerstone of individual development. Yet more must be done if an individual leader's learning is to be turned into *knowledge*, a permanent part of that leader's intellectual repertoire as well as an integrated element of the organization's collective knowledge base. As noted by Ikujiro Nonaka,

> In an economy where the only certainty is uncertainty, the one sure source of lasting competitive advantage is knowledge. When markets shift, technologies proliferate, competitors multiply, and products become obsolete almost overnight, successful companies are those that consistently create new knowledge, disseminate it widely throughout the organization, and quickly embody it in new technologies and products.[29]

Converting learning to knowledge, both individual and organizational, demands an additional step in the leadership development process, one we will call "linking."

Linking

As discussed earlier in this book, traditional leadership development stopped at the point of individual learning. The idea of linking learning to the workplace often was ignored, with the occasional exception of performance appraisal systems or process-oriented organizational development interventions. New approaches to leadership development pay close attention to this critical step, leveraging individual learning by providing opportunities for leaders to put their "newfound" perspective to work within the organization.

When linking opportunities are individual-based, the individual grows as a leader. However, when linking is team-based, individual learning is shared across team members and applied to the resolution of defined organizational challenges. This type of team-based leadership development helps convert individual learning into a collective base of organizational knowledge, thereby contributing to organizational growth and development. Techniques for linking learning to the workplace include

- Performance appraisal
- Teaching/training/facilitating
- Task force/project team assignments
- Action learning

Performance Appraisal. With current leadership development expenditures in the billions of dollars, it would appear logical for organizations to take pains to link development to the immediate work environment. Performance appraisal processes are a readily available and powerful technique for doing so. Reporting on a recent study, C. Longnecker and D. Gioia noted:

> Although executive appraisal is a challenging and frequently delicate proposition, it is clear that executives benefit from systematic reviews. Appraisal has long been shown to be effective for letting people know where they stand, improving productivity, enhancing growth and development, and making training, promotion, and compensation decisions.[30]

Based on their research, Longnecker and Gioia listed several key myths about executive performance appraisal processes, perhaps the most important of which was the myth that executives neither need nor want structured performance reviews. In fact, every executive who participated in their structured interview process dismissed that notion and indicated that systematic feedback in some form was crucial. Despite the critical nature of performance appraisal processes, the previously mentioned Penn State study of executive development trends found that reliance on performance appraisal as a leadership development technique had declined dramatically between 1982 and 1992.[31] Similarly, in a more recent survey of more than 400 managers, Longnecker found only about one-quarter of the participants indicated a level of satisfaction with their organization's appraisal process.[32] Longnecker and Gioia further found that, the higher a manager rises in an organization, the less likely he or she is to receive quality feedback about job performance. They noted:

> One of the most frequently cited concerns of neophyte and even journeyman executives was the fear of taking executive action not understanding that their actions were considered to be a mistake by superiors.
>
> Making mistakes might be acceptable; not knowing they are mistakes is not. Naturally, the ambiguous executive environment breeds situations where criteria for such judgments are not easily established. And that is exactly the reason that executives want regular feedback, so that they can get on track, stay on track, or if necessary, get back on track.[33]

It is clear that performance appraisal processes have the potential to be a major tool for leadership development which can help shape performance and link that performance to the reward and development systems of the organization. It is equally clear that performance appraisal and related performance management processes merit much deeper consideration by organizations designing strategic leadership development systems.

Teaching/Training/Facilitating. Another very effective way to help developing leaders link their individual learning to the workplace is to require those leaders to teach others what they have learned. The discipline needed to structure a "lesson plan" forces leaders to take stock of what they know and apply it to improved performance on the job. At the same time, by transferring the individual learning of a leader to his or her "classes," that learning is shared throughout the organization, creating powerful opportunities for organizational development.[34] For example, when Motorola made expansion into Asian markets a priority, 100 senior executives were immersed in the analysis of how to move forward, then were charged with passing along the lessons of their analysis to the next 3,000 managers throughout the company.[35] Clearly, this technique can be a very effective mechanism for both individual and organizational development.

Task Force and Project Assignments. Temporary assignments such as task forces and special projects provide a valuable source of linking opportunities. Although such assignments are often met with a less-than-enthusiastic response by those chosen to participate, they can be very effective developmental experiences.[36]

The previously mentioned CCL studies on the lessons of experience reported that task force and project assignments give organizations a chance to expose developing leaders to different types of leadership situations, thereby enhancing their potential for development. These experiences also benefit developing leaders by helping them realize that they cannot be experts on everything, that there are others within the organization with complementary capabilities who are essential to both personal and organizational success. Such insights not only promote individual development, they also lay the foundation for internal leadership networks,[37] so crucial to the transfer of knowledge throughout the organization.

Action Learning. Although task force and project assignments can create a foundation for the creation and transfer of knowledge throughout an organization, action learning can help institutionalize the process. C. Wick and L. Leon noted that action learning helps make experiential learning intentional and deliberate.[38] According to V. Marsick and colleagues, action learning involves "learning by doing, but it is not a simulation. . . . It is 'training' that takes the form of an actual business problem for teams of learners to solve together."[39] The authors noted that the basic characteristics of an action-learning initiative are:

- Working in small groups to solve problems
- Learning how to learn and think critically

- Building skills to meet the training needs that emerge during a project
- Developing a participant's own theory of management, leadership, or employee empowerment—a theory that is tested against real-world experiences as well as established tenets

Tracing the evolution of action learning from its roots in the United Kingdom, Louise Keys added that action learning should involve problems that are current and "live," that there should be often a set advisor present throughout each team's life, to assist in their progress, and that the clients—often top executives—should agree to attend an evaluation meeting and listen to the teams' results.[40]

Team-based action learning initiatives can be a very powerful mechanism for linking learning both to the workplace and to the strategic agenda of the firm. Through action learning, an organization can convert individual learning into organizational knowledge through the hands-on resolution of real business problems. Because the projects are conducted in teams, learning is shared across members, networking is reinforced, new perspectives are encouraged, and leadership skills are practiced. All of this takes place within the context of the organization's strategic imperatives, helping to bring those imperatives to life and give them meaning throughout the company. In addition, action learning can help resolve business issues related to the pursuit of strategic imperatives, creating an additional return on investment for the company.

The examples of ARAMARK and Cartech discussed in Chapter 3 demonstrate this power. Both organizations have developed a set of strategic imperatives that is being used to initiate change and reinvigorate the competitive nature of the company. These strategic imperatives provide the context for action learning–based development. Both organizations have created leadership development programs for their senior leaders. Both are committed to building internal networks and promoting cross-organizational interaction to leverage the firm's resources. In addition, both companies have demonstrated the courage to use their own business issues as "live case studies" around which these interactions are developed. These case studies have taken the form of action learning initiatives that involve teams of leaders working together to address critical organizational opportunities within the context of the newly developed strategic imperatives.

As a result of their use of action learning techniques, both companies have enhanced face-to-face interactions among their managers, increased understanding of and commitment to current business directions, and provided hands-on leadership development experiences. Through these interactions and experiences, each company has leveraged the commitment and involvement of its managers in setting and implementing business policy decisions. The companies themselves have become learning laboratories, with the success of current business initiatives the "test" of how well the organization and its leaders have learned their lessons.

To maximize the impact of action learning techniques, each company has devised a process whereby the lessons to be learned are effectively developed by the program participants themselves. Although each company has developed a "program," complete with faculty and content, the faculty and content are there to stimulate corporate leaders to rethink the effectiveness of their organization and its business processes. The formal program is thus a means, not an end in itself. The end is the hands-on resolution of critical business challenges by teams of leaders. This type of developmental process, complete with the tension and contention it generates, becomes a source for continuous creation and dissemination of organizational knowledge, the next stage of the cycle.

Knowledge

Nonaka noted that "making personal knowledge available to others is the central activity of the knowledge-creating company. It takes place continually and at all levels of the organization."[41] When groups of individual leaders have had the opportunity to work together, share personal learnings, and solve real business problems, they have developed frameworks for creating new organizational knowledge. In effect, they have collectively crafted new ways of thinking, operating, and performing for the organization. This new knowledge can serve as the basis for transforming an organization's culture and operating perspective by making the organization what Stan Davis and Jim Botkin called a "learning business."[42]

Strategic leadership development initiatives are geared not only to developing individual leaders, but also to creating opportunities for leaders to share their experiences across the organization in order to grow the overall "intellectual capital" of the business. Through strategic leadership development processes that include team-based action learning activities, organizations are able to leverage their intellectual capital and thereby enhance organizational development. When these team-based organizational development initiatives are tightly linked to the strategic agenda of the firm, an organization can create incredible momentum for transformation and change. The leadership development processes of the many benchmark companies discussed throughout this book are good examples of this form of knowledge creation.

Challenge

To continue the creation of new knowledge—in effect, to become a learning organization—organizations must continue to provide new challenges to leaders.[43] These challenges include new opportunities to learn, through

- Rotational assignments
- Stretch assignments
- Developmental assignments (startups, turnarounds, international, and staff-line)

The list covers the full range of experiential opportunities suggested by M. McCall and colleagues.[44] Engaging leaders in a continuous learning process that includes new experiences and new opportunities to gain perspective stimulates new individual learning, new linking opportunities, and ultimately new opportunities to create organizational knowledge. This, in turn, facilitates ongoing renewal throughout the organization.

PUTTING THE CYCLE TO WORK

Leadership development initiatives can be a key mechanism for revitalizing a company and crafting organizational competitiveness. By combining an understanding of the knowledge creation cycle with the focus of an organization's strategic imperatives, the stage can be set for purposeful leadership development. Westinghouse Electric Corporation presents an interesting case study of a company engaged in such a process.

For decades, Westinghouse has been a pillar of American industry. Although the company has seen some ups and downs over its lifetime, it has remained a well-known, well-respected business entity. Then, in 1992, disaster struck. The Financial Services unit of Westinghouse had moved well beyond its traditional role as an internal financing arm of the company and had dramatically and profitably expanded its portfolio of loans, particularly in the then-booming U.S. real estate market. When that market collapsed in 1992, Westinghouse was left with billions of dollars of bad loans, a plunging stock price, and impending disaster.

As a result of this chain of events, Westinghouse CEO Paul Lego resigned and was replaced by Michael H. Jordan in June of 1993. Jordan, a 19-year veteran of PepsiCo and 10-year veteran of McKinsey & Company, mounted a transformation effort to position Westinghouse to regain much of the luster lost during the tumultuous period that preceded him. To create an engine for this turnaround, Jordan and Westinghouse coupled a focus on strategic revitalization with a commitment to leadership development, in an effort to transform the operating culture of the company. A model depicting the process they created appears in Figure 5.2.

One of Jordan's first initiatives was to define a set of five strategic imperatives for Westinghouse. These imperatives, listed in Figure 5.2, focused on both financial stability and business growth. A leadership competency model was developed to ensure that Westinghouse leaders had the necessary skills and capabilities to achieve those strategic imperatives. Assessment processes were revamped to profile the company's leadership talent pool. A set of leadership development initiatives was designed to help communicate the strategic imperatives and competencies throughout the organization and to address critical skill or perspective gaps that existed within the talent pool. These initiatives included topical workshops, executive education programs, discussion sessions with the CEO, and action learning initiatives. The entire process was reinforced by linking it to the company's performance review and compensation systems.

Although Westinghouse is still in trouble, and although the company will be splitting up into separate operating units, the company's leadership development initiatives played a critical role in the reorganization efforts by serving as a communications medium and as a mechanism for engaging leaders in discussions of the strategic context of the firm.

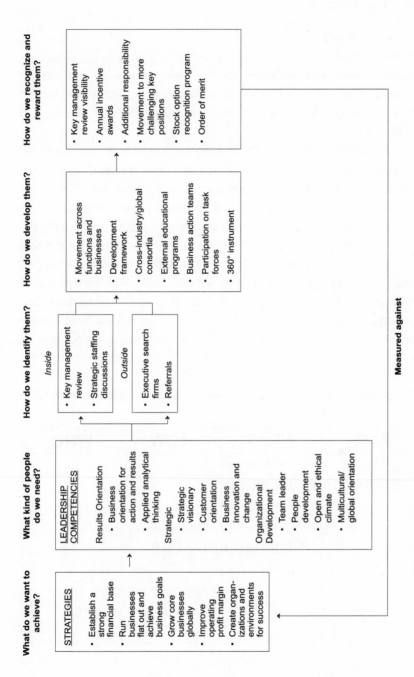

What do we want to achieve?

STRATEGIES

- Establish a strong financial base
- Run businesses flat out and achieve business goals
- Grow core businesses globally
- Improve operating profit margin
- Create organizations and environments for success

What kind of people do we need?

LEADERSHIP COMPETENCIES

Results Orientation
- Business orientation for action and results
- Applied analytical thinking

Strategic
- Strategic visionary
- Customer orientation
- Business innovation and change

Organizational Development
- Team leader
- People development
- Open and ethical climate
- Multicultural/global orientation

How do we identify them?

Inside
- Key management review
- Strategic staffing discussions

Outside
- Executive search firms
- Referrals

How do we develop them?

- Movement across functions and businesses
- Development framework
- Cross-industry/global consortia
- External educational programs
- Business action teams
- Participation on task forces
- 360° instrument

How do we recognize and reward them?

- Key management review visibility
- Annual incentive awards
- Additional responsibility
- Movement to more challenging key positions
- Stock option recognition program
- Order of merit

Measured against

Figure 5.2 Leadership Development: An Integrated Approach at Westinghouse

Moving Forward

The Westinghouse case illustrates the power of linking an organization's strategic agenda with leadership development processes. It also surfaces the need to link various methodologies together to address the "why," "what," "how," and "who" of strategic leadership development, as noted in Figure 5.3.

As the model suggests, perspective-building activities involving various conceptual, skill-building, feedback, or personal growth approaches seem to be most effective in addressing the "why" and "what" of strategic leadership development. These activities provide excellent forums for outlining challenges, presenting information, discussing and clarifying issues, and comparing ideas, practices, and processes—for creating awareness of *why* individual leaders and their organizations need to change in order to perform effectively. In addition, they provide a good first-stage opportunity to discuss *what* needs to be done if an individual or an organization is to succeed, as well as *what* leaders have learned from their experiences. As discussed previously, these activities provide leaders with opportunities to gain perspective on themselves and their organizations.

Although perspective building is an effective method for addressing

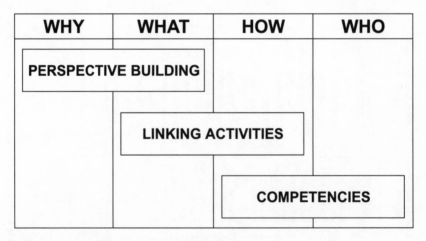

Figure 5.3 Elements of Executive Development

Source: A. A. Vicere, "The Knowledge Creation Cycle: A Framework for Assessing Executive Development Techniques," working paper 96-001, Institute for the Study of Organizational Effectiveness, University Park, PA, 1996. Reprinted by permission.

the "why" of organizational and individual development, and although it can introduce leaders to "what" needs to be done for them and their organizations to maintain effective performance levels, transferrable learning is more likely to occur if discussions of "what" needs to be done are linked to actual hands-on practice in critical thinking and problem solving. Performance appraisal systems and action learning projects, such as those in the Cartech and ARAMARK examples, are very effective vehicles for ensuring that the lessons of programs are linked to the real-world work environment. In addition, these activities provide organizations with an opportunity to assess the "how" of strategic leadership development by providing a forum in which particular skills, concepts, or capabilities can be applied to leadership decision making in a guided fashion and thereby can be readily integrated into individual and organizational management practices.

Leadership competency models like that developed by Westinghouse take the process a step farther by helping to clarify "how" an organization expects the leadership process to be carried out, providing even greater specificity to performance expectations. In addition, the creation of organizational competency models addresses the question of "who" is most likely to succeed in a leadership position, contributing greatly to the appraisal and succession planning processes. This bridge to selection and appraisal helps to link the leadership development process to HR systems within the organization, giving it greater credibility, accountability, and opportunity for impact. In addition, analysis of the database created during competency assessment can help frame the objectives and directions of next-generation leadership development programs, bringing the process full circle.

Because competency modeling is rapidly gaining attention as a leadership development technique, we will discuss the process in more detail below.

The Role of Competency Models

Companies today are spending an enormous amount of time and money developing leadership competency models. Esque and Gilbert noted:

> The idea is to define a set of competencies for each job in the organization—a list of things the job holder must be able to do. These job specific

competencies become the basis for hiring, developing and compensating employees within those jobs.[45]

To say that the development of competency frameworks is big business is an understatement. Organizations like the Center for Creative Leadership in Greensboro, North Carolina, Hay McBer in Boston, Personnel Decisions, Inc. (PDI), in Minneapolis, KGC in Rancho Santa Fe, California, and others do an incredible volume of business helping organizations develop competency models. These models often are translated into 360-degree assessment processes and serve as the heart of the sponsoring company's leadership development strategy.

Competency models can be invaluable. They can help organizations profile the nature of effective leadership and effective performance. They can serve as a basis for performance assessment, appraisal, and 360-degree assessment tools. They can assist in profiling both jobs and potential candidates for those jobs. They can be the basis for assessing and profiling an organization's leadership talent pool, providing an ongoing needs assessment for future leadership development initiatives. All of these contributions are significant.

But, despite the potential benefits of competency modeling, the activity has many critics. T. Esque and T. Gilbert noted that "the danger is that the term 'competencies' can lead people to err by focusing on behaviors instead of on accomplishments."[46] Doug Ready of the International Consortium for Executive Development Research goes even further:

> Companies that place too great an emphasis on leadership competencies run the risk of developing a "programmatic framework" that often results in their doing a very good job of training *yesterday's* leaders. Companies would be well served to adopt a "competitiveness framework," which focuses on both today's *and* tomorrow's challenges. The process of exploring competencies should be directed toward one goal: creating competitive capabilities and a sense of preparedness for the future.[47]

Ready defined three types of competencies:

1. *Enduring competencies* related to a sense of identity and purpose within the organization.
2. *Contextual* competencies related to the strategic agenda of the firm.

3. *Process* competencies related to the ability of both the individual leader and the firm to continuously learn, improve, and grow.

Based on these classifications, Ready crafted an *International Competitive Capabilities Inventory* which blends an assessment of the strategic organizational capabilities essential for competitiveness in the global marketplace with an assessment of individual leader capabilities that are essential to the organization's ability to craft those competencies.[48]

Such a strategic approach to competency modeling can make a major contribution to the development of an organization. For example, Allen-Bradley, a highly profitable division of Rockwell International and a world leader in the design and manufacture of automation and process controls, has used competency assessment as a tool for implementing strategic change. CEO Jodie Glore has launched the company on an ambitious growth plan driven by four key imperatives: quality, reduced cycle time, globalization, and leveraging alliances. Ready's *International Competitive Capabilities Inventory* is being used by Glore and Mary Eckenrod, director of Human Resources Development, to link leadership development to the strategic imperatives of the firm through the creation of a strategic "learning plan" for the organization.[49]

Similarly, the Westinghouse competency model discussed previously was used to define a new set of leadership behaviors. These behaviors were part of a dramatic culture change taking place within the firm. The Westinghouse competency model was developed by an internal task force to set new organizational standards for leadership performance. It served as the basis for the company's Key Management Review process (selection and succession planning) and for portions of the appraisal process. In effect, the model was being used as an instrument of influence, linking the firm's new strategic imperatives to the new set of performance standards for managers. As such, the framework was a powerful engine in the Westinghouse reorganization process.[50]

Competency modeling can be of tremendous value to an organization. The issue is whether the competency model takes on a life of its own, or whether an organization uses the model to define and craft opportunities for building competitiveness. When carefully worked into the strategic leadership development process, competency models can be a powerful tool for defining leadership roles and expectations, clarifying organizational directions and directives, and linking leadership development to other HR processes such as appraisal, succession, and compensation. Used ineffectively, competency models can be a symbol of the status quo, an anchor in past behaviors that have rapidly become bad habits in a changing marketplace.

SUMMARY

Executive education and leadership development, when viewed from the strategic context described in this chapter, can have powerful, positive impacts on corporate performance. For that to happen, however, an organization must have a well-defined, well-aligned set of strategic imperatives that frame how it plans to build competitive advantage in the marketplace. This strategic agenda must then serve as the basis for the establishment of developmental processes that facilitate progress toward the future.

From our analysis, it appears the leadership development demands of an organization's strategic agenda are best addressed through a balanced portfolio of methods that address both individual and organizational development. Within benchmark companies, there is a clear understanding of the role each of these methodologies plays in the leadership development process. Work experience is seen as the key driver of individual development. Programs are designed to help build perspective and outline the "why" and "what" of continued individual development. Linking activities such as performance appraisal and team-based action learning projects are used to provide hands-on practice, clarifying the "what" and facilitating the "how" of development, ultimately promoting knowledge creation and organizational development. Competency models are created to help the organization institutionalize the "how" as well as define and delineate "who"—who is likely to succeed in a leadership position, how will they perform their duties, and how the company will assist them to develop to their fullest potential. Together, these elements comprise the basic tool kit for creating a strategic leadership development process.

6

Company-Specific or External Programs?

ONE OF THE MOST hotly debated issues in leadership development today is the role of the classroom in leadership development. Although most people would agree that classroom training adds an important dimension to leadership development, it is far more difficult to get agreement on when, where, and how to use classroom initiatives in the process. The growing interest in company-specific educational programs discussed throughout this book has further confused the issue, creating intense debate over the role and potential contribution of external open-enrollment programs like those traditionally offered by university business schools. Some critics have charged that company-specific programs provide greater benefits to the organization and are therefore more appropriate investments than external open-enrollment programs. Others are beginning to challenge the wisdom of a company's spending too much time "talking to itself" in company-specific initiatives. This chapter attempts to address those charges.

The discussion is built on a central premise; that is, that programs designed for a general audience serve a different purpose and generate different outcomes than do company-specific programs. As such, both can contribute significantly to leadership development when used in an appropriate manner. To facilitate this discussion, we will use a case study approach. We will address the objectives, process, and outcomes of a traditional open-enrollment program by analyzing a four-week, residential general management program offered by the Smeal College of Business Administration at the Pennsylvania State University. Then we will analyze a custom-designed program developed and managed by

Johnson & Johnson. We will compare and contrast these analyses in order to discuss the opportunities, outcomes, and potential of each type of program, as well as guidelines for deciding whether to go internal or external with a particular leadership development initiative.[1]

THE EXECUTIVE MANAGEMENT PROGRAM

The Executive Management Program (EMP) is a four-week general management program offered several times each year by the Smeal College of Business Administration on the campus of Pennsylvania State University. EMP is typical of many multiweek general management programs offered by major business schools around the world. The following 42 universities offered similar programs in 1996:[2]

Ashridge Management College

Banff School of Advanced Management

Carnegie Mellon University

Columbia University

Cornell University

Cranfield University

Dartmouth College (Tuck)

Duke University (Fuqua)

Harvard University

Henley Management College

INSEAD

International Institute for Management Development (IMD)

International Marketing Institute

Irish Management Institute

London Business School

MacQuarie University

Massachusetts Institute of Technology (Sloan)

Monash Mt. Eliza Business School

Northwestern University (Kellogg)

Ohio State University

Pennsylvania State University (Smeal)

Simmons College

Smith College

Stanford University

Templeton College

University of California at Berkeley

University of California, Los Angeles

University of Hawaii

University of Houston

University of Illinois

University of Michigan

University of Minnesota

University of New Mexico

University of New South Wales

University of North Carolina at Chapel Hill

University of Pennsylvania (Wharton)

University of Pittsburgh (Katz)

University of Tennessee

University of Texas at Austin

University of Virginia (Darden)

University of Washington

University of Western Ontario

Source: Bricker's International Directory 1996. Reprinted by permission of Peterson's, P.O. Box 2123, Princeton, NJ from Bricker's International Directory: University-Based Executive Programs 1996. Copies are available by calling the publisher at 1-800-338-3282.

The program, launched in 1956, is attended by international audiences of high-level corporate executives. Nearly 35 percent of the approximately 30 executives who attend a session of the program reside outside the United States, with the remainder from throughout the country. The typical participant is 43 years old, with over 11 years of management experience. The majority of the participants are upper-middle managers—heads of functional areas in corporations, or general managers. All of the participants have been identified as key players in their organization's future development. To ensure integrity in maintaining this profile, each candidate's application is subject to an admissions screening process. Because interaction with a diverse group of peer managers is a key benefit of EMP, the screening process also enables the sponsoring business school to maintain the diversity of the group in terms of companies, industries, and geographic location.

Background

As a general management program, EMP has a strategic focus presented from the perspective of a senior corporate officer. The program is designed to both challenge and broaden participants by exposing them to the leading-edge management thinking of faculty, as well as the values and viewpoints of successful executives from different companies, cultures, and industries. Through a carefully designed sequence of experiential exercises, lectures, discussions, case exercises, and business simulations, the program attempts to foster an educational environment that enables executives to break out from their usual routine and develop a more comprehensive, more global orientation to management. As such, the program utilizes a number of approaches and techniques to facilitate the greatest possible opportunity for development to take place.[3]

Program Process

The brochure for EMP describes it as a developmental experience. The intent is not to engage in "skill building," although there are several elements of the program, particularly in the areas of finance and accounting, that do lend themselves to skill-based development. Rather, the intent is to challenge participant assumptions about their company, their career, and their role within the organization. As such, the program may be classified under what Conger labeled "conceptual approaches" to leadership development.[4] To achieve their objectives, EMP designers have developed a process they call "paying the *piper*," a five-step process that helps participants maximize the value of the educational experience.[5] The *piper* process can be described as follows.

Prepare. The EMP learning environment is intense, and preparation for daily sessions is critical. In addition to their full-day classroom sessions, participants are encouraged to devote several hours each evening to preparation of daily assignments. These assignments can include reading articles or case studies, completing various diagnostic instruments, or meeting with a discussion or simulation team. EMP participants report the month-long schedule of academic activities can be grueling.

Interact. Program designers note that, in an EMP-type experience, participants will learn as much from each other as they do in the formal classroom sessions. Interaction with a diverse group of peers from different companies, cultures, and industries provides EMP participants with the opportunity to broaden their perspectives and increase their awareness of external issues and trends. The development of a closely knit learning community is therefore of paramount concern. EMP utilizes an outdoor leadership development experience at the beginning of a session, as well as other experiential exercises, to promote interaction and involvement among participants. This element of the program's design incorporates an element of the personal growth approach to leadership development, but does so more from a team building perspective than from a personal development perspective.

Participate. EMP coordinators report that session leaders purposely are not called teachers, professors, or instructors. Rather, they are called "faculty leaders" because their job is not to lecture the participants, but to facilitate discussion of a particular agenda to which they contribute their academic expertise. Active classroom participation is a key element of the program experience, and there is frequent utilization of small group discussions and other forms of dialogue and idea exchange. This type of process takes advantage of the participants' experience base and promotes a much higher level of networking among them.

Expand. As a general management program with a developmental focus, EMP is designed from a futuristic perspective. The program is intended to help leaders bridge from their current mindset toward a more strategic perspective on leadership. Participants are encouraged to discuss ideas among themselves and debate their applicability to organizational and leadership effectiveness in a rapidly changing global economy. This expansion of thinking encourages a heightened awareness of the leadership challenge.[6]

Reflect. The program makes extensive use of simulation and structured feedback to bring new concepts to life for participants. At least one 360-degree assessment instrument is used to provide participants with feedback on their performance as leaders. This type of experience and feedback is perhaps one of the greatest benefits of attending an EMP-type experience, as well as having a concentrated period of time away from daily work demands. This type of sabbatical enables participants to take stock of their experience, capabilities, organization, and career. It also can provide participants an opportunity to rethink their approaches to leadership and to develop personal action plans for future growth and development. Participants are encouraged to make use of the university's resources to help them in this process.

Program Outcomes—Participant Reactions

Most of the participants' reactions tend to focus on three particular outcomes: (1) *confidence building*, (2) *broadening/developing an external perspective*, and (3) *network building*. Each of these general themes is discussed below.

Confidence Building. Most EMP graduates began a discussion of the impact of their experience from a pragmatic perspective. Said one participant, "I was looking for an opportunity to reexamine my own views on business in a controlled, structured setting with opportunities to relearn and discuss the issues." For many participants, this opportunity for reexamination was viewed as having "a positive effect on my performance and my level of confidence." Said another participant, "The difference is in my confidence to deal with whatever comes along." This increased confidence was often perceived as a major force in continued career development. Noted one EMP graduate, "I am confident that the knowledge, skills and contacts gained from the EMP program were a significant factor in making the move from middle management to upper corporate management."

Broadening and Developing an External Perspective. Participants also discussed the impact of EMP in terms of the development of a broadened, more externally oriented perspective. One participant said, "EMP showed me how much I have to learn." Another noted, "Sometimes positive effects are measured in what you are able to do for the careers of others. The program enabled me to pass much on to my employees and my children." Said another, "By developing a better understanding of myself, I can manage changes in the business environment more easily." Finally, one participant commented, "The interaction with different people from different industries and countries was exceptional in giving me a much broader view of national and international dimension of management."

Networking. In a survey of corporate users of university programs, a key perceived value of experiences like EMP was found to be opportunities for participants to network with colleagues from other companies, industries, and cultures.[7] EMP participants made frequent reference to this idea. Noted one participant, "Our group had participants from all over the world. . . . It gave us an opportunity to understand our countries and our businesses from the point of view of people from other countries, and it added a [real] dimension to the program." Said another, "We opened up our thoughts, our minds, and our hearts to each other— diverse people, different cultures. It really was impressive." Another participant summed it up: "Now when I'm in Europe or Asia or just about anywhere, I have a friend nearby to call on. When I need help figuring out how to deal with customers in certain industries, I have a contact who can help me out. The connections I've made are invaluable."

Transfer of Learning

Although these participant reactions appear to be very positive, sponsoring companies still must determine the likelihood that the individual learning and personal growth they suggest actually transfers back to the workplace. Based on his experience with open-enrollment leadership development programs, Conger noted, "ultimately . . . , the encouragement and development of leadership skills rests with the individual's own motivation and talent and with the receptiveness of their organizations to support and coach such skills. This leaves a lot to chance."[8] It is this element of chance that may be the biggest problem with external open-enrollment programs like EMP. In surveys investigating the reasons why companies use external programs like EMP, opportunities to broaden participant perspectives and help them develop external networks topped the list.[9] In research where participants were asked about the impact of attending an external program on their career, most characterized their experiences as powerful catalysts for encouraging the transition from management into leadership.[10] However, as Conger suggested, the degree to which this transition actually progresses is directly related to the effort put into the development agenda by both individual participants and their companies.

In a recent study, researchers found that, of the companies they surveyed, slightly over 70 percent of those that university programs reported made it a practice to brief participants before they actually attended a program. This number was *down* from 76 percent five years previously.[11] To make matters worse, when the same researchers polled participants enrolled in the EMP program described above, *less than 30 percent* of the participants recalled having been briefed. Despite their company's view to the contrary, most said they came to the program with very little knowledge of the purpose of their attendance. With that as the case, is it any wonder that sponsoring companies are struggling to see the relevance of external programs? Only the most motivated individuals are likely to benefit personally from the experience. Furthermore, only the most fortunate organizations are likely to get a return on their investment, as it appears that very few had any tangible objectives for sending people to the programs, or any plans for capturing the learnings and experiences of their participants.

This relates back to our previous discussion of systems thinking in Chapter 2. If external programs are looked to as ends in themselves, they will have value for an individual only by chance, and value for the organization only by accident. If they are looked to as a *means* to address a particular element of the development agenda, then they have far greater potential. Several years ago, in the foreword to *Bricker's International Directory: University-Based Executive Programs*, the leading guidebook in the field, it was noted:

> There are critical times in an individual's career, particularly when he or she is moving into a position of expanded scope and/or responsibility, when an external program can help to break the mold of an organizationally or functionally influenced mindset by promoting a greater openness to ideas and a greater awareness of the general management perspective.[12]

At such critical points, an appropriately selected and managed external program can help broaden perspectives, boost confidence, and stimulate a deepened conceptual understanding of leadership. This has a much better chance of happening when the developmental context is managed, when participants are briefed and objectives for the experience set, when assignments are given to be completed during the program, and when participants are expected to return and share their learnings and experiences with their staff and colleagues. It seems today, however, that briefing is haphazard, few participants are given assignments (less than 10 percent of the companies in the previously mentioned study reported doing so with participants they sent to university programs),[13] and even fewer require the sharing of experiences. Based on these facts, one must wonder whether a powerful source of leadership development is being squandered.

To avoid wasting these opportunities, users of external experiences would be wise to take advantage of the following guidelines for selecting and utilizing external programs developed by *Bricker's International Directory: University-Based Executive Programs 1996:*

Guidelines for Selecting Executive Programs

Unlike investing in real estate—where the three most important criteria are said to be location, location, and location—making the right choice about executive education relies on careful investigation of a variety of factors. Location does happen to be among them: weighing the relative advantages of programs offered nearby, in other parts of the country, or around the world. But scouting sites is only one step. Whether you're looking to send one executive or many, you want to receive a high return on the investment. That means narrowing the field to programs that can accommodate individual learning needs, meet your expectations for quality, and are aligned with your organization's management philosophy and strategic goals.

These guidelines highlight several key factors in making the right choice. In general, the more thorough the selection process, the better the opportunity for getting the performance results you want.

Learning Objectives

- *Identify critical business issues* that need to be addressed through an executive program, both organizational goals and those of immediate concern and directly relevant to individual executives.

- *Clarify both personal and organizational expectations*, including whether the primary objective is to build skills, enhance subject matter knowledge, or initiate a change in mind-set.

- *Match the program to the executive's learning style*, for example, one with an experiential component for an executive who responds better to hands-on activities rather than pure lecture or case discussions.

Faculty

- *Assess the level and nature of the faculty's business experience*, including the type and size of companies they've worked with and in what capacity.

- *Find out whether the faculty has experience teaching executives* as compared to strictly undergraduate or graduate-level business students.

- *Compare the faculty's management orientation to that of your organization* by reviewing faculty publications, bios, and other background information.

- *Observe the faculty* in action if possible by visiting classes, attending speaking engagements, or viewing videotaped presentations.

- *Determine the availability of faculty* for consulting or coaching participants on individual issues.

Content

- *Ask for a detailed program schedule*—not just an overview of topics addressed—to see how time is allocated.

- *Get a sense of how the subject matter will be approached* by speaking to the program director; different programs often treat the same content in different ways.

- *Gauge how much exposure participants will have to state-of-the-art management practices and theories*, for example, by reviewing a syllabus or bibliography to see how recent the teaching and study materials are.

- *Consider the level, nature, and relevance of assignments*, including in-class exercises, individual homework assignments, group projects, and any pre-program preparatory work.

- *Check on any high-tech aspects of the program*, for example, to assure a comfort level for executives unaccustomed to working with computers, or conversely, access to up-to-date tools for the technologically adept.

- *Evaluate activities that involve individual psychological assessments and/or counseling* to discover whether they will be conducted by qualified professionals and are suitable for particular executives.

Participant Mix

- *Find out whether the program attracts largely a regional, domestic, or international participant base*, especially if your organization is looking to foster a cross-border or cross-cultural perspective.

- *Consider the industry representation* to assess the relative advantages of having an executive interact with others from the same industry or from a broad industry mix.

- *Determine the average age, experience, and career level* of typical program participants and other such factors relevant to productive peer group exchange.

Teaching Methodologies

- *Gauge the level and nature of interaction between faculty and participants* that is facilitated by the program format, including opportunities for informal exchange outside the classroom.

- *Evaluate the type and variety of teaching methods and technologies used,* which may include case studies (ask how current they are); lectures by faculty and outside experts; directed discussion; role plays; performance feedback tools; group projects; individual exercises; participant presentations and reports; games and business simulations; self-assessment/diagnostic instruments; and instructional or interactive videos. A variety of methods can be important, especially in long programs, to enhance learning and ward off boredom.

- *Determine the opportunities participants will have to implement or practice the skills they learn* both in class and back at work—for example, action learning activities focused on current business issues of participants and their organizations, or action plans outlining specific steps participants intend to take after the program is over to apply what they have learned.

- *Assess the value of outdoor or other physical learning activities* with regard to whether they are appropriate for individual executives and transferrable to the business environment. Also be sure such activities are supervised by individuals with proper qualifications/credentials and pass muster with your organization's legal department regarding insurance liability.

- *Find out if followup activities are part of the program,* either formal or informal, as a means to reinforce learning over time or to support an ongoing network among faculty and participants.

Quality Control

- *Look for clear and detailed program learning objectives* that describe specific ways in which attendees will benefit from their participation.

- *Evaluate sample program materials* both for substance and with regard to the overall written quality of the documentation.

- *Contact previous users of the program* for their views about the strengths, weaknesses, and ultimate value of the program, both colleagues at other organizations who have sent participants as well as the participants themselves.

- *Visit program sites and audit individual programs* whenever possible, particularly when you are considering sending several executives or using the program on an ongoing basis.

Reprinted by permission of Peterson's, P.O. Box 2123, Princeton, NJ, from *Bricker's International Directory: University-Based Executive Programs 1996.* Copies are available by calling the publisher at 1-800-338-3282.

Summary of EMP

It can be noted from this analysis that an open-enrollment program like EMP may be best characterized as a developmental experience; one that challenges the beliefs, skills, and values of participating managers and creates greater awareness of the leadership challenge. Through this type of experience, participants are given the opportunity to rethink their values and views across many dimensions. Through their interaction with a diverse group of peers, they are encouraged to broaden their perspectives and develop a greater openness to diversity and change. Perhaps these outcomes were best summarized by one EMP graduate: "EMP will go down as an experience of a lifetime. I am back at work invigorated, ready to take on the world."

EXECUTIVE CONFERENCE II AT JOHNSON & JOHNSON

When CEO Ralph Larsen of Johnson & Johnson (J&J) was planning a leadership development effort for the top 700 people at his firm in 1992, he was driven by the importance of thinking about the future along with the dangers of trading on past successes. Faced with a similar challenge in 1988, Larsen had appointed a committee of key executives, gave them access to information on the future of J&J gathered through interviews with over 100 of their colleagues, and charged them with developing a plan for his proposed initiative. Their work resulted in the company's first Executive Conference, a very successful initiative built around the theme "Setting the Competitive Standard." This highly interactive series of programs was coordinated by the Center for Executive Development, a consulting firm from Cambridge, Massachusetts.

Background

Based on the success of the first Executive Conference, J&J decided to launch a second initiative in 1993. The program director, Dr. Myron Goff, interviewed representatives from approximately a dozen university-based business schools and independent consulting firms to find a partner for the initiative. Goff decided to create a network of independent providers (both individual university faculty and independent consulting firms) rather than select a single entity because of what he perceived as opportunities for greater flexibility and responsiveness to demands for a high degree of custom work. One of the authors was selected as course manager and selected professors from two U.S. and two European universities, as well as one independent consultant, to work on the program.

Through the interview process and a series of wide-ranging discussions, a number of ideas and issues were brought to the fore of the agenda for Executive Conference II. The program steering committee eventually evolved the four most important objectives for the initiative, which they titled "Creating Our Future":

1. To acquire the tools to create a future full of new opportunities for success.
2. To challenge basic assumptions.
3. To reflect on feedback from self and others that can lead to personal change.
4. To develop the competence and courage to lead changes that bring about a successful future.

Goff was insistent that some of the principals who designed the program also be involved in the delivery of the content. The faculty members conducted interviews with J&J executives in six countries and helped develop the course design and materials. These included computer-assisted discussion exercises; an original future scenario case called "J&J 2002"; a comprehensive, integrative "Merlin Exercise" (described later) which resulted in presentations to the CEO or member of the J&J Executive Committee; and individualized 360-degree feedback sessions conducted by professional psychologists based on leadership profiles completed by peers, subordinates, and superiors. Because of the extensive involvement of university-based faculty members, the developmental cost for this program was at the upper range of costs reported in surveys of the field. Yet faculty members agreed to participate in the development process at half their usual billing rates because of the opportunity to participate in an extensive number of programs over a three-year period—a total of 23 sessions in all—in the unique format described below.

Program Process

The content and flow of the program were designed to build on what preceded it. Consequently, faculty members were not allowed to switch days because of their own convenience. All 23 iterations of this program were conducted with exactly the same program design and content. A designated faculty coordinator began each day by leading the group in a discussion around some of the major learnings of the preceding sessions. This provided integration and gave the program a seamless design.

The program design called for an integrative exercise to tie the various aspects of the program together. The challenge was met through the creation of a "Merlin Exercise," which involved participants each day in applying course concepts to the creation of a future vision of the firm.[14] In addition to integration, the Merlin Exercise also provided an opportunity for participants to interact, through a series of presentations at the conference conclusion, with the CEO or vice chairman. Traditionally, participants had been given the opportunity to challenge the company's most senior officers with questions about the present status or future direction of the firm. Their concerns often were presented in a somewhat critical manner and sometimes put the respondent in a defensive mode. The Merlin Exercise provided an opportunity for people to describe a future they would recommend to senior management, one that they would feel fully committed to supporting with their own efforts. Senior management could then engage in an open discussion around these future scenarios, helping to eliminate defensiveness while challenging the basic assumptions of the firm.

In addition, the firm had recently begun to use Lotus Notes as a communications/networking tool. The J&J Information Systems Group saw the program as an opportunity to demonstrate the power of the network and offered their expertise in the development of exercises to enhance the team-based interaction called for in the program design, including providing coaches to teach the system to participants with relatively little computer proficiency. Ultimately, ten computer-assisted discussion exercises were created and built into the conference design. Coupled with a futuristic "J&J 2002" case, these exercises helped participants develop scenarios for the future of the company and perspectives on how J&J could capitalize on those future scenarios to carry on their legacy of success.

A unique feature of the conference was that each person had an individual session with a professional psychologist who helped interpret data from a 360-degree feedback assessment. These individuals also helped participants develop personal action plans for improvement. Many of these "coaches" were involved in over 100 feedback reports and thus were extremely sensitive and helpful in their interpretation of the feedback. The ability to place the issues in a practical and meaningful context for individual participants was seen as a key element of the program's objective of not just talking about the future, but also taking action to create it.

Program Outcomes

Participants in the Executive Conference were asked to evaluate the degree to which the program met their expectations as well as the stated objectives of the program. After the first ten sessions had been conducted, an outside firm was engaged to survey previous participants in order to determine the real and lasting value of the program. The category clusters were

- Widened horizons for thinking and planning
- Personal feedback about areas for change
- Overcoming the complacency often associated with long-term success

More important than the participants' comments were reports of three new businesses generated as a result of the Merlin presentations and the use of tools acquired in the conference at lower levels within the organization.

Widened Horizons. Many participants reflected on the fact that the program provided an unusual opportunity for them to step out of the day-to-day pressures of their operating responsibility and think about the truly critical responsibility for creating a future for the company. One participant wrote, "The session was successful in allowing me to begin declaring a future and understanding what is needed to achieve this vision." Another participant wrote that the high point of the conference was "an opportunity to envision J&J unencumbered by the constraints of our world today." This unrestricted way to "declare" the future was invigorating and thought-provoking. The interaction with other companies outside the franchise group was also very informative. Many participants describe Merlin as "a unique way for dealing with future possibilities." Another participant wrote that the significance of participation in Executive Conference II was "understanding the tools of anticipatory learning and being given very vivid examples of how breakthroughs can direct markets and completely change the way we do business. These breakthroughs then create new standards that become widely accepted. A real challenge for us."

Personal Feedback. An important part of any change initiative is recognizing the need to make revisions. Individualized feedback based on data collected from peers, subordinates, and bosses provided participants with real data about how they were perceived by others. Some had difficulty in recognizing that, even at the top of the organization, there are variations in performance and behavior. All of the participants could not be above average in their peer group. One participant wrote, "It was the best personal feedback I have had in 21 years with the company. It was relevant given the way it was structured." One participant commented on the importance of being able to "see the boss's feedback, unadulterated and undiluted." Another appreciated "getting feedback from direct reports. This motivation for positive change by a personal action was invaluable."

Overcoming Complacency. One of the chairman's original objectives for setting up Executive Conference II was the fact that Johnson & Johnson had been consistently successful for such a long period of time.[15] While the company had a wonderful heritage, Ralph Larsen had seen industry leaders like IBM and General Motors begin to founder and lose ground because of what was perceived by outside observers as arrogance or complacency. In fact, former CEOs at these firms served on his board of directors. Participants were given opportunities to discuss what dangers they saw in various parts of the Johnson & Johnson family of companies. One participant described the need to "always look at yourself as others see you. You can become complacent when you are doing well. Always challenge your strategy. Make sure that you are looking forward and don't get lost in the present."

Each participant was expected to interview a customer about the perceived future of their industry before coming to the conference. These interview profiles became a database for reference by other participants. One participant said he "enjoyed the discussion relative to the successes and weaknesses of tomorrow . . . and also the discussion of products and the perceived value of our customers was informative." A summary of the value of these concepts was captured by a participant who wrote about the "important concepts of how past successes can easily predispose an organization to future failures. We must avoid this."

Transfer of Learning

Comments from participants captured some of the ways that a custom program design can address specific challenges which address an already successful organization. The program allowed for important dialogue to take place from various parts of almost 200 separate companies within the J&J organization. It provided exposure to "cutting-edge" ideas and an opportunity to apply those directly to the entire company as well as to the specific portion which each participant represented. One participant wrote, "This course is well-designed, well-taught and well-managed." More significantly, the same person concluded, "It is obvious that J&J upper management is taking these topics and executive development very seriously." A colleague summarized his experience by reporting, "Forcing us to look out in the future is clearly the right direction. This should be used at the individual company level to help develop a common vision and identify the core competencies required to achieve it. This can then be shared with other business groups to explore opportunities."

Perhaps the most important conclusion about the success of this initiative came when the faculty coordinator congratulated a former participant on a very significant promotion. The response was "It took six months to make it happen, but I finally got my Merlin." This individual had seen the final conference presentation as more than an intellectual exercise. He continued to push for the establishment of an integrative health care system that was broader than anything within the current company portfolio. By leveraging the work done in the conference, an important new business began, and a significant promotion was the personal reward for applying program concepts to the competitive environment.

Techniques for selecting partner providers to assist in the design and delivery of programs like Executive Conference II are outlined in Chapter 7.

A COMPARATIVE DISCUSSION

By analyzing the brief cases presented above, one can begin to grasp the impacts and implications of both open-enrollment and company-specific executive education/leadership development experiences. The traditional open-enrollment program, typified by EMP, is a broadening experience. It enhances participants' confidence, challenges their assumptions, encourages them to rethink their own and their organization's traditional values and viewpoints, and makes them more aware of the leadership challenge. Appropriately designed and presented, it is a perspective-building experience that can revitalize a leader's career and position him or her for continued development.

However, an open-enrollment program is less likely to develop specific skills or reinforce specific corporate values or operating styles. Rather, the experience often serves as a catalyst for change and innovation in individual management styles and perspectives, and as a tool to aid in the transition from a managerial mindset to a leadership mindset. As may be noted from the comments of EMP participants, the experience challenges the individual to look beyond the routine elements of his or her job toward a more comprehensive view of the leader as strategist.

Company-specific programs, typified by Executive Conference II, generate somewhat different outcomes. Perhaps the most significant of those outcomes are the encouragement of teamwork, the development of new lines of communication, and the clarification of organizational style, strategy, and culture. Participants learn more about their respective companies, more about their competitive strategies, and more about each other, but focus less on issues apart from the specified corporate agenda. Thus they are less likely to have experienced a challenge to their organization or its operational status quo unless that challenge was planned for or orchestrated through action learning projects or some other technique.

Appropriately designed, a company-specific executive program is also a perspective-building experience, but for different reasons than an open-enrollment program. The company-specific program assists managers at all levels to develop a working understanding of an organization's current and desired strategy and culture. It helps managers to feel better informed and more aware of the internal workings of the firm. As such, they are better prepared to provide leadership and direction and to facilitate desired organizational changes. Comments made by Executive Conference II participants show how this type of program can serve as a conduit for organizational communication, as well as a catalyst for team building and organizational transformation. Furthermore, the applications and action planning focus typified by Executive Conference II can help initiate dialogue and action that can transform the sponsoring organization.

Based on this analysis, we believe that internal and external programs generate different kinds of outcomes and clearly are not substitutes for each other. Whether they are complementary or in conflict depends on an organization's ability to understand and acknowledge their respective contributions to leadership and organizational development and to appropriately choreograph their use. At the right times in an individual's career or in an organization's developmental cycle, each can have a dramatic effect on individual or organizational effectiveness. A better understanding of the impacts and implications of both types of programs can ensure that each type of educational experience is more effectively matched with the executive development objectives of individual managers and the organization as a whole.

SUMMARY

The debate regarding the use of internal versus external programs rages on. Our research shows that both types of programs have their strengths, both have their place in the arsenal of tools for leadership development. By understanding the nature of both experiences, companies should be in a better position to maximize the contributions of each approach. External programs can provide a rich developmental sabbatical for participants, through which they are exposed to leading-edge thinking, multiple approaches to doing business, and a potential network of diverse colleagues. Although most participants find such experiences stimulating and refreshing, the benefit to both the individual and the company will be greatly increased through the kind of briefing, preparation, and followup discussed in this chapter.

Internal programs can be an engine for transformation, a vehicle for changing the way an organization operates. By helping people develop a deeper understanding of the organization as a whole, and by helping to form and maintain internal networks, these programs can play a critical role in the organizational development process. But, for that to happen, senior managers of the company, like those at Johnson & Johnson, must play an active role in the process. And to truly leverage the experience, the company and its providers must work in partnership to create the most effective, relevant experience possible. The following chapter is focused on the assessment and selection of provider partners.

7

Selecting
Providers

CORPORATE EXPENDITURES FOR various forms of leadership development have grown to over $45 billion during the past decade. Arthur Andersen spends well in excess of $300 million a year on its learning initiatives. Motorola invests more than $100 million each year on its various educational activities. Many corporations have multimillion-dollar budgets for educating their key managers, and many programs are targeted at more than 1,000 executives in a single firm.[1] With the stakes in the corporate leadership development marathon so high, it is surprising that so little systematic work has been done on the process of evaluating potential providers and the programs they offer. This chapter deals with that challenge.

THE SELECTION PROCESS

Word of mouth still appears to be the major means by which specific providers fall into consideration for involvement with a leadership development initiative. Universities still have an edge in the process, because alumni from their regular degree programs and public executive education courses are apt to nominate their alma mater for consideration. Was it coincidence that, in 1995 when Jack Snow, CEO of CSX and a University of Virginia (UVA) alumnus, announced plans for a "World Class" commitment to organizational learning, UVA's Darden School was designated as the principal provider of a two-week leadership development program for its top 500 executives?

It also appears that being mentioned in print as one of the leaders in executive education has an undetermined but very real impact on increasing credibility and generating opportunities for providers of leadership development initiatives. Marshall Goldsmith reports that, after having been identified as one of the top ten independent executive education consultants in the *Wall Street Journal*, the number of inquiries his office received tripled almost immediately. Universities report similar results when they are listed at the top of various rankings of executive programs.

The "systems approach" discussed in Chapter 4 offers insight into how the process of selecting providers typically works. A "virtuous cycle" is created when a provider has been involved in a successful leadership development program. This is crucial for new providers trying to break into the competitive arena of high-level executive programs. Until a provider has delivered a successful program, no one knows for certain if that provider has the capability to do so. An individual who has been successful in delivering portions of a program as a platform presenter or facilitator may have some credibility. Yet the ability respond to client requests, develop or select appropriate materials for a larger-scale initiative, then manage the logistics of the people and materials required to successfully deliver that initiative on a repetitive basis require a totally different and much broader set of capabilities.

Thus there evolves a virtuous cycle that can be described as follows: "Experience builds success . . . success builds a reputation." Few users are going to trust a new provider with a major initiative or with groups of experienced leaders. Consequently, the selection of providers can become a process of an organization's continually repeating what has always worked in the past, either for it or for other clients of an experienced provider.

If an organization is not careful, it can find itself in the business of buying "programs" from "proven" vendors as opposed to selecting provider "partners" who work to understand the organization, its strategic imperatives, and its developmental objectives. Therefore, to ensure the creation of purposeful leadership development initiatives that are driven by the strategic imperatives of a firm, careful attention must be given to crafting a process for selecting provider partners.

THREE KEY QUESTIONS

The process of narrowing the field of potential providers for a major initiative can be viewed as three hurdles represented by the following questions:

1. What Have You Done?

Almost every "request for proposal" (RFP) asks about previous projects, solicits specific examples of program design, and requires a list of previous clients served. Respondents who give evidence of having done interesting work of a comparable scope are considered worthy of further consideration and moved on to the next hurdle.

2. What Else Can You Do?

This question is used to examine the depth and potential of providers. Some corporations may want a provider to conduct a needs assessment. Others may want detailed development of original program materials, including cases, simulations, or other exercises. Clients often are (and should be) concerned about "back office support." Is the potential provider or an associate likely to be available or accessible to respond to questions and handle problems given the travel and time demands of their work?

It is also important to examine what the provider is really good at. Some firms have a specialty they pursue with great dedication and excellence. They have, by choice, decided not to compete on a wide range of topics or projects. A group that specializes in outdoor adventure learning or in providing 360-degree feedback may not be a viable candidate for a broad-scale program on global competitiveness. On the other hand, some relatively small firms are able to offer a wide range of program designs due to their extensive network of contacts and their knowledge of the industry.

For example, even after downsizing his organization to two full-time people, Jim Bolt's Executive Development Associates is still considered a potential provider for a wide variety of programs because of its network of intellectual resources. As mentioned previously, Global Access Learning, with less than a dozen full-time employees, talks of having utilized 60 academics from 25 institutions for programs on six continents. Universities tend to have broad networks as well. The network into which a prospective provider can tap can be a very valuable resource to a client.

3. What Will You Do for Us?

The issue addressed by this final question is flexibility. Academic institutions and established consulting firms often have distinguished track records and the resources to do almost anything a company needs. Yet, because of conflicting pressures on principals and/or faculty resources, they may exhibit a lack of responsiveness to program initiatives that require a significant degree of customization.

Universities are often seen as being best at making minor adaptations to relatively successful public programs which can be offered to a large number of executives in a single firm. For example, the Darden School of the University of Virginia will offer "Creating the High Performance Work Place" four times each year as an open-enrollment program. A similar version of the program will be offered a comparable number of times to specific company groups.

Perhaps due to their success in public programs or in adaptations of existing course offerings, some universities do seem to lack the flexibility required to respond to requests from clients who may ask for the creation of original cases, computerized exercises, video vignettes, or integrative exercises to tie a program together. Not all universities are so constrained, however. The Kellogg School at Northwestern, the Smeal College at Penn State, the Darden School at the University of Virginia, the Wharton School at the University of Pennsylvania, the Fuqua School at Duke, the Kenan-Flagler School at the University of North Carolina, Ashridge and Cranfield in the United Kingdom, and INSEAD and IMD in Europe, among others, have all developed impressive portfolios of custom program clients.

The real issue here is whether the provider is willing to work with the organization to develop an initiative that is tailored to the needs and demands of the organization—whether the provider is really willing to be a partner with the sponsoring firm.

FORMAL PROPOSALS

In order to ensure some degree of objectivity, as well as to focus their own thinking, many firms have developed a formal "request for proposal" (RFP) process. Creating an RFP can be an arduous assignment in itself. It is difficult to think through, in advance, all of the factors likely to be important in making the decision about a program designer/ deliverer.

At least in the early stages of a selection process, most corporate clients have a sense of the providers with whom they would be most comfortable. They have had successful experience working with some of them in the past, or they have received good reports on them from colleagues in other firms. Most HRD professionals have well-developed networks of contacts that they utilize regularly to gather information about the perceived strengths and weaknesses of various potential providers. Many corporate executives maintain one or two memberships in networks created as forums for sharing "best practices" and concerns with colleagues. For example, Jim Bolt of Executive Development Associates created and still maintains a client network in addition to his own consulting practice. One of his purposes is to bring together prospective buyers and sellers to discuss the evolving marketplace for his firm's services.

While one of the authors was Director of Corporate Management Development at AlliedSignal, he regularly talked with colleagues at AT&T, IBM, GTE, Combustion Engineering, Beatrice Foods, Borg-Warner, and Coca-Cola. Representatives of these firms agreed to meet for one or two days every six months with an almost-unstructured agenda and no outsiders present. The first meeting of what came to be called the Executive Education Exchange was conducted at the AlliedSignal Pleasantdale Farm facility. Six months later, the group reconvened for a day and a half at the GTE Conference Center in Norwalk, Connecticut. Typically, the host institution began the session by outlining the scope of their program offerings, problems, and plans. In open, candid discussions, members outlined the challenges they faced, reviewed successes with particular vendors, or highlighted problems that other members might need to address. The meetings typically involved only one night away from home and office and provided an uncensored opportunity to share ideas and concerns, along with best practices, with a select group of peers.

Universities often create and maintain networks, frequently through business school–sponsored research institutes, that can be veritable fountains of information for HRD professionals. The Executive Development Forum at Babson College, the MIT Center for Organizational Learning, the Cornell Center for Advanced Human Resources Studies, the Center for Effective Organizations at the University of Southern California, the Penn State Institute for the Study of Organizational Effectiveness, and many others provide corporate sponsors access to leading-edge information as well as knowledge of potential resources. In addition, more formal networks, like the International Consortium for Executive Development Research (ICEDR), based in Lexington, Massachusetts, are engaged in facilitating think tank–type interaction among leading researchers in the field and corporations. In fact, ICEDR has emerged as one of the most valuable sources of information on trends in executive development.

A MODEL REQUEST FOR PROPOSAL

Regardless of the amount of networking done by an HRD professional, the creation of a formal request for proposal (RFP) process will add clarity to the design and selection process. The inserts "Criteria for Selection of External Providers" and "Specific Selection Considerations" provide some details from an unusually comprehensive RFP developed by Ron Meeks at Hoechst Celanese Corporation. An interesting factor in this RFP is the company's quantification or weighing of several key selection criteria. Meeks would admit, however, that a great deal of subjectivity goes into the assignment of the various weights.

Criteria for Selection of External Providers

Overall Expectations: The consultant(s) will assist HCC define its specific purpose and scope for the Continuing Leadership Education Forums, and will provide the following expertise:

A. A structured "needs analysis" methodology for 1) identifying the key business issues and challenges, 2) the related leadership behaviors, skills and knowledge required to meet those business challenges, 3) identification of the segments of the leadership levels requiring those competencies, and 4) the "gap(s)" which, in general, need most emphasis.

B. Methodologies for designing specific "interventions" targeted at each priority issue (priority to be defined by HCC). Such methodologies will be subject to context, cost and time considerations to be managed at HCC.

C. Access to "leading edge faculty." Will help identify the appropriate choices, will guide in selection, and will serve to orient the faculty initially to HCC's needs, expectations, and opportunities. Will manage the contractual arrangements between the external faculty and HCC.

D. Program evaluation methodologies to determine effectiveness of the interventions in both "participant reaction" level as well as "application and behavior change" level.

Hoechst Celanese and its representatives (specifically HRD personnel, Leadership Development Steering Committee) will be responsible for the following:

A. Guiding consultant(s) in the expectations of Continuing Leadership Education, and in specifying "operating and design parameters" such as time, cost, frequency, etc. for both design activities and delivery.

B. Leading processes for setting priorities on Continuing Leadership Education forums, in defining "target audiences" and in establishing communications to target participants.

C. Approving the methodologies and content of the forums once a scope and context have been agreed to.

D. Soliciting and orienting "internal expertise" to be used, as well as arranging specific HCC information and materials incorporated in the design.

E. Arranging logistics and administration of meetings related to design and delivery of the forums.

F. Assessing overall program interest and effectiveness.

Source: L. Ronald Meeks, Director, Leadership Development, Hoechst Celanese Corporation, 1994.

Specific Selection Considerations

Reputation: (A)
Experience in Executive Management Education: (A)
Teacher/Faculty Access Process: (A)
Time Availability: (A)
Cost/Cost Effectiveness: (B)

Support Resources: (B)
Geographic Proximity/Ready Access: (B)
Support Resources: (B)
Serves as Faculty Sometimes: (C)
Flexible but Systematic: (A)
Ability to Adapt to HCC Cultural Expectations: (A)
Industry/Business Experience: (B)
Creative/Innovative Methodologies: (B)
Commitment to HCC—Existing "Supplier": (B)
Willingness to Confront Customer When Needed: (B)

(A) = *Major importance, weighted value of 3 points*
(B) = *Would significantly improve our confidence, weighted value of 2 points*
(C) = *Would be nice to have this attribute, not critical, weighted value of 1 point*

Source: L. Ronald Meeks, Director, Leadership Development, Hoechst Celanese Corporation, 1994.

A system similar to Hoechst Celanese's could be used to compare provider proposals using the format shown in Table 7.1. In today's competitive world it is not uncommon for two consulting firms to be considered as potential providers along with two or more business schools. A visible comparative process can help clarify which provider would make the best partner, thereby adding a bit more objectivity to the process.

Most of the selection criteria listed in this example are self-explanatory. The first two items deal with the experience and reputation of a provider. Teacher/faculty access refers to the degree to which an individual supplier is willing to utilize the best available person for a program module regardless of institutional affiliation. For example, in their Middle Management Leadership Program, Hoechst Celanese attached a great deal of importance to one provider's willingness to use independent consultants as well as professors from a variety of academic institutions, rather than being restricted to the faculty of a single business school. This may or may not be a critical issue for a company in the selection process. The weighing of this factor can then be adjusted accordingly.

TABLE 7.1 Proposed Selection Model

On a scale of 1–5 (1 = weak, 5 = strong), rate each resource against the parameter. Multiply the rating by the weighting factor for the total rating of each parameter.

			PROVIDERS				
Decision Parameter (weighting)	1	2	3	4	5	Total Score
Reputation: (3)							
Experience in Executive/ Management Education: (3)							
Teacher/Faculty Access Process: (3)							
Time Availability: (3)							
Cost/Cost-Effectiveness: (2)							
Geographic Proximity/Ready Access: (2)							
Support Resources: (2)							
Serves as Faculty Sometimes: (1)							
Flexible but Systematic: (3)							
Ability to Adapt to HCC Cultural Expectations: (3)							
Industry/Business Experience: (2)							
Creative/Innovative Methodologies: (2)							
Commitment to HCC— Existing "Supplier": (2)							
Willingness to Confront Customer When Needed: (2)							
TOTAL POINTS:							

Source: L. Ronald Meeks, Director, Leadership Development, Hoechst Celanese Corporation, 1994.

In addition, some program providers like to view program modules as interchangeable parts. Others take the view that each component should build on the others. Consequently, modules scheduled for Wednesday cannot be shifted to Monday in order to accommodate presenters' schedules, as it might undermine the integrity of the original program design. This challenge can be addressed in one of two ways, both of which have been utilized in Johnson & Johnson's Executive Conference series. During the first three-year initiative (built around the theme "Setting the Competitive Standard"), program design and sequence were sacrosanct. The Center for Executive Development developed a core faculty for this program but coached alternative faculty members who were available in the event that a particular instructor was not available for a particular session. In the second Executive Conference ("Creating Our Future"), 23 sessions were conducted over a three-year period with exactly the same instructors in the same sequence utilized in every session (except for one half-day module in the beginning of the series). Instructors and facilities were scheduled one to two years in advance, and the program operated like clockwork.

"Time Availability" refers simply to how important the client will be to a provider. Every client would like to believe that its project is the most important program the provider has to deal with. At the same time, the most successful providers are likely to be involved with several projects simultaneously. The best potential provider organization may not get a project if the client lacks assurance with regard to access to key resources throughout the project. A respondent in our field interviews reported an experience with a business school. When a particular program was first offered, "world-class" faculty members were utilized. During the second or third iteration of the program, experienced presenters were used, but the "superstars" were less likely to be available. This observer concluded, rather cynically, that by the time a program was a couple of years old, the business school was struggling to get junior faculty members involved. We encountered similar stories about the involvement of consulting firm principals in various projects.

An issue like the one above is addressed in the model RFP under "Commitment to HCC—Existing 'Supplier.'" A consultant or business school that has worked with the client previously has already moved up the learning curve. They know something about the culture of the organization and the expectations of the client, and they are more of a known quantity. As a result, if there is ongoing access to key provider faculty and other intellectual resources, it can be a great advantage to clients. On the other hand, a provider that has become too familiar with an organization can become too much like "one of the gang" and not challenge participants enough. One of the major themes discussed at the 1996 conference of the International University Consortium for Executive Education was the need for providers of leadership development to focus on developing deeper relationships with a few corporate partners rather than attempting to be generalists who provide limited engagements for large numbers of clients.

For consulting firms, support resources, or "back office" staff, are an important issue. A client wants to know that the less glamorous, but essential jobs of preparing notebooks and getting materials to the appropriate place on time will be adequately handled. Although this is typically a strength of university providers, it is often a major challenge for a smaller firm. In addition, some companies prefer that a particular provider be totally involved in the design of a program and contract out to other individuals for delivery. Conversely, some clients want to be sure that the person or people who coordinate the project have the ability to design as well as to deliver. These expectations must be clarified if a working partnership is to develop.

Finally, many customers of leadership development programs will speak openly about the "chemistry test." Despite the credentials offered by some providers, the decision maker knows, almost intuitively, that certain providers will mesh with the corporate culture—that there will be "good chemistry" between the two organizations. This is seldom just a matter of liking a principal's personality. It usually is intuition based on years of experience in attempting to articulate what it is that makes programs successful or unsuccessful within a given organization.

CAN UNIVERSITIES DELIVER?

Universities have always been a major provider of executive education/leadership development programs. Even with today's proliferation of providers, a relatively small group of universities still controls over 25 percent of the highly fragmented market for leadership development services.[2] Yet, throughout our research, it has become clear that there is a significant movement away from external open-enrollment programs toward customized programs. It is also clear that an increasing amount of corporate executive education and leadership development dollars (approximately 75 percent) is being spent internally or on nonuniversity providers. In Appendix A, we quote Jim Baughman of Morgan Guaranty, who said, "University programs are too long. They are not flexible enough. They are too expensive, and they lack action learning."[3] *Fortune*'s Brian O'Reilly encouraged his readers to:

> Ask a lot from the business schools, colleges and professors that do work for your company. Plenty are greedy, lazy, or incompetent. Because executive education is so profitable for universities, many have rushed into the business. The teachers they provide may be academic drones without the temperament of solid consulting experience needed to satisfy veteran executives.[4]

In a recent article, it was noted that, although highly regarded as providers of strategic leadership development, universities have yet to achieve their full potential as critical components of the corporate leadership development process, a state resulting from unintentional collusion between the supplier and customer communities.[5] It was further argued that a "market economy" was developing in the field.[6] This market economy should yield substantial improvements in both university-based and corporate-directed executive education/leadership development over the next few years. It was further suggested that these improvements would be directly related to a steadily increasing degree of corporate sophistication in the use of executive education/leadership development as a vehicle for organizational development.

In a longitudinal study on executive development practices, researchers at Penn State's Smeal College of Business found that a growing percentage of the corporate community were approaching universities to become partners in the development and dissemination of state-of-the-art research and knowledge that impacts organizational performance (see Table 7.2).[7] These findings reflected a dramatic shift over the fifteen-year interval of the study—away from traditional views of universities as centers of undergraduate education and academic research, toward a more collaborative role in business and organizational development.

The authors also noted that although a small percentage of respondents felt universities were ineffective in their provision of state-of-the-art leadership development programs (Figure 7.1), less than 25 percent viewed them as effective. The majority, 68 percent, felt effectiveness varied by institution. In a recent study, Doug Ready, executive director

TABLE 7.2 Perceived Roles of Universities in Developing Management Talent (percentages)

Role	1982	1987	1992	1997
Develop and present state-of-the-art research and issues	32	45	58	52
Provide quality instruction and faculty	27	10	25	31
Revitalize, challenge, and stimulate in environment of reflection	7	10	21	43
Broaden and develop managers for the future	7	43	21	60
Respond to needs of business as partner, consultant, and resource	14	15	21	55
Provide external contacts and dialogue exchange	8	14	15	7
Be pragmatic and relevant through experiential learning	—	10	10	36
Teach specific or functional skill	5	12	8	16
Provide background prior to employment	18	2	4	5

Respondents could indicate more than one role or responsibility.

Source: A. A. Vicere, "Changes in Practices, Changes in Perspectives: The 1997 International Study of Executive Development Trends," University Park, PA: Institute for the Study of Organizational Effectiveness, 1997. Reprinted by permission.

of the International Consortium for Executive Development Research, similarly found corporations desired stronger linkages between executive education/leadership development programs and the realities of work. In addition, these same companies were interested in new and innovative approaches to teaching and learning, and were demanding that university programs and services be more responsive and customer focused.[8] Interviews conducted by Alan White of MIT supported these findings and further encountered a perception that, in general, universities had been far too slow to change. It was perceived that many universities were continuing to use outdated materials or were simply out of touch with the realities of competing and managing in today's environment.[9]

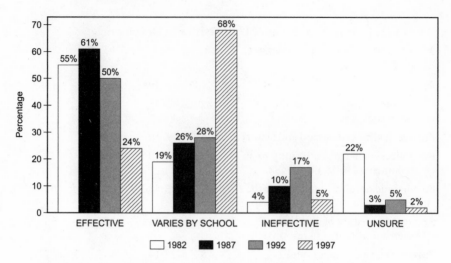

Figure 7.1 Perceived Effectiveness of Universities in Management Development

Source: A. Vicere, "Changes in Practices, Changes in Perspectives: The 1997 International Study of Executive Development Trends." University Park, PA: Institute for the Study of Organizational Effectiveness, 1997. Reprinted by permission.

Two related corporate behaviors and conditions seem to have contributed to prolonging these undesirable conditions:

1. Until recently, corporations have tended to lack the internal capability to provide a viable alternative to university-based programs.
2. At the same time, there has been a steady to growing expenditure rate on university programs by corporations that may have sent the wrong message to universities.

These factors created an unintentional collusion within the marketplace, with no incentives for universities to change because their traditional programs were operating at full capacity.

As executive education and leadership development have emerged as important levers for competitive advantage, companies have increasingly begun to pay more attention to the function. They have hired professionals to run it and asked them to calculate returns on investment in it. This has resulted in a significant professionalization of the field over the past decade, along with a corresponding increase in the internal executive education and development capabilities of many companies.[10] As a result, a growing sense of corporate dissatisfaction, coupled with a marked improvement in internal program development and delivery, has led to a visible decrease in the use of open-enrollment, university-based executive education programs over the past several years.[11]

This is not meant to suggest that all institutions were blind to the need for change or to the importance of being focused on the customer. To the contrary, one study found that, although the overall perception of university effectiveness in developing management talent was declining, the percentage of those indicating that perceived effectiveness varied by institution was steadily increasing (see Figure 7.1).[12] This assertion was clearly supported by other researchers.[13]

These conditions suggest that a strong potential exists for a shakeout among universities in the strategic leadership development business over the next few years. Institutions with carefully crafted strategies that focus on leveraging their core competencies, coupled with a fierce dedication to quality, teaching excellence, innovation, and *measured* market responsiveness, will not only survive, but will be very likely to flourish in partnership with the corporate community. This perceived opportunity for the university community is the cornerstone of the authors' second observation: that a market economy is emerging within the field.

At its core, a market economy is characterized and driven by supply, demand, price, and competition. Changes in any of these variables usually stimulate changes in the dynamics of the market—in this case, the executive education market. When markets are efficient, there is a reasonable amount of stability among these variables. When they are inefficient, there is a significant amount of instability.

A variety of factors support the proposition that an inefficient market currently exists in the field of executive education/leadership development. Many indicators point to a significant increase of institutional suppliers or competitors.[14] *Bricker's International Directory: University-Based Executive Programs 1996* reported that 52 new executive programs were offered in 1996, up from 41 in 1993.[15] This proliferation of offerings came at a time when demand for such programs seemed to be waning. On a practical level, corporate practitioners have indicated to us that it is becoming increasingly difficult to distinguish the serious players from the opportunists because so many new providers have entered the market in the recent past. This does not even take into account the additional private-sector competitors that have emerged.

If demand were reasonably stable for university-based programs, this increased competition could be explained as a response to unmet customer needs. However, several researchers have identified a clear shift away from external programs toward internal, company-specific programs.[16] Furthermore, one study indicated that only a fraction of that shift would likely become business for universities as customized programs.[17]

Despite this, many universities seem to be shedding their portfolio of open-enrollment programs in favor of custom programs, in hopes of capturing what appears to be the only growth segment of the market. This shift toward customers' (companies') controlling channels of distribution (running their own internal programs) reflects a classic for scenario planners in that the customer has become one of the supplier's most formidable competitors.

Corporations today seem to be looking less for programs and more for educational process partners to help create development systems that promote continuous improvement, continuous innovation, and continuous learning for both individual leaders and the organization as a whole. This emerging demand provides a challenge to universities and a window of opportunity for other providers.

COORDINATING THE PROCESS: THE AT&T APPROACH

AT&T has made as strong a commitment to ongoing leadership development as any organization in the world. The following brief discussion outlines the company's strategy for coordinating an impressive investment in executive education and how the company attempts to develop partnerships in program development and delivery.[18]

Background

AT&T has had longstanding commitments to in-house education and training for all levels of employees; tuition support for out-of-hours study; release-time programs for specially selected individuals (typically, executive MBA programs or advanced technical degree programs); executive education programs conducted internally using university faculty, consultants, and corporate executives; and sending high-potential managers to university-sponsored executive education programs. Annually, approximately 300 middle and upper-middle managers attend strategic leadership development programs designed and administered by AT&T. In addition, approximately 500 managers at the same levels and higher (directors and officers) attend university-based programs.

There are three components of AT&T's human resource management system that have direct bearing on involvement in strategic leadership development and what form it will take:

1. *Performance management.*

This is a process for assuring that corporate and organizational goals are defined and communicated, and for determining the basis for setting individual objectives; how performance should be measured against those objectives; and the developmental needs of the individual which must be addressed in order to enhance achievement of current objectives and ensure long-range professional growth.

2. *Career planning.*

Although defined as the primary responsibility of the employee, career planning at AT&T is viewed as a "three-legged stool": the employee defines his or her values, goals, and interests; the supervisor provides instruction, support, and feedback; and the organization defines longer-term needs and provides education and training resources.

3. *Leadership identification.*

Based on defined leadership competencies or dimensions, individuals are identified by their organizations as having potential for accelerated movement to higher-level positions. Typically, organizational "round-tables" are used for review of candidates. Once identified, high-potential managers are viewed as the primary (but not the exclusive) group from which to select executive education participants.

Corporate policies and programs in support of these three aspects of career development are defined and made available to individual business units. The units have full cost responsibility and can "buy" or not as they see fit. Typically, all business units participate, modifying approaches to suit their own business needs. One area where they have somewhat less freedom is in the use of university-sponsored executive education programs, as will be explained below.

Development Philosophy

The preferred executive education route for the high-potential individual is participation, first, in an internal AT&T program early in his or her career. Working with a class of 30 to 40 colleagues from all parts of the corporation, these individuals learn more about AT&T, gain insight into synergies that exist across organizational lines, and have the opportunity to develop internal networks. After the individual has completed this internal experience, further developmental initiatives rely heavily on university-based programs and the AT&T School of Business (discussed later). In this respect, AT&T is unlike many corporations that have pulled away from open-enrollment university programs. AT&T sees great value in having its high-potential managers work alongside peers from other industries and countries as a way to expose these individuals to alternative organizational structures, leadership styles, and business development approaches.

While executive education is managed at the corporate level, business units are also involved in leadership development. Change seems to be a dominant issue in the management literature today, and AT&T is no stranger to the process. Because change dominates the agendas of business units, programs related to change are the responsibility of those business units. Typically, these involve week-long experiences attended by all managers at a particular level or within a particular group. These programs are conducted in addition to, not in place of it, corporate-managed executive education.

Organization of the Executive Education Function

Responsibility for executive education policy, liaison with schools, enrollment, administration, and program evaluation rests with a manager at the corporate office, referred to here as the "corporate manager." Within each of the business units (approximately 40), one person is designated as the executive education coordinator (referred to here as the "coordinator") for his or her unit. Responsibility for conducting in-house executive education programs resides in the AT&T School of Business; however, admission to such programs is overseen by the corporate manager. The AT&T School of Business provides all internal general management and skills training for AT&T employees worldwide. Programs are offered for clerical- through director-level employees. The School of Business coordinates its educational offerings with those of other functionally oriented AT&T training organizations. Programs are designed in partnership with providers, usually external, who develop specific programs which are marketed throughout the organization. These providers may be individuals, consulting firms, or universities.

Process

Annually, the corporate manager runs a conference for the business unit coordinators at which the internally generated AT&T executive education course catalog is reviewed. The catalog is sent to all officers, human resource heads, and coordinators. Its prefatory material explains basic philosophy and linkages to performance management, career planning, and leadership. It lists both internal and university programs available for the next year, their broad content, and the intended audience, along with costs and session dates. Over 75 general management and 60 functional programs were listed in the 1996 catalog. Business units are allocated a rough number of seats based on the size of the unit and historical participation in various programs. With respect to university programs, AT&T (like university executive education program directors themselves) does not want to dominate sessions numerically, and thus limits the number of participants who can attend any one session at a given school. Such factors are taken into account when seat allocations are made.

Coordinators return to their organizations and, working with line executives, line managers, leadership and development staff members, and high-potential employees, develop the list of people whom the unit will support for education during the following year, as evidenced by an officer's approval. The coordinators submit applications to the corporate manager, usually suggesting up to three programs that appear to match the developmental needs of each nominated individual.

The corporate manager and staff review the applications to ensure that candidates appear to be appropriately matched with programs, and then attempt to allocate seats based on coordinators' recommendations. Formal notification is given to the organizations, listing which programs candidates have been approved to attend and providing instruction to line supervisors as to how they should brief each individual before and following the program.

The corporate manager also notifies the universities as to how many AT&T candidates they can expect for the following year's approved programs. Arrangements have been worked out with most universities to accept the AT&T executive education application form in lieu of having the student make separate application to the university. This is because AT&T has agreed with the universities it uses that all contacts with the individual school will be through the corporate manager or his or her staff. This relieves universities of having to deal with multiple business units. It also facilitates discussion of program evaluation, as discussed below. A database is used to manage all administrative and valuative aspects of the process.

Program Selection and Evaluation

Major universities around the world have programs included in the AT&T internal catalog. The corporate manager determines which programs will be listed. He or she bases selection on the school's reputation as well as on the experience of AT&T managers who have participated in previous sessions. New programs usually are added in one of two ways. As new offerings are made by universities, the corporate manager asks a coordinator to identify someone who might benefit from the experience and who would be willing to provide the company with a detailed evaluation of the program. The second approach is involvement in consortium programs where AT&T participates with other companies in the development and guidance of a program for managers from member companies.

The corporate manager attempts to visit as many schools as possible each year. In addition, regular contact is maintained with university representatives to ensure that the company stays abreast of new programs or revisions to existing programs. More important, the feedback from individuals who have attended programs is taken very seriously. Each student is asked to complete a multipage evaluation which covers program content, level of fellow participants, faculty, facilities, and so on. The ratings by students are entered into a database and are used to provide feedback to university representatives. If a program receives consistently low ratings, it is dropped from the catalog. Additionally, if programs included in the catalog draw little interest, they also are dropped.

The AT&T example demonstrates the value of developing both a strategy for executive education and leadership development, as well as a well-defined process for implementing that strategy. Because of their orchestrated approach, AT&T is able to catalog information about both potential providers and potential participants. This leadership development database enables AT&T to maintain both focus and quality in its leadership development initiatives. Individuals are more likely to be placed in appropriate programs. There is a greater likelihood that learning from the program will be bridged back to the workplace. Sound data can be collected on potential providers or resources for internal programs. Better relationships can be built with university providers. Better internal programs can be developed. All of this information enhances the value of leadership development to the organization.

Making the Final Selection

There is little question that the common ingredients for provider success in the new, emerging paradigm for executive education and leadership development include quality, teaching excellence, innovation, and market responsiveness. However, we believe the most effective providers are likely to be those that have mastered the process of defining and optimizing their core capabilities. Providers must build from their strengths in order to meet customer requirements effectively. If a provider enjoys a worldwide reputation for research in technology development and manufacturing, then a more plausible scenario for its success might be to leverage those strengths by finding a set of customers with needs for such capabilities, instead of trying to launch a "finance for nonfinancial managers" program because a company asked it to do so.

Providers, like the corporations they serve, have limited resources and therefore decreasing opportunities for investment in the future. It is vital that those investments be made strategically. Being market responsive and customer focused should mean more than a willingness to try to deliver a service. It should also mean that the provider is actively engaged in becoming one of the world's leading suppliers in its areas of expertise. By applying these and other standards, providers can make great strides in developing executive education/leadership development programs and other services. By holding providers to those standards, corporations enhance the capability and capacity of the entire field.

Moving Forward

In assessing the opportunities and challenges of creating initiatives in strategic leadership development, users *and* providers of executive education/leadership development may wish to keep several observations in mind:

- Users are turning "internal" to meet executive education/leadership development needs. However, they seem unsure as to what activities are needed and often question their ability to develop and deliver those activities in an effective, timely manner. This suggests that the need for process consulting services from the top providers may be growing, providing new opportunity for those providers willing to share both their educational *process* and their *content expertise* with the user community.

- Users are sure that courses on issues such as change management, leadership, and process and performance management are needed quickly to help adjust to the demands of a changing world. They are less sure of what their leadership development needs will be in the future. Universities are being asked to look into their crystal ball of research to help organizations define and address emerging opportunities. The demand, however, is less for basic research and more for outcome-oriented applications—processes that contribute to change and transformation. This is a challenge to universities who have tended to view themselves as the *creators* of new knowledge and ideas, and not consultants on the *implementation* of those ideas in the corporate world. The dramatic growth of corporate/university research consortia in recent years suggests that universities may be slowly but steadily learning to better blend societal needs for essential basic research with corporate needs for rapid applications of that research to the solution of real-world problems. Meanwhile, consulting firms are demonstrating that they, too, have the ability to do research and publish, as witnessed by the recent wave of best-selling books emanating from consulting firm authors.[19]

- Users are increasingly interested in educational experiences that are tied to the work environment and are growing more convinced that the action learning model is a powerful framework for leveraging investment in executive education. At the same time, users must not forget the need to continue to build strong individual skills among high-potential key managers even while faced with the need for overwhelming organizational reforms. There is danger that leadership development processes could become too insular if focused only within a particular organization and only on its current competitive environment. Careful consideration should be given to whether the pendulum may have swung too far in the direction of targeted educational interventions, and whether there is a need to promote more debate on the appropriate balance between open-enrollment and company-specific executive education experiences.

- Providers must recognize that key supply and demand partnerships will be established over the next decade. It appears that comparative advantage will (and should) go to those providers willing and able to develop innovative mechanisms for establishing such partnerships with both the corporate community and fellow providers who can add complimentary capabilities or additional capacity.

- Finally, users must demand that providers practice what they preach. Providers must be required to identify their core competencies, focus on those areas where they can leverage their value and uniqueness in the marketplace through partnerships, establish those partnerships, and help their clients rethink the meaning of executive education and leadership development for the twenty-first-century economic environment. They must help their clients plan for success in a world where continuous learning is the ultimate competitive advantage.

8

Evaluating
Impacts

THE EVALUATION OF LEADERSHIP development programs is one of the most perplexing challenges facing human resource development (HRD) practitioners. Most of the work that has been done on evaluation has focused on lower-level training initiatives, where it is easier to quantify learning. Although the challenge of assessing programs for corporate leadership is greater, many of the same principles apply.

W. J. Rothwell and H. C. Kazanas defined evaluation as the process of assigning value and making critical judgments about the impact of leadership development on organizational, group, or individual performance. They suggested that evaluation should answer the following questions:

- What changes resulted from the program or its various methods?
- How much change resulted from the program or its methods?
- What value can be assigned to those changes?
- How much value can be assigned to those changes?[1]

In a presentation to the National Society for Sales Training Executives (NSSTE), J. P. Huller of Hobart Corporation noted that the ability to document impact was directly associated with the credibility and therefore the influence of the HRD function. Huller outlined the value of such credibility:

When you are accepted, trusted, respected and needed, lots of wonderful things happen:

- Your budget requests are granted.
- You keep your job (you might even be promoted).

- Your staff keeps their jobs.
- The quality of your work improves.
- Senior management listens to your advice.
- You are given more control.[2]

If all these wondrous things can happen when there is an effective design for evaluating leadership development efforts, there should be great interest in enhancing the caliber of evaluation techniques. Without doubt, program assessment is a source of considerable stress in HRD departments. One of our interviewees commented, "A provider of programs that are well received is 'managerial Sominex'—if the evaluations go well, I can sleep at night." In a more serious vein, initiatives are evaluated to determine whether they should be supported, or whether a particular session or facilitator should be changed, eliminated, or given an expanded role. Credible evaluation processes also help identify ways future leadership development initiatives can be even more effective, and help justify the continuance or expansion of development efforts. Perhaps most important, in an age of continual cost cutting and relentless expenditure justification, continued corporate investment in leadership development is predicated on credible assessment data that verify the positive impact of those investments on individual and organizational performance.

Two approaches to evaluation are essential:

1. *Formative* evaluation is conducted before and during an initiative, to ensure that it stays on target. This includes ongoing reviews of objectives; assessments of methods, approaches, and materials; previews and pilot testings of programs, providers, and techniques; and benchmarking "best practices" for comparative purposes.
2. *Summative* evaluation occurs after the fact, either following each aspect of an initiative in progress and/or at the conclusion of the overall experience.

Although most evaluation efforts are devoted to summative evaluation, it is formative evaluation that ensures the integrity of an initiative's initial design. We discuss both approaches below.

GETTING STARTED

Leadership development initiatives are mounted, not to "run programs," but to address potential gaps in leadership skill sets that could impair an organization's ability to achieve its strategic imperatives. Therefore, it is essential that evaluation and assessment focus on performance—both individual and organizational. The first step in the evaluation process, then, should be an assessment of the leadership development task at hand. A plan of action should draw heavily on our discussion of systems frameworks for leadership development. Those frameworks root leadership development in the firm's strategic imperatives. Objectives are then created for development efforts that facilitate progress toward the strategic imperatives. Based on those identified objectives for development, methods and providers are selected, initiatives developed, and linkages made with corporate human resource management systems in order to reinforce the process. Finally, techniques for assessing and evaluating effectiveness are built in throughout the system to ensure its integrity.

Thus far in this book, we have devoted considerable discussion to linking leadership development with strategic imperatives. For the purpose of this chapter, then, we will assume that the firm's strategic imperatives have been identified and that broad-based objectives for development have been formulated. We will begin our discussion of evaluation at the stage of assessing opportunities for creating leadership development initiatives.

A Framework for Assessment

Figure 8.1 presents a simple framework for the upfront assessment of leadership development initiatives.[3] The framework starts with a set of agreed-upon objectives for development. Various ways to address those objectives can be considered by working through the model.

The first level of assessment involves determining whether the best way to address a defined objective is through some form of instruction, or through alternative techniques like coordinated job experiences, task force/project team assignments, or coaching/mentoring. If instruction seems to be the most viable solution, then the next level of assessment involves consideration of whether the classroom is a viable delivery mode. If the classroom is found to be viable and appropriate, then ways to enhance the classroom experience can be assessed. If the classroom does not seem viable, then feedback, personal growth, or action learning approaches can be contemplated. Once all of these issues have been considered, plans for leadership development initiatives can then be

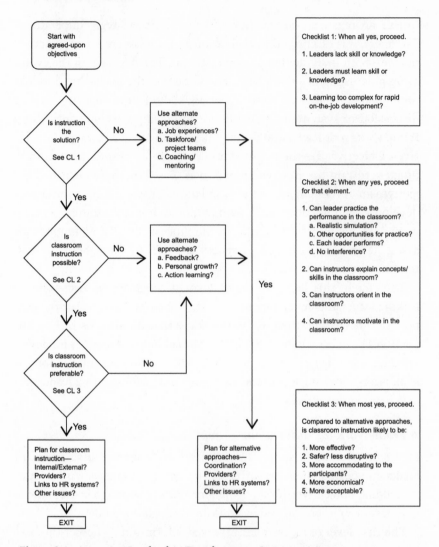

Figure 8.1 Assessing Leadership Development Opportunities

Adapted from: S. Yelon, "Classroom Instruction," *Handbook for Human Performance Technology*, ed. H. Stolovitch and E. Keeps (Washington, D.C.: The National Society for Performance and Instruction, 1992), 385.

crafted to include methods for linking the initiatives to human resource management practices within the firm, as well as methods for evaluating the effectiveness of those initiatives in addressing the core objectives for development.

Benchmarking

Either in advance of designing a leadership development initiative, or in an effort to keep an ongoing initiative vital, benchmarking best practices can be an effective tool for enhancing the effectiveness of the effort. Jac Fitz-Enz, president of the Saratoga Institute, defined *benchmarking* as:

> An investigative process that seeks out high-performing business units, inside or outside the company, for the purpose of learning how they have achieved their exceptional results.[4]

When Westinghouse decided to redesign its leadership development process, it made extensive use of benchmarking. The company had a well-defined leadership development process in place, but Jack Murphy, former director of education and development, described that process as "traditional and low risk." Although the company had a highly mechanized succession planning process, and although candidates for executive education and leadership development programs were selected using that process, there was a lack of accountability for actual performance compared with development plans. In addition, the company had no reliable method for measuring effective behavior and performance in leadership positions. As a result, Murphy noted, "the corporation didn't really enjoy much behavior or performance change. It was a case of information transfer coupled with 'ticket punching.'"[5]

To assess opportunities for rectifying this situation, Murphy launched an effort to identify and benchmark best-practice companies in the areas of succession planning and leadership development. He drew on his extensive network of contacts both within and outside of Westinghouse to identify a group of target companies to visit. He then identified a group of high-potential leaders, organized them into a task force, and set out on the project. Through this benchmarking process design, Murphy in a sense, initiated Westinghouse's first foray into action learning.

Ultimately, the task force visited 13 companies in the United States and Europe, and developed a set of "lessons learned" that heavily influenced the development of the integrated model we discussed in Chapter 5. According to Murphy, the four most critical lessons were:

- The quality of leadership development is directly proportional to the level of interest and involvement of senior management. CEO commitment is essential.
- Most learning comes from actual experience on the job. As a surrogate for experience, many companies are experimenting with "action learning" in a variety of forms.
- We must identify and develop employees with high potential early in their careers in order to create a "talent pool" within the organization.
- Performance reviews should be frequent and focused, potentially involving the use of 360 degree assessment.[6]

Armed with these lessons, Westinghouse set out on a course to revamp its executive education/leadership development process. The information gleaned from the benchmarking study was used to determine what the company was doing right, in addition to what it could do differently to improve its process. Interestingly, when disaster struck in 1992 and the massive reorganization described in Chapter 5 began, the information from the benchmarking study was very useful in assessing how the company could use executive education and leadership development as an instrument of its transformation process.

MOVING FORWARD

Once assessment has been conducted, benchmarking accomplished, and an initiative designed, methods for ongoing evaluation must be developed. The standard system for classifying approaches to evaluation was developed by Donald A. Kirkpatrick. In 1959, he wrote a series of four articles entitled "Techniques for Evaluating Training Programs," published in *Training and Development Journal.*[7] These articles described the four levels of evaluation he developed while working on his Ph.D. dissertation. Although Kirkpatrick's focus was on "training," he argued that the system he outlined applied to all "courses and programs designed to increase knowledge, improve skills and change attitudes, whether for present job improvement or for development in the future."[8] Kirkpatrick's early work is still cited regularly, and his four levels have become a standard model for the evaluation process.

The remainder of this chapter will focus on the four levels of evaluation, with examples of how each can be utilized more effectively. The levels should be viewed as a sequence of increasingly sophisticated approaches to evaluation, each with its own role and importance. Moving from Level I to higher levels becomes increasingly challenging and time consuming. Yet higher levels of evaluation provide more credible data on the real returns on leadership development investments. The four levels of evaluation to be discussed are:

Level I   Reaction Evaluation

Level II   Learning Evaluation

Level III   Behavior Evaluation

Level IV   Results Evaluation

LEVEL I: REACTION EVALUATION

The most common and basic technique for evaluating programs is assessing the reactions or critiques of participants. In essence, this approach is a "customer satisfaction index." It lets the program designer know whether participants are satisfied with the program's content and methods of delivery. Many individuals refer to reaction evaluations as "smile sheets." This label could be related to the phenomenon discussed in Chapter 10, in which program designers enlist speakers who are good "closers" in order to ensure that participants leave the program "happy." As a result, participant evaluations are often influenced by a "recency effect"—if the most recent speaker was good, the program was just fine.

Because of this, and because of the simplicity of the method, reaction evaluation sometimes is not viewed seriously, despite its almost universal use. Yet monitoring participant reactions to an initiative and its various components does provide valuable feedback which helps assess the perceived value of that initiative. If people are not satisfied with the learning experience, they probably will not use what they have learned and are likely to advise others that the program has little value. In order to maximize the impact of this kind of evaluation, it is important to articulate what participants really are expected to learn or accomplish. If there are stated program objectives, it may be more helpful to ask participants about the degree to which this session or program met those objectives than it is to ask about "enjoyment" or even perceived relevance. Figure 8.2 is an example of a daily evaluation sheet that related

"Leadership in Transforming Organizations"

1. Listed below are the key objectives for this segment of the program. You are asked to evaluate how well the presenter fulfilled these objectives.

Objective A: Be able to discuss the nature of effective leadership in the company.

Excellent _____ Good _____ Fair _____ Poor _____

Objective B: Be able to articulate the challenge of building competitive capabilities within your business.

Excellent _____ Good _____ Fair _____ Poor _____

Objective C: Be able to describe the leadership implications of the life cycle stage of your business.

Objective D: Excellent _____ Good _____ Fair _____ Poor _____

Be able to profile the organizational development challenge faced by your business using the High Flex Organization model.

Objective E: Excellent _____ Good _____ Fair _____ Poor _____

Be able to articulate the key strategic leadership issues you face in today's environment of change.

Excellent _____ Good _____ Fair _____ Poor _____

2. What points were made in the presentation that were the most valuable or meaningful to you?

3. Presenter's effectiveness

	E	G	F	P
• Presented subject matter clearly; explained, illustrated key points				
• Kept session moving and on track				
• Knowledge of subject matter				
• Visuals (slides/videographs) readable and clear				
• Instructional materials (handouts/ exercises/case studies) useful				
• Encouraged participation and answered questions satisfactorily				
• Overall opinion				

E = Excellent   G = Good   F = Fair   P = Poor

Additional Comments:

Figure 8.2 Sample Daily Evaluation Sheet

presenter performance to both session objectives and traditional performance indices. "Sample Feedback, Level I" gives examples of reaction feedback that has been quantified according to whether the objectives of a program or various segments of a program were met.

Sample Feedback, Level I (Quantified)

MONDAY

Monday's activities were to focus you on thinking about our long-term future in nontraditional ways.

1. Relevance of the content to the
   challenges facing GHP   MEAN SCORE = 4.07
2. Value of the content to you   MEAN SCORE = 4.07
3. Quality of presentation and group
   discussion   MEAN SCORE = 3.94
4. Effectiveness of the case, GHP 2002   MEAN SCORE = 3.85

360° FEEDBACK REPORT

The report and your one-to-one meeting with the coach-psychologist were to provide you with insights into your leadership strengths and opportunities for personal improvement.

1. Relevance of the 360° Feedback survey
   to the challenges facing GHP   MEAN SCORE = 4.23
2. Value of the 360° Feedback survey to you   MEAN SCORE = 4.32
3. Quality of Tuesday's presentation of the
   survey report   MEAN SCORE = 3.91
4. Effectiveness of the one-to-one meeting
   with the coach-psychologist   MEAN SCORE = 3.77

OBJECTIVES

There are four major objectives of the conference. Rate the extent to which each objective has been achieved.

28. To acquire tools to create a future with
    new opportunities for success   MEAN SCORE = 3.96

29. To be able to challenge basic
    assumptions   MEAN SCORE = 4.13
30. To reflect on feedback from self and
    others that can lead to personal change   MEAN SCORE = 4.17
31. To develop the competencies and
    courage to lead changes that bring about
    a successful future   MEAN SCORE = 4.03

CONFERENCE OVERALL

32. The overall quality of instruction   MEAN SCORE = 4.26
33. The quality of the instructors'
    interaction with participants   MEAN SCORE = 4.07
34. The quality of the support staff's
    responsiveness to participants' needs   MEAN SCORE = 4.55
35. The quality of the educational facility   MEAN SCORE = 4.42
36. The effectiveness of the Executive
    Conference overall   MEAN SCORE = 4.26

MERLIN

The Merlin exercise is intended for you to experience a process of creating breakthrough business opportunities and to communicate them to top management.

1. Effectiveness of the Merlin process as a
   tool for stimulating discussion of
   breakthrough thinking   MEAN SCORE = 4.23
2. Effectiveness of your Merlin group
   focused on our long-term future   MEAN SCORE = 3.91
3. Quality of the presentation by the
   Merlin group   MEAN SCORE = 4.29

A good reaction evaluation form should quantify as many measures as possible, but still provide an opportunity for open-ended input from participants. Simple questions, such as "How could this session have been improved?" or "What were the most valuable aspects of the session?"

are examples of typical queries that provide focused, but open-ended responses. Analysis of these open-ended responses can add useful context to numerical evaluations, helping to explain discrepancies or clarify concerns.

To avoid the problem of nonresponse bias, every participant should submit an evaluation. Most practitioners agree that insisting that evaluation forms be completed before participants leave a session is the best way to ensure this will happen. It seems that, despite their best intentions, individuals who suggest that they want to spend more time on the evaluation and then return it by mail are not likely to do so once they have returned to the hectic demands of their regular schedules. One way of dealing with this challenge is to encourage people to complete a portion of the evaluation at the end of each day. In this way, impressions are still current, and when the program comes to a close, only a small portion of the assessment remains to be completed. Information collected on an ongoing basis can be more current and can be useful for formative evaluation of an experience. However, frequent collection of data can make the experience routine and mechanical for participants, further encouraging the "smile sheets" mentality.

Some organizations have experimented with either daily or end-of-program critiques, or open discussion sessions with participants. Most have found these sessions to have more negative than positive consequences. Some of the negative consequences are that quieter people tend not to get involved in the discussions, participants' true feelings seldom emerge, and the critique can turn into a "bashing" session. As a result of these and other concerns, the value of this technique is uncertain.[9]

Following from this, there is always a question about how to use the information generated by reaction evaluation. Certainly, managers who are responsible for a program need access to the data. The faculty or facilitators should be given a summary of the information that pertains to their part of a program. Most companies provide facilitators with a quantitative evaluation of questions pertaining to their sessions, as well as a complete transcript of related written comments, both positive and negative. Many program directors utilize this information as a way to help facilitators improve their delivery. This is particularly important when the program is to be repeated a number of times. Some program directors set a minimum level of acceptability. If a program session does not achieve an overall average of 4.0, for example, the instructor may be given a couple more opportunities to meet that standard before being replaced. Some organizations use participant reaction as a quality control or customer satisfaction measure. For example, because of GTE's organizational commitment to quality, management development offers participants (and their departments) a complete refund of the tuition charged for any program that does not meet a participant's expectations. Participants are allowed to make that judgment independently and do not have to "justify" a negative response—even if other people in the program view it as being successful.

LEVEL II: LEARNING EVALUATION

Level II evaluation attempts to add an increased level of sophistication to the process by determining whether or not participants have actually learned what a program was designed to teach, whether participants have internalized the prescribed content, and whether they have mastered the material at the level of some prescribed standard. It is typically administered through some form of testing, demonstration, or role-playing technique. Level II evaluation can be viewed as "quality assurance" for the program.

D. Kirkpatrick asserted there were three things that instructors could teach: "knowledge, skills, and attitudes."[10] He added that it was important to measure learning, because behavioral change was not likely to take place unless new knowledge had been acquired, new skills developed, or attitudes changed in some way. Moreover, it is difficult to assess the meaning of a lack of behavioral change (Level III evaluation) unless there is knowledge about the degree to which learning has occurred. In other words, if a program results in little or no behavioral change, it is important to know whether that was a result of lack of learning or whether something in the environment prevented participants from applying new concepts to their work.

It is inherently more difficult to measure the knowledge gained during a leadership development experience than to determine whether a person has improved his or her ability to apply methods of statistical process control to his or her job. However, certain programs, such as "Finance for the Nonfinancial Manager" or "Quantitative Tools for Decision Making," can lend themselves to Level II evaluation. Most university credit courses use this type of assessment in the grading process. Because of the subjectivity associated with Level II evaluation, this may be the most difficult part of being a university professor. Douglas D. Anderson, managing partner of the Center for Executive Development, contrasted his experience as a member of the Harvard Business School faculty with that as a principal with a major consulting firm by referring to Shakespeare's line "The test of a vocation is the love of its drudgery." Anderson added:

> I can't say that I always passed that test at HBS; for although I loved the teaching, learning and colleagueship of the university, I did not love the grading of exams, the attending of committee meetings, and some of the other duties associated with the academy. Now, I don't have to do any of those things. I feel like I have found the Shangri-La of teaching.[11]

Assessment centers focus on the bridge between Level II and Level III. Assessment centers are "competency demonstrations" which provide learners with an opportunity to demonstrate what they have learned while being observed by an evaluator. Robinson and Robinson described this as being similar to "auditioning actors for the cast of a stage production."[12] In auditions, actors are usually given pages of script to read and deliver in a believable manner, thus demonstrating their acting skill. Similarly, simulations or activities that require participants to demonstrate how they would respond to specific situations requiring knowledge of concepts discussed in an earlier part of a program can provide concrete evidence of learning. Additionally, the simulation may serve as a reinforcement for the concepts that were taught.

An added level of sophistication for assessing performance involves using a scale with behavioral anchors. In this system, each anchor describes a particular level of competence. A *behaviorally anchored rating scale (BARS)* provides a means of assessing the differences in skill levels possessed by learners. This technique can help eliminate some degree of subjectivity from the observer evaluation and can be used as a feedback tool for participants. An example of a simple BARS scale is shown in "Behaviorially Anchored Rating Scale."

Behaviorally Anchored Rating Scale

For "Listening and Responding," the learner demonstrated the level of skill indicated.

5   Learner accurately identified the feelings of the other person, indicated what those feelings were, provided a summary of what the other person had just said, and asked if his or her understanding of the message was accurate.

4   Learner accurately identified the feelings of the other person, indicated to the other person what those feelings were, and provided a summary of what the other person had just said.

3   Learner provided the other person with a summary of what the person had just said.

2   Learner gave an answer to the other person without summarizing what the other person had just said.

1   Learner interrupted the other person and gave his or her own point of view.

Source: Reprinted with permission from Dana Gaines Robinson and James C. Robinson, *Training for Impact: How to Link Training to Business Needs and Measure the Result*, p. 198. Copyright © 1989 Jossey-Bass Inc., Publishers. All rights reserved.

The quest for objectivity in assessment center evaluation is an elusive goal that has challenged university professors and HRD professionals alike. Most organizations that use assessment centers use a multirater format in which several experts evaluate participants' performance. Some organizations videotape simulation exercises so that program managers can go back to review and verify their assessments of individual participants.

An organization that wishes to use Level II assessment would do well to think through the design of the evaluation process while developing the program. Some corporations have found that specialized firms are able to offer objective assistance in building Level II evaluation into a program design. For example, Johnson & Johnson has utilized Clark, Martire and Bartolomeo of Englewood Cliffs, New Jersey, to evaluate its

Executive Conferences, and Hoechst Celanese employed Helios Custom Training of Haydenville, Massachusetts, to assess its Leadership Development Programs. In both instances, the outside firm provided experienced observers to critique the program itself and to construct evaluation protocols to use with a sample of program participants and their sponsors. A detailed assessment by an experienced outside specialist offers a degree of credibility and objectivity that is hard to duplicate from within the sponsoring organization.

LEVEL III: BEHAVIORAL EVALUATION

A critical question for any leadership development program is "Did the behavior of participants change?" When assessment focuses on behavioral change, it has advanced to a Level III evaluation process. The acquisition of knowledge or skills does not guarantee that the acquired knowledge or skill will actually be used. Level III assessment attempts to address this issue by determining whether or not an individual has actually changed his or her behavior as a result of attending a program. Ideally, Level III evaluation compares behavioral change within a control group with similar change experienced within the group that participated in the learning experience. This can be difficult to do, as it is almost impossible to find two groups that are equal in all the factors that could have an impact on behavioral change.

Level III evaluation relies heavily on pre- and postmeasures for evaluation, because impressionistic reports of changed behaviors are less reliable than those that have some type of quantitative standard associated with them. However, sometimes preprogram assessment is neither feasible nor possible. When that is the case, it is possible for organizations to interview or survey participants after a program to determine whether they felt the experience had any perceived impact on their behavior. This can be useful, but it is far less reliable than pre- and postmeasures. Reliability can be increased if the participants' bosses, colleagues, and subordinates are surveyed to ascertain whether they have perceived any observable changes in the participant's behavior that might be attributable to the developmental experience. Another consideration is that there must be enough time for the change to take place. A six-month followup is a generally reliable standard and fairly easy to manage.

One of the most impressive approaches to assessing behavioral change, discussed briefly in Chapter 5, is 360-degree feedback. Recently, a *Fortune* headline asserted, "360° Feedback Can Change Your Life."[13] Author Brian O'Reilly described 360-degree feedback as being essentially synonymous with "feedback from co-workers or multi-reader assessment." Some observers believe that, for feedback to truly represent a 360-degree radius, it must include a personal assessment, the rating of a boss, and assessment from peers, subordinates, and key customers. Most formal programs involving 360-degree feedback utilize all of these perspectives—although many omit responses from customers.

When the Scottish poet Robert Burns penned the words "Oh wad some power the giftie gie us / To see oursl's as others see us! / It wad frae monie a blunder free us" ("To a Louse"), he could have been talking about 360-degree feedback. People seldom have an opportunity to see themselves in such detail as when they are assessed by peers and colleagues on values, competencies, and behaviors that are seen as extremely important to their effectiveness and success. The assessment instrument is likely to gather opinions on indices such as the person's listening skills, whether the person demonstrates a long-term perspective, whether the person is trustworthy, whether the person tends to be abrasive, and so on. The forms are usually computer scored and summarized at an outside agency, and a computer-generated report identifying perceived strengths and weaknesses is provided. Some companies collect copies of the analysis for the individual's career development dossier, whereas others choose to let participants "own" the data and share it with the company only if they wish to do so. Often participants are debriefed one-on-one by an expert on the instrument. These debriefing sessions sometimes include the individual's boss or a corporate HRD staff member.

The Center for Creative Leadership in Greensboro, North Carolina, is probably the largest provider of 360-degree feedback instruments and programs. Their "Benchmarks" assessment tool is one of the most highly regarded in the field. With separate specialized forms that are prepared for executive, midlevel, and supervisory participants, CCL provides an extensive database against which to compare responses and profile participant strengths and weaknesses. In addition, CCL has extensive experience in delivering programs around 360-degree feedback, and a reputation for unparalleled objectivity.

An Example of Level III Evaluation

Keilty Goldsmith & Company is a firm that specializes in programs that provide Level III pre- and postcourse assessment. The firm also has conducted some of the most significant research on the impact of feedback and followup on leadership effectiveness. Their research began with a Fortune 500 company that had conducted a "Leadership and Values Course" for its top 100 executives. As part of the program, each executive received feedback from his or her direct reports using a custom-designed behavioral assessment. Based on this feedback, participants were encouraged to

1. Pick one to three areas for improvement.
2. Develop an action plan for desired change.
3. Respond to direct reports concerning areas for improvement and ask them for help in changing.
4. Follow up with direct reports to check on progress and to receive further assistance.

Some 18 months later, the direct reports were asked to rate these same executives on their increased or decreased effectiveness as leaders, and on how well they had responded to and followed up on concerns raised in the assessment. This 18-month Followup Questionnaire is shown below. This same methodology was repeated with several other firms to generate a database of over 5,000 managers.[14]

18-Month Followup Questionnaire

LEADERSHIP INVENTORY SUPPLEMENT
FOR DIRECT REPORTS

1. Do you feel this individual has become more effective (or less effective) as a leader in the past 18 months? (Please rate this person on her/his effectiveness concerning aspects of leadership she/he can con-

trol. Please do not consider environmental or organizational factors that are beyond this person's control.)

Less Effective		No Perceptible Change					More Effective		
−5	−4	−3	−2	−1	0	+1	+2	+3	+4	+5

2. Did this person discuss what he/she learned from his/her previous leadership inventory feedback with you?

_____ Yes

_____ No

_____ Not Sure

_____ This person did not receive prior feedback from me.

3. How has this person followed up with you on areas that he/she has been trying to improve?

_____ Consistent (Periodic) Followup

_____ Some Followup

_____ No Perceptible Followup

___

An additional 18 months after the initial feedback evaluations were completed, 60 percent of the direct reports still had the same reporting relationship with their managers. These individuals were asked to once again complete the form shown above. The responses from direct reports who did not have the same managers after 18 months were not included in the study.

Research Findings

The results of a 36-Month Followup Questionnaire shown on the following page indicate that, 18 months later, over 74 percent of the managers who attended the session were perceived by their direct reports as having responded to their feedback. It is possible that some managers in the "did not respond" group actually did respond, but their response had so little impact that their direct reports did not remember it. For those managers who did respond to the feedback, only 11.4 percent of their direct reports noted that there had been no followup on progress. The most common response was "some follow up" (41.5 percent) with a substantial group being seen as conducting "consistent/periodic followup" (21.1 percent). The analysis indicates that participants who responded to their direct reports after receiving feedback were very likely to follow up concerning areas in which they were trying to improve. Moreover, leaders who both responded and followed up were more likely to be perceived as having significantly improved their effectiveness.

Results of 36-Month Followup Questionnaire

DIRECT REPORTS (18 MONTHS' EXPERIENCE)

My manager responded after program	74.1%
My manager did not respond after program	25.9%

DIRECT REPORTS (OF THOSE MANAGERS WHO RESPONDED AFTER THE PROGRAM)

My manager did no followup	11.4%
My manager did some followup	41.5%
My manager did consistent/periodic followup	21.1%

These results reflect the power of Level III evaluation. This type of detailed assessment makes it possible to evaluate the impact of an ongoing initiative while shaping future initiatives for improvement. The implications of this particular example may have an even more profound significance for evaluation and assessment efforts: if a leader receives feedback, develops an action plan, and follows up periodically, he or she will almost invariably be perceived as more effective by direct reports. This reinforces the point that a program itself is not the answer. Each leader in the Keilty Goldsmith study attended the same program, taught by the same instructors, and received feedback from the same inventory. Although most leaders were seen as benefiting from the experience to some degree, a few were seen as wasting their time. However, the major variable for change was found not to be the program, but the followup process that took place after the program.

Organizations tend to spend a great deal of time planning programs, but almost no time on planning followup. Yet followup seems to be an approach that not only enhances the outcomes of a leadership development initiative, but also provides an ongoing mechanism for measuring progress or improvement associated with that initiative.[15]

Item Analysis

Another value of the accumulated data generated by 360-degree feedback is the use of item or cluster analysis to create categories for benchmarking or development. These types of analysis provide objective, statistically based methods for uncovering clusters of similar individuals or patterns of similar behaviors within a larger population. One Fortune 50 firm used this technique to analyze data from over 500 participants in a senior leadership development initiative. While maintaining individual anonymity, the analysis of the data revealed six categories or profiles of leaders who had similar patterns of strengths and weaknesses. These included

- Highly skilled leaders who use moderate pressure to get results
- Highly skilled, supportive, team-oriented leaders
- High-pressure, business-focused leaders
- Underskilled leaders with moderately effective problem-solving skills
- Generally underskilled leaders
- Underskilled leaders who apply high pressure[16]

Figure 8.3 provides an example of the information generated by this type of analysis. The data suggest that approximately 10 percent of the participants in the sample could be described as supportive and team oriented. Their weaknesses were in market knowledge and willingness to take risks. Their strengths were in basic "people skills." The bottom of the table suggests potential areas for personal development. Individuals in this category were viewed as being better candidates for mentoring and helping develop younger colleagues than for startup or turnaround assignments. By similarly analyzing and reviewing all six clusters, the

BRIEF DESCRIPTION

Supportive, team-building executives

COMPOSITION

	n	Percent Breakdown within Group 4-R	Percent of Each Level Falling into Group 4-R	Percent of Whole Population
Senior level	14	30%	6%	10%
Mgt Board Level	33	70%	13%	(n = 47)

SKILL PROFILE

	Low	Average	High
Leadership Vision		√	
Risk Taking/Venturesomeness	—		
Marketplace Awareness	—		
Organizational Awareness		√	
Managing Complexities		√	
Employee Development		√	
Team Development			+
Information/Data Support		√	
Standards of Performance		√	
Push/Pressure			+
Coping with Stress			+
Sharing Credit			+
Cultural Appreciation			+

CHARACTERISTICS

- Show a combination of high, average, and below-average skills.
- Are especially strong in the people-oriented areas of management.
- Probably manage internal, day-to-day motivational processes well.
- Show weaknesses in knowledge of the market and willingness to take risks.

IMPLICATIONS

- Need to develop externally oriented skills.
- Need to develop greater long-term and visionary planning skills.
- Need to become more effective with the implementation and organizational processes which are more cognitive, analytical, and planning oriented.

Figure 8.3 Group 4-R: Perceptions by Reports

sponsoring company crafted a well-targeted leadership development initiative, complete with appropriate measures for effectiveness. In addition, this information was shared with the entire human resource department and was especially helpful in refining the performance evaluation and succession planning systems.

LEVEL IV: RESULTS EVALUATION

After assessing the degree of behavioral change, the next logical question is "How have these changed behaviors impacted the business?" Line executives want to know if productivity or quality has improved, or if the change in behavior is consistent with the organization's strategy and objectives. Just as in evaluating the benefits of an investment in new equipment, this level of assessment often requires numerous "before" and "after" organizational performance measures, along with some difficult calculations.

Some common techniques for evaluating results include pre- and post-measurements of indices such as productivity, customer complaints, cycle times, employee turnover ratios, and employee attitudes. If there is improvement in these indices following a leadership development initiative, then it can be assumed that the initiative contributed in some way to the progress made. Unfortunately, there are many intervening variables in the environment that can affect these same indices during the measurement interval, and it is nearly impossible to control for all of these variables. In order to deal with this challenge, Rothwell and Kazanas noted that a results-based evaluation process must:

- Identify important measures, on the basis of organizational needs/plans, to be changed as a result of leadership development initiatives.
- Clarify the degree of change sought.
- Control for intervening variables to the extent possible.
- Compare organizational performance after the leadership development initiative to those existing before the initiative took place.[17]

The ultimate evaluation objective of most human resource development programs is to prove that the activity has generated a significant return on investment for the sponsoring organization. Jack J. Phillips suggested that a fifth level of evaluation should be added to the Kirkpatrick model, focused specifically on return on investment (ROI).[18] Programs that affect "the bottom line" are certainly more significant and more credible than those that simply produce people who "enjoyed" the experience. However, as with Level IV evaluation, success in business performance is usually related to a combination of variables. Consequently, it is difficult to determine what portion of any type of performance improvement might be directly related to particular developmental initiatives.

Rothwell and Kazanas's four suggestions for creating results-based evaluation systems seem equally applicable when attempting to calculate some form of ROI.[19] The difference is that not only do critical measurements need to be identified, targets for improvement set, and pre- and postmeasurements made, but these numbers must be converted to financial indices. For example, no company has made a greater effort to track its return on investments in learning than Motorola. The board of Motorola University regularly has a third party audit team assess whether or not specific programs produce a return for the business. Motorola University President Bill Wiggenhorn justifies an expenditure of over $100 million by citing a conclusion recently reached by the company's vice president of finance, who reported that the reduction of floor space in Motorola factories and labs can be attributed to skill enhancement programs that reduced corporate costs by $2.2 billion between 1987 and 1992.

> Those audit reports show that when we train the right people, transfer the knowledge and skills back to the [work] environment, the managers change their own behavior by reinforcing the use of these skills, we got a $30–35 return for every training dollar spent. This is the best return on capital that we get in any of our investment schemes.[20]

Determining such financial returns of a leadership development program requires careful planning and computation. The first step is to identify the impacts of the program in some measurable way. Methods that can be used in leadership development ROI analysis include customer assessments, control group comparisons, and time series analyses. Additionally, program participants as well as their supervisors, subordinates, or outside observers can provide an assessment of the impact of developmental initiatives. When these data have been quantified, it is necessary to convert them to financial values. Hard data, such as quantity, quality, cost, or time, can be converted directly. Softer data—such as assessments of the impact of programs taken by participants or observers on issues like productivity or morale—are more difficult. Some firms have outside auditors prepare analyses of cost savings or increased profit or revenue due to leadership development. Some have their own finance group do the analysis. Others are content with the analysis provided by the leadership development staff.

To calculate leadership development ROI, it is first necessary to calculate the total cost of the initiative. The cost calculation should incorporate all out-of-pocket expenditures for the program, along with participant time, travel, and other related expenses:

- *Direct costs*, such as materials, meals, provider fees, related travel, lodging, and meal expenses

- *Indirect costs* associated with development efforts but not tied directly to a specific initiative, including administrative support and marketing

- *Development costs* for program and content design, faculty preparation, and pilot testing

- *Overhead costs* associated with corporate charges and facilities/ equipment use

- *Compensation costs* for participants' time while involved in the initiative

Some firms do not include this last cost in their calculations, and for many others, participant travel and lodging expenses are the responsibility of the sponsoring unit and therefore not included in ROI calculations.

The ROI formula, then, is the net program benefits, as assessed in the analysis of changes in critical financial indices, divided by the program cost. A simple way of expressing this formula is:

$$\text{ROI (percentage)} = \frac{\text{Benefits} - \text{Costs}}{\text{Costs}} \times 100$$

Table 8.1 summarizes attempts that several organizations made to calculate the return on investment of various training and development initiatives. Some of these examples are focused on lower-level training. Many, however, are parts of initiatives that have "cascaded" through an entire organization.

A Systems Perspective on Evaluation

As mentioned previously, the levels of evaluation described above should be viewed, not as an individual approach, but as a cascading process of increased sophistication. Each level provides useful and important information. An overall evaluation process that makes use of techniques from each level is more likely to generate useful data that verifies the impact of leadership development on the organization and its members. Figure 8.4 describes how CIGNA provides an overall assessment and evaluation of its programs utilizing the four levels of evaluation.

Chain of impact		Research tool		Time period
Opinions	↓	Trainee self-report	↓	Throughout training and at three-month followup
Learning	↓	Trainee self-report	↓	At end of training
Behavior	↓	Survey of trainee's subordinates	↓	Before training and at three-month followup
Results	↓	Trainee's work unit records, action plan, and objectives review	↓	Tracked from three months preceding training to three months following training

(Difficulty — vertical label between columns 1 and 2; Power — vertical label between columns 3 and 4)

Figure 8.4 CIGNA Impact Model

Adapted from: D. Kirpatrick, *Evaluating Training Programs*, p. 194. Reprinted with permission of the publisher. Copyright © 1975 by D. Kirpatrick, Berrett-Koehler Publishers, Inc., San Francisco, CA. All rights reserved.

TABLE 8.1 Return on Investment for Learning Initiatives

Setting	Target Group	Program Description	Evaluation Process	Results
Electric and gas utility	Managers and supervisors	• Applied behavior • Management focusing on achieving employee involvement to increase quality, productivity, and profits	• Action planning (variety of projects) • Performance monitoring	• 400% ROI • Benefit/cost ratio 5:1
Bottling company (Coca-Cola)	Supervisors	• Eight half-day workshops covering supervisory roles, settling goals, developing the team, etc.	• Action planning • Followup session • Performance monitoring	• 1.447% ROI • Benefit/cost ratio 15:1 • Variety of measures
Paper products company	Managers, supervisors, and hourly employees	• Organizational development program (workshops, action study teams, skill building programs)	• Followup with interviews • Survey • Performance monitoring	• Variance from standard: +$106,000 • Waste 36% improvement • Absenteeism 35% improvement • Safety 25% improvement
Health maintenance organization (HMO)	All managers and all employees	• Organizational development program (team building, group meetings, customer service training)	• Performance monitoring • Management estimation	• 20,700 new HMO members • 1,270% ROI • Benefit/cost ratio 13.7:1

Organization	Target group	Program	Evaluation	Results
Large commercial bank	Consumer loan officers	• Two-day sales training program (focus on increase in service training)	• Followup • Performance monitoring	• 30% increase in consumer loans • 2,000% ROI • Benefit/cost ratio 21:1
Information services company	Supervisors	• Twelve 2.5-hour sessions on behavioral modeling	• Followup with surveys	• 336% ROI
Bakery (Multi-Marques, Inc.)	Supervisors/administration services	• 15-hour supervisory skills training (including the role of training)	• Action planning (work process analyses) • Performance monitoring	• 215% ROI • Benefit/cost ratio 3.2:1
Avionics (Litton Industries)	All employees	• Self-directed work teams	• Action planning • Performance monitoring	• Productivity increased 30% • Scrap rate reduction 50% • 700% ROI
Truck leasing (Penske Truck Leasing)	All supervisors	• 20-hour program on supervisory skills, utilizing behavior modeling	• Performance monitoring	• Turnover reduction 6% • Absenteeism reduction 16.7%
Trucking (Yellow Freight System)	Managers	• Redesigned performance appraisal with training on interpersonal skills, communication, and coaching	• Followup interviews • Performance monitoring	• 1,115% ROI • Benefit/cost ratio 12:1
Federal government	New supervisors	• 5-day introduction to supervision course covering eight key competencies	• Followup questionnaire	• 150% ROI • Benefit/cost ratio 2.5:1

*These cases appear in Jack J. Phillips, ed., *Measuring Return on Investment* (Alexandria, Va.: American Society for Training and Development, 1994).

SUMMARY

The approaches to assessment and evaluation discussed in this chapter should not be seen as independent of one another. Instead, they should be viewed as a "chain of impact" for leadership development investments. First, learning intervention must be rooted in the strategic imperatives of the firm. Then it must be designed to take full advantage of the various techniques, methodologies, and providers available. The design should be benchmarked against "best-practice" companies. It must be accepted and embraced by participants. It must change participants' knowledge and attitudes. It must help them to change their behavior back on the job. It must show that these changed behaviors have led to improved results for the organization.

Nicholas S. Merlo of Hughes Aircraft Corporation reported that his firm had generated returns of over 3,000 percent from performance improvement related to training. Although his numbers are challenging, Merlo felt that the approach used to obtain them was conservative and pragmatic,[21] and suggested that the findings call for HRD professionals to reorient their thinking. Perhaps our primary concern should move beyond what is being taught and how many managers are being developed, to the more productive question "Is what we are teaching impacting performance?"

PART 3

The Future

9

The Leading Edge

IN THIS CHAPTER, we present six leading-edge examples of new paradigm approaches to leadership development. Although we cannot claim to have benchmarked every best-practice organization in the field of strategic leadership development, we do believe these five exemplar initiatives to be among the most innovative approaches we have found. We offer them as an opportunity for readers to do their own benchmarking and as detailed examples of how prominent organizations are responding to the challenge of strategic leadership development.

Although each of the exemplar initiatives is grounded in well-conceived, systemic approaches to the process, each addresses a particular dimension of strategic leadership development.

1. The Center for Creative Leadership's LeaderLab Program exemplifies innovative approaches to program design.
2. AT&T's Leadership Development Program for Middle Managers exemplifies innovative approaches for developing key middle management talent.
3. ARAMARK's Executive Leadership Institute exemplifies comprehensive, action learning–based approaches to leadership development.
4. The World Bank's Executive Development program exemplifies consortium-based, experientially driven design.
5. The new leadership development initiatives at Johnson & Johnson exemplify emerging strategic approaches to the process.
6. MIT's Center for Organizational Learning exemplifies emerging approaches to university/corporate collaboration in leadership and organizational development.

INNOVATION IN PROGRAM DESIGN

The Center for Creative Leadership's LeaderLab program was launched in 1991.[1] Since its inception, it has run over 30 times for well over 500 participants. According to program designers Victoria Guthrie and Bob Burnside, the stated purpose of LeaderLab is "to encourage and enable leaders to take more effective actions in their leadership situations, actions which develop themselves and others in pursuit of goals that benefit all." This statement embodies a belief that, in the future, leaders need the resources to act, and not just reflect, in order to effectively confront the serious challenges that await them.

LeaderLab's content falls into three basic categories:

1. Review of the significant generic challenges faced by leaders today
2. Development of the competencies necessary to deal with those challenges
3. Assessment and development of skills and knowledge to help participants understand their specific leadership situation and take action

A fourth category, the information and personal awareness that each participant generates by means of item 3, is developed during the course of the program and is unique for each individual.

LeaderLab expands on the center's traditional model of a self-awareness program by providing mechanisms for support and accountability over an extended period of time (six months), to help participants transmit course learning back to the workplace. Extensive precourse preparation is required, including qualitative analyses of the individual's personal and work situations, as well as a variety of feedback instruments that are thoroughly explained during the program to help the individual gain a deeper understanding of him- or herself. Participants spend time at the center learning ways to lead in a variety of situations and developing the processes and tools to achieve lasting behavioral change. They create an action plan to implement in their own work environment with the help of a center staff person called a process advisor (PA), a "coach" who maintains frequent contact with the participant via telephone. During the program itself, and back in the workplace, the participant is supported by several "change partners." These are fellow program participants or individuals personally selected by the participant back in the workplace who act as resources to encourage, coach, and give honest feedback to participants on their work.

Several unique, action-oriented techniques created for LeaderLab are used in concert with more conventional training methods like discussion, exercise, simulations, and use of learning journals. Two of the guiding principles of the program are that learning should be connected to the back-home leadership situation and that learning should occur over time. LeaderLab makes this happen through two time-phased training sessions, implementation of action plans back in the workplace, and continuous work with the process advisor and change partners. The program methods and their rationales are summarized in Table 9.1.

Program Process

Based on the program's objectives, different elements of instruction are combined in a unique and potentially powerful experience. Following Table 9.1, the basic components of the program are outlined.

TABLE 9.1 LeaderLab's Program Methods and Rationales

Method	*Rationale*
Action learning over time	Intervening and learning over time leads to change; addressing real issues helps transfer learning to leadership situation
Developmental relationships: process advisor (PA), change partner	Support for change-feedback challenges; provides wisdom/advice
Reflective learning journals	Connects participant to program over 6 months to distill patterns, key lessons; encourages self-analysis; provides content for process advisor phone calls
Visioning and action planning	Provides process and structure of targeting changes and improvements; emphasizes positives or "ideals" to guide change process

Nontraditional activities
  Acting
  Artistic activities
  3-D problem solving (group sculpting)
	Taps creative, emotional sides of learning; helps get "outside the box" of linear thinking; emphasizes importance of using affective and behavioral domains as well as cognitive

Intervention over Time. The program begins with a six-day classroom session culminating in each participant's development of an action plan for improving his or her leadership. Participants then return to their jobs for three months, during which time they work to carry out the plan. Following that intervening period, a second classroom session of four days takes place. At that time, participants review how their action plan progressed and modify it based on their experiences and learnings from the first three months. A revised action plan established at the end of the second classroom session is then implemented over the remaining three months. Thus the program duration is six months. This type of intervention over time is a critical factor in the program's approach to ensuring lasting behavioral change. The program is structured to accommodate the full adult learning cycle (planning, doing, and reflecting).

Program Activities in an Action-oriented Format. The focus on learning to learn and relating learning to the individual participant's unique leadership situation call for classroom activities in addition to traditional lectures. These include discussion, exercises, simulations, use of a learning journal, and nontraditional activities. Discussions promote cross-fertilization of ideas among participants, allowing them to bring their experience and expertise to one another. Exercises serve as the first safe place where new ideas and behaviors can be put into practice. The simulation is an extended exercise (known as a "simmercize" in Leader-Lab) which puts participants into the organizational roles of a fictional company, dealing with rapid change and difficult issues while wrestling with seemingly conflicting individual and divisional values. The daily learning journal provides a vehicle for reflection on learning and gives the individual themes or patterns of behavior that can be useful in taking more effective actions in one's own situation.

Process Advisor. This staff person meets with the participant during both weeks of training and helps construct his or her action plan. The advisor also contacts the participant monthly by phone during the three-month intervals. The advisor's purpose is to continually prod and encourage the participant to address issues and blocks in his or her development.

Change Partners. The main task for each participant in this program is to create and follow through on an action plan for his or her leadership situation. A system of support, both in the program (change partners) and in the workplace (back-home change partners), is set up to support the participant in this goal. In LeaderLab, a diverse, three-person, in-course work group collaborates to encourage the individual. At home, each participant must also establish a group of change partners in the organization to help him or her with leadership improvement.

Diversity of Participants and Trainers. Because diversity is one of the challenges of the future, LeaderLab classroom composition is a mix of genders, ethnic groups, and work situations. A working actor and artist-facilitator serving as trainers have added an important element of experiential diversity.

Nontraditional Learning Activities: Art, Acting, and Sculpting. A number of additional components which have not traditionally been part of a leadership development program are presented in LeaderLab. Frequently, being in a management position develops one's abilities to intellectualize and verbalize, but not to use other methods of expression. Art is used to address this issue. In one segment, the participant draws with pastel chalks to communicate a particular situation in his or her life. In another, participants create a "Touchstone" sculpture that communicates a metaphor for their approach to leadership. They are asked to think back on their experiences of the week and put on the touchstone whatever they want most to remind themselves of back in the daily chaos of their work environment. They may select from a pool of materials that includes leaves, wood, stones, string, and numerous other materials. One participant explained his touchstone as follows:

> This piece of plywood is me. See, it's right angled at one end—that's where I'm coming from, very analytic and hard edged. This big, open shell is my analytic side. No problem with that, it's well developed and I rely on it a lot. But here, next to it is my emotional side. It's a lot smaller, only open a little way, and it's pretty well covered up. These other two shells here at this end are more equal in size. They represent my analytic side and my emotional side more in balance. That's where I want to go. But how am I going to get from here to there? There's a straight path here at

the right-angled end. It's fast and smooth, but if you notice, it doesn't get me all the way to the other end. The other path, the twisty, turning one, does go all the way. It'll take me longer. It's winding and rough, but it will get me there.[2]

The acting component was designed and is trained by a working actor and incorporates methods used in acting instruction. Its focus is on awareness of the participant's physical self-presentation (tone of voice, body posture, gesture) and its effect on others. The "Acting Leader" is the first of the nontraditional segments to be presented in the program. It comprises two classroom sessions in week 1 of the program, plus the trainer's personal assessment of each participant's behaviors as observed during the opening "simmercize." In a brief individual session, each participant is given a "suggesture" (from suggested gesture), based on what he or she typically tends to do, that would make the participant more effective. Two more sessions take place in week 2, which focus more on group interaction based on the same principles.

The body-sculpting component was designed by a practicing family therapist and makes use of the pioneering work of Virginia Satir in identifying and working with family dynamics issues nonverbally. This session occurs on the second day of week 1. In its adaptation to the leadership development context, participants work with an issue or situation that has caused difficulties at work, using classmates to stage a scenario, representing first a problem situation, then creating a scenario representing a possible solution. The scenarios are verbally debriefed in depth. A second session occurs during week 2, during which time participants form groups to create scenarios representing problems they have faced in meeting their action plans; they then create scenarios representing resolution of these difficulties. Because the participants are using their bodies as "clay" to construct their own unscripted scenarios, these exercises are relatively unstructured. They require skilled facilitation, both in the process and in the debrief, which involves being able to translate a nonverbal experience into terms relevant to the participants' work environment.

Impact of the Experience

Participant comments from the final essay prepared at the conclusion of LeaderLab provide insight into the unique nature of the experience.

LeaderLab provided me with a more clear sense of purpose and a plan for moving forward. The competencies and holistic model provided context within which to identify options and develop strategies. Conversations with my process advisor, coupled with the journaling process, helped me stay focused on that sense of purpose and start to find a balance between short and long term issues and goals.

LeaderLab reinforced the importance of continuing my team leadership approach while thoroughly assessing situations and developing very specific and measurable action plans. The most significant impact of my LeaderLab experience is the importance of viewing results as learning events and to reflect on the experiences.

Dianne Young at the center recently completed a rigorous followup study of 37 LeaderLab participants from three different programs to assess the impact of the experience 9 to 12 months following attendance.[3] Although the participants were very high on the experience, perhaps the most telling finding was that individuals who worked with the participants noted substantial (statistically significant) positive change in them. In particular, participants were found to have made tangible progress in coping with difficult, stressful situations; developing and maintaining personal relationships; and perhaps most impressively, initiating changes in organizational practices. The participants themselves cited as the most helpful aspects of the course the extended time interval (six months), coupled with the emphasis on action planning. In addition, the coaching aspects of the program received high praise as a mechanism for maintaining a focus on development and ensuring followup. Perhaps most interestingly, although the artistic aspects of the content (Touchstone exercise) were often evaluated more critically by participants during the program, they actually received much higher praise in the followup research. This may reflect the longer-term value of a "stretch" or personal awareness exercise for participants, when that exercise is linked with an action plan for personal growth.

Summary

LeaderLab is a unique experience that combines aspects of conceptual, feedback, and personal growth approaches to leadership development with coaching and action learning. By drawing from several steps of the knowledge creation cycle (Chapter 5), the program appears to be a more holistic, well-rounded approach to individual development. Based on the followup research, the program seems to have a powerful positive impact on the personal development of participants.

BUILDING LEADERSHIP DEPTH

Earlier in this book, we discussed the critical role of middle managers in today's flatter, more networked organizations and the importance of targeting leadership development initiatives to this group. We stated our belief that the battered and bruised middle managers of today's organizations may hold the key to future competitiveness. In the aftermath of significant downsizing and restructuring, the importance of middle management in creating competitive advantage is being rediscovered. AT&T's Leadership Development Program for Middle Managers (LDP), a two-week residential program delivered five to six times each year to groups of approximately 45 high-potential middle managers from throughout the company, is a benchmark attempt to deal with that challenge. Program director Deepak (Dick) Sethi helped design the experience, which is delivered using external experts at the company's new headquarters-based learning center in Basking Ridge, New Jersey.[4]

Always noted for its commitment to executive education and leadership development, AT&T launched LDP in 1988 in a format that might best be described as a traditional, "mini-MBA" executive education experience. The company took a radically different approach to the program when it was redesigned in 1992. The redesign was driven by the vision of CEO Bob Allen, who had just dramatically reorganized the company into strategic business units and committed it to a core set of strategic imperatives, including emphases on customer focus, globalization, diversity, total quality, and innovation. The goal was to make AT&T a fleet-footed world leader in the telecommunications industry— or, in AT&T terminology, the world's best at bringing people together. Allen and the AT&T HRD staff realized that this new way of operating, far removed from the traditional perspective of a huge regulated monopoly, would require a new style of leader—one that would combine strong general management skills with the drive of a change agent (see

Figure 9.1). The Leadership Development Program for Middle Managers was recreated to help meet this requirement.

The core objectives for the redesigned LDP are to transform middle managers into general managers and leaders, and to create agents of change who can transform AT&T's culture, starting with themselves. The program relies heavily on experiential and action learning techniques to address the critical dimensions of leadership in the new AT&T environment. Although classroom discussion sessions are utilized to present concepts and ideas important to the direction of the program, these discussions are intended to add dimension and perspective to its real thrust—learning through dialogue, networking, and action planning. The program takes a holistic approach to leadership development, addressing hard and soft business issues, as well as issues in wellness, fitness, and work-family balance.

Program Process

LDP is rooted in two basic philosophies:

1. *Unlearning* is a prelude to new learning.
2. Learning has not taken place if behavior has not changed.

The program is designed to create a climate of safety, trust, and learning where participants learn from and with each other in a manner that impacts both knowledge and performance enhancement. Risk taking, entrepreneurship, and influence skills are emphasized, and even making

FROM		TO
Functional	→	General manager perspective
Risk averse	→	Innovative
Responsive	→	Take-charge/Responsible/Accountable
Internal/Individual	→	Customer/Market/Team collaboration
Upward/Transactional	→	Relationships
Domestic	→	Global
Power over	→	Power with/Power under
Controls	→	Coaches
Manager	→	Leader-manager
Reacts to change	→	Leads change

Figure 9.1 Leadership Transformation at AT&T

a mistake is championed—as long as someone learns from it. During the program, participants are encouraged to speak their minds and get involved. Nothing is reported back to their supervisors.

Precourse Work. About eight weeks before to the start of a session, the 45 managers who will be attending are asked to document the key business challenge they face. As the participants will learn, these business challenges then become a key focal point of the program. In a recent enhancement to the program, each participant discusses the issues with the supervisor prior to attending the program, in preparation for the experience, as well as after the program in an effort to apply the learning that has taken place.

"Gap" Group Process. At the outset of the program, participants are assigned to "gap" groups of six or seven people—"gap" referring to the difference between where they currently are and where they need to be in addressing their predefined business challenges. Each day, a different participant spends two hours discussing his or her challenge with the gap group. Group members offer ideas, advice, and pushback to their colleague. Program director Sethi and an outside consultant act as group facilitators when needed. Sethi refers to the outcomes of this approach as "compound organizational learning," in that each individual can use group feedback to better frame personal issues and generate creative solutions to problems, while at the same time, each gap group member learns from the experience of colleagues. The gap group participants often maintain their network following the program.

Classroom Discussion. In addition to the gap group process, participants engage in discussion and dialogue with leading business school professors and consultants, who discuss issues identified as critical for the company. These sessions address issues like industry trends, change management, financial management, and global business development. Rather than focusing solely on lectures and case studies, however, the experts facilitate discussion and dialogue around the actual issues of concern to the group and the company. These sessions help promote a greater awareness of the general management challenge among the participants, as well as a deeper understanding of the key roles of leaders in a changing organization. Discussions with senior AT&T executives and major customers also take place during the program, giving participants an opportunity to further broaden their perspectives on the company and its business. CEO Bob Allen typically joins each of the groups for a discussion session.

Learning Circles. At the end of each day, participants engage in "learning circles," small groups, different from the gap groups, that discuss what happened during the day and what learnings were generated. These debriefings help participants to clarify what they have learned and apply the learning to their work situation.

Leadership Laboratories. Another feature of the program involves the use of "leadership laboratories," experiential exercises in which participants have a chance to work in teams to solve unique problems. For one assignment, the group simulates a "production process" by tossing tennis balls within and between three circles of people. The object is to place a tennis ball in a basket after everyone in all three groups has touched it. The group gets $1 million for each ball it successfully places in the basket, but loses $3 million for each ball dropped. Teams representing investors, customers, marketing, and management are selected to help "coordinate" the process, with all other participants being designated as "production workers." Typically, after 30 minutes of nearly chaotic activity, the exercise ends with skeptical investors, concerned customers, worried management, unhappy workers, and a bunch of dropped balls. At their conclusion, exercises like this are thoroughly debriefed to help participants gain greater insight into the leadership process. In the instance above, management may have crafted a well-developed plan for completing the exercise, but often has failed to communicate the plan to production workers or execute it with due quality and a sense of urgency. The results are disastrous, just as in the real world. These experiences help bring basic principles of leadership to life, and facilitate feedback and dialogue around critical leadership skills.

Holistic Activities. In addition to business issues and leadership dimensions, the program endeavors to address what program designers call "mind and body" issues. Activities such as hour-long daily exercise periods, mild aerobics, relaxation, and discussions on personal well-being and work-family balance are built into the program to complete its holistic approach.

Action Plans. Participants leave with a documented action plan at the conclusion of the course, in addition to having addressed their business challenge in the gap group process. They are also encouraged to develop a second action plan to enhance their personal effectiveness and leadership skills.

Impact of the Experience

Participant reactions to LDP tend to praise its highly engaging, interactive approach and its action orientation. The program is consistently seen by participants as having made a difference in their approach to both leadership and their jobs. In addition, the peer coaching and "learning laboratory" aspects of the program are viewed very positively, as is the opportunity for cross-organizational unit networking. The following comments are typical:

> Excellent group process. Allowed members to not only learn/relearn skills, but to put them immediately into action.

> The gap process touched and taught me one of the most important learnings of the course: everyone brings value and a great perspective to any task—everyone should be heard.

> There was more interaction . . . and respect shown for the intelligence and talent of participants. [It provided] real insight into leadership skills.

> The program brought together some of AT&T's sharpest minds . . . the intellectual stimulation was a sheer delight.

> In that room I had to force myself to articulate my problem to folks who don't know anything about it. I came back with such solid ideas.

AT&T has built several reinforcement elements into the program to ensure its transfer to the workplace. They include postprogram meetings with participant supervisors to discuss transfer, and followup calls to participants from program staff and coaches following completion of the program to discuss the experience and the individual's ongoing development. One of the most lasting benefits of the program may be that the gap groups continue to meet long after the program ends. In addition, the documented action plan prepared during the course provides an opportunity for immediate implementation of ideas generated during the course. Taken together, this hands-on, holistic approach does seem to have the potential to make a real impact on both the participants and the organization.

Although AT&T believes that such positive impacts result from the program, the company is seeking hard data to verify its perceptions. In a study completed in 1993, appropriately referred to within AT&T as "Beyond the Smiles," over 70 past program participants were interviewed, along with their superiors and a group of peers and subordinates. The study found that over 75 percent of the participants had followed through on their action plans, most quite successfully. It also included an in-depth analysis of which elements of the program had the most impact on the participants in their professional and personal lives.[5] These data were then used to further refine and enhance the experience. A similar followup study conducted in November 1995 found that 87 percent of the participants felt that they had become more effective leaders, and 85 percent felt that they had increased their effectiveness in managing change, several months after the experience. AT&T believes that, if it can verify whether individual leadership behavior has been positively impacted by the program, it also can verify whether the program has met one of its core objectives: creating change agents who can transform AT&T's culture, starting with themselves.

With the trivestiture of AT&T in September 1995, the LDP program was refocused in 1996 to meet the needs of the new AT&T. Dick Sethi and his team have made the design even more aggressive, inculcating a greater sense of urgency. Participants are encouraged to actively practice new leadership behaviors that will help enhance AT&T's business performance. There is much more focus on AT&T issues, and the company's new strategies are presented to the group in open-forum discussions by senior AT&T executives. Participants and executives are encouraged to engage in a healthy dialogue as owners of the company. A 360-degree feedback instrument has also been added and participants are given feedback and counsel. The program continues to exhort the participants to lead through ownership, accountability, speed, and clarity.

Summary

The AT&T LDP is an excellent example of the creative adaptation of classroom, experiential, and action learning approaches to leadership development. In effect, LDP has been established as a learning laboratory where participants have an opportunity to interact with external experts, customers, corporate officers, and one another in an effort to gain deeper understanding of leadership principles and their application within AT&T. The gap group process helps link this understanding to each participant's work environment, thereby leveraging the experience and contributing to organizational development and effectiveness. AT&T's continued efforts to assess the impact of LDP are impressive, reflecting the need for organizations to continually strive to ensure that investments in leadership development contribute to enhanced performance of both individual participants and the organization as a whole.

ACTION LEARNING–BASED LEADERSHIP DEVELOPMENT

In Chapter 3, we discussed the ARAMARK Executive Leadership Institute (ELI), a strategic leadership development initiative targeted to the seniormost leaders of the company. ELI, jointly developed by ARAMARK and Penn State Executive Programs, was designed to help the company's senior leaders address the organization's core strategic imperatives: achieving a high level of profitable growth by becoming the world leader in managed services. Thus far, over 200 senior executives have completed a version of ELI, including CEO Joe Neubauer and his fellow corporate officers. Specific objectives for the program follow:[6]

- Create a shared vision for growth.
- Share "best practices" throughout ARAMARK.
- Encourage innovative thinking.
- Embrace change in order to continue success.
- Increase analytical skills.
- Enhance risk taking.
- Promote individual leader development

ELI is a unique, nine-month leadership development experience consisting of four program "modules" and an action learning experience. In addition, an accompanying 360-degree assessment process using the Center for Creative Leadership's *Benchmarks* instrument is conducted over the duration of the program by RHR Associates of New York. The end product of this assessment is a personal development plan for each participant, jointly agreed upon by the individual and his or her boss. The database developed through the 360-degree assessment process also has become the basis for the development of an ARAMARK leadership competency model, which is guiding the redesign of selection and appraisal systems in the company.

Program Process

The overall structure for the program is presented in Figure 9.2. The first module of ELI is a one-week, classroom-based program which features a specially designed series of discussions on critical issues and core analytical frameworks deemed essential to ARAMARK's future success. These discussions make extensive use of ARAMARK case studies and hands-on application exercises, including an outdoor leadership development experience. Participants also are introduced, on the final day of the module, to the 360-degree assessment process. Faculty for the week include professors from major universities who have been well versed on the history of ARAMARK and its current strategic objectives.

The ideas, techniques, and skills learned during the first module make up the basic tool kit for use in an action learning assignment called an "Action Project." The objectives for ELI's Action Project process are

- To give participants the opportunity to apply the concepts of the Executive Leadership Institute to real-world situations
- To give participants the opportunity to work with individuals from other business units and to build internal networks
- To share best practices across business units
- To have fresh eyes investigate and analyze opportunities for business development and revenue growth
- To institutionalize the practice of fact-based analysis among ARAMARK senior managers

At the conclusion of module one, participants are assigned to an Action Project team. Those teams then engage in an experiential exercise in which they address the above objectives by analyzing and resolving a

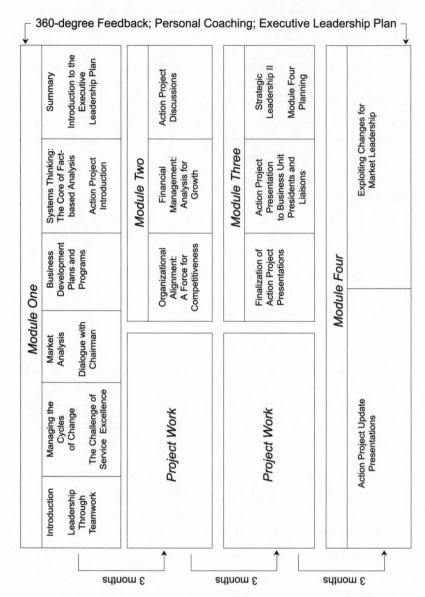

Figure 9.2 ARAMARK Executive Leadership Institute

critical company concern. Those concerns have been identified and submitted to the ELI staff by ARAMARK's business unit presidents and approved by CEO Joe Neubauer to ensure their importance and relevance. The only stipulation with regard to the Action Project teams themselves is that no participant can work on a problem within his or her own business unit. This helps in achieving ARAMARK's objectives for the initiative, particularly with regard to enabling the organization to get a "fresh eyes" perspective on resolving difficult organizational problems. It also provides powerful opportunities for internal networking, an additional objective of the institute.

For the next six to eight weeks, participants work on their projects, balancing the demands of their regular jobs with the challenge of the Action Projects. Although the time commitment involved can pose a problem for some participants, for most it does not. During this interval, the groups have frequent contact with a "coach," an external resource who serves as a consultant and sounding board to the team. Although the coach plays a critical role in the process as a facilitator, he or she does not do any of the work on the project.

At the conclusion of this interval, the entire class gets back together for module two, a three-day classroom-based program. Two days of that program involve additional presentations on critical skills and concepts that ARAMARK leaders will need in order to be successful in the future. Not coincidentally, those same skills and concepts are also becoming more critical to the completion of the Action Projects. The final day of this module is spent in project team meetings with the coach present.

A second six- to eight-week interval ensues, in which the Action Project teams, working with their coaches, finalize their analyses and presentations. The presentations themselves are delivered during module three of the program. On the first day of this two-and-a-half-day module, teams have an opportunity to polish their presentations and to brief project sponsors on their final analysis. On the second day, the presentations are made to the entire ELI class, as well as to project sponsors. ARAMARK senior officers attend the presentations and are actively involved in the question-and-answer process.

On the final morning of module three, participants are given an opportunity to suggest ideas for module four, the final component of the program. During this concluding two-day module, typically conducted three to four months following module three, project sponsors are given an opportunity to meet with the Action Project teams to debrief the project and update the team on what has been done with their recommendations. Although Action Project sponsors are not required to conduct a debriefing session, few have refused to do so. In addition to the debriefing session, the class participates in one final classroom session to cap their experience, and they engage in a well-deserved celebration of their achievements.

Action Project Roles

ELI designers have delineated a set of critical roles in the Action Project process, several of which have been mentioned in this discussion.[7]

Action Project Sponsor. Generally, this role is filled by each project's sponsoring business unit president. Its purpose is to demonstrate support of the Action Project team and provide sufficient preliminary information for the team to begin meaningful work on the project. The sponsor receives periodic progress reports from the team and attends the team's formal presentation during module three.

Business Unit Liaison. This role is the critical link between the Action Project team and the sponsoring business unit. The liaison's role is to provide the team with access to the "inside" information that they need to complete their project work. The liaison is also responsible for keeping the Action Project sponsor apprised of the team's work on the project. Like the sponsor, the liaison receives periodic progress reports from the team and attends the team's formal presentation during module three.

Coach. The coach is an external resource who acts as a process consultant for the Action Project team. This role includes serving as a "sounding board," questioning and critiquing the team's assumptions, and providing analytical guidance. The coach is a facilitator only and does not do any of the actual project work.

Corporate Support. Individuals in this role provide support by giving direction and assistance to teams seeking access to critical information, such as financial or market data.

Executive Leadership Institute Staff. The individuals in this role oversee and monitor the entire program, including the Action Project process, ensuring that the entire initiative stays on track. In addition, they provide special assistance when needed by the teams.

The Action Project Process

Teams, typically made up of six individuals, each representing a different business unit or department of the company and all from units other than the one sponsoring the project, are given their project assignment on the final day of module one. The team has some time that day to begin to structure its work, but the bulk of its efforts occurs between the formal sessions. Ultimately, the teams make fact-based presentations to their business unit sponsors and liaisons during module three.

The sponsoring business unit president is asked to compose a "memo" to the Action Project team explaining the business unit's view of the project. The purpose of this memo is to provide the team with a framework from which to work, demonstrate that the sponsoring business unit is in support of the team and its efforts, and identify the Action Project liaison. The sponsoring business unit is also asked to provide essential background information to the team: history of the issue, courses of action taken on this issue in the past and their outcomes, information regarding marketplace trends, relevant financial information, and any other pertinent material. The basic guideline is that anything that the organization would supply to an external consulting firm hired to work on the project should be supplied to the Action Project team before it commences work.

Milestones/Progress Reports. The first task of the teams is to select a contact person and formulate milestones for the completion of their projects. The contact person maintains responsibility for providing the coach, the liaison, and the sponsor with periodic progress reports. Those reports can be one-page summaries but should provide specific information, including an update on the group's progress, details on goals that are on or off track, reasons for variations, milestones achieved, and any revisions to the group's work structure.

Process Suggestions. In an introductory session at the end of module one, coaches provide team members with a short (90-minute) orientation to the Action Project process and give them a three-page set of guidelines for organizing themselves and moving forward with their analysis. The guidelines include a set of initial considerations for addressing their project and a brief set of expectations for the kinds of analysis they are expected to perform. Beyond this brief orientation to the process, the teams are on their own to structure themselves and move forward.

Fact-based Presentations. Teams deliver their final analysis and recommendations during module three. They are allotted approximately 20 to 30 minutes for their formal presentation, with an additional 20- to 30-minute period for questions. The presentations are to include commentary on all pertinent issues, including personal benefits attained from project work. A final written report is also to be provided to the sponsor, liaison, and ELI staff. This report is to include copies of overheads or slides used in the final presentation, an outline of recommendations, and all supporting analytical information.

Followup. An opportunity for debriefing, updates on progress, and followup on team recommendations are provided during module four. As mentioned above, project sponsors are not required to conduct a debriefing session, although most are quite willing to do so.

Impact of the Experience

The success of ELI can be measured in a number of ways. On their evaluations at the end of module four, a full 100 percent of the ELI participants felt that the overall program met or exceeded their expectations. Additionally, nearly 95 percent of the participants felt that the Action Projects were a meaningful process for their own development as well as the development of ARAMARK. In followup interviews, ELI participants indicated that the program had a very positive impact on self- and company awareness, internal networking, a more collaborative leadership style, and increased risk taking and "out-of-the-box" thinking. Typical comments on the impact of the experience were:

> One of the truly valuable outcomes of ELI is that you see a shift from resistance to change to desire to change. . . . A willingness to change only

comes about when the culture fosters risk taking and allows you to take risks in order to improve. . . . I think ELI did a very good job fostering that willingness to take risks which allows us to make change.

The Action Project gives you new ideas. In fact, we started an action project within our division . . . using the format we learned in ELI. It was very beneficial with regard to the specific Action Project as well as a way to use it in my own business.

Interaction/networking was a big plus for me. It's increased my understanding of our business and our people, and also given me personally more confidence in how I fit into the organization.

In addition to participant reactions to the program, CEO Neubauer is even more specific in his critique of ELI:

We could not even dream of Mission 10-5 [the company's five-year growth plan] without the foundation of the Executive Leadership Institute. The market focus and organizational momentum we gained from the education and Action Projects has been the basis of conceiving that we actually could grow the company 10% for each of the next five years.

Finally, ARAMARK has an additional tool for assessing the impact of ELI—the results of the Action Projects. Although, as it should be expected, some projects had more impact than others, the company can point to several instances in which an Action Project team's recommendations had significant impact on the company. These include a role in the decision to merge two business units to gain operating efficiencies and leverage customer relationships, the identification of opportunities for better utilization of information technology in another business unit, and a decision not to engage in a particular plan for cross-selling initiatives across business units. In all these instances, the company has generated results that clearly demonstrate the impact of ELI.

Summary

ELI has played an enormous role in the revitalization of ARAMARK, and seems to have added a spark to the already successful and profitable company. The initiative itself was so meaningful to the 200 senior-level participants that they have commissioned the design of a version of the program for the next 400 to 500 managers in the company.

A CONSORTIUM-BASED, EXPERIENTIALLY DRIVEN APPROACH

For over 50 years, the World Bank has been committed to helping its borrowers reduce poverty and improve living standards in developing economies throughout the world. To promote sustainable economic development, it has supported more than 6,000 development projects in over 140 countries, with more than $300 billion in financing. However, the world in which the World Bank Group operates is changing dramatically. The process of economic development is being revolutionized by two major trends: the decline in development aid and the dramatic increase in private capital flows. As a result, in a world of increasing conflict and growing poverty, the need for a global development agency is crucial. Leadership is needed to help developing countries become integrated into the new global economy, transfer cross-regional experience, and manage global regional initiatives to fight poverty and environmental degradation.

Providing this type of leadership has always been the mission of the World Bank. Yet World Bank management recognized that changing the internal culture of the bank was an essential prerequisite to strengthening its contributions to global economic development. The bank's president, James Wolfensohn, emphasized the need to break the bureaucratic gridlock that had evolved within the bank over the years, in order to restore the bank to its position as an international leader in promoting economic development. To do this, he recognized the need to improve client relationships, make a quantum leap in bank managers' financial analysis skills, and develop a culture committed to performance and results.

Changing the Bank's Culture

Changing the culture of the bank would be a major undertaking, in which executive education was seen as critical. Bank staff who had participated in executive education programs felt that a high-level educational experience could make a difference in the organization. Furthermore, there was overriding consensus on the importance of giving managers throughout the bank an opportunity to step out of their daily environment and interact with a diverse group of peers from outside their normal base of contacts. As a result, the bank's leadership proposed a program that would

- Show the bank's willingness to learn from other organizations.
- Underscore the fundamental importance of client focus and results.
- Illustrate processes for change in large organizations, particularly those in the public sector.
- Demonstrate the importance of leadership and accountability as forces for change.
- Develop a learning organization.

Program Process

Following these discussions, Wolfensohn decided to commission a special executive education program to be designed and delivered by five partnering graduate schools: the Harvard Business School, INSEAD (France), the Stanford Business School, Harvard's John F. Kennedy School of Government, and IESE (Spain). The objective over two years is for up to 400 World Bank executives to participate in this program. Christened "The Executive Development Program (EDP)," the experience is designed to equip executives to meet tomorrow's leadership challenges. Through creatively designed lectures, case discussions, study groups, and team workshops, participants learn and apply new approaches to building the bank's capabilities.

The comprehensive program is residential and delivered in three two-week academic modules, each separated by a break of up to two months. The first module is held at the Harvard Business School, with the second and third modules held at Lansdowne Conference Center in Virginia. Between modules, participants return to the workplace to begin applying what they have learned. Upon returning to the program, participants reassess their own business strategies and refine their action plans based on their experiences and their interactions with participants and faculty. In fact, all participants must immediately apply their learning to a specific issue or challenge for the bank and its clients. These group projects, presented at the end of the course to Wolfensohn, are a critical link between learning and results.

Addressing Critical Issues. Although the specific curriculum is continuously refined and adjusted, the basic program content includes the following broad topics:

MODULE I: STRATEGY AND COMPETITION
—Poverty and Environmental Sustainability
—The World Bank in Context
—Customers and Customer Focus
—Crafting Strategy in a Competitive Environment
—Finance
—The Role of the General Manager
—Integrative Exercise on Strategy and Competition

MODULE II: STRATEGIC MANAGEMENT OF OPERATIONS AND SERVICES
—Analysis of Service Delivery Processes
—Finance
—Analysis of Resource Allocation Systems
—Management of Large Scale Projects
—Business Process Reengineering
—Relating Performance Measures and Incentive Systems to Strategy
—Team Effectiveness
—Managing Alliances and Partnerships
—Integrative Exercise on Organizational Effectiveness and Design

MODULE III: LEADERSHIP, CULTURE, AND THE LEARNING
ORGANIZATIONS
—Leadership as a Force for Change
—Crafting Effective Corporate Culture
—Managing and Capitalizing on Diversity
—Behavioral Change versus Structural Change
—Integrative Exercise on Sustaining Change

The Poverty Module: An Action Learning Experience. One of the innovative aspects of this program is a nonacademic experience called "The Poverty Module." The Poverty Module is designed as an integral component of the EDP. Its purpose is to encourage the application of the analytical and strategic skills gained during the academic weeks of the program to the bank's mission of poverty reduction. The intense classroom sessions provided by the intellectual exposure of the first three modules are designed to sharpen awareness of global competition and the vital importance of being client focused. The Poverty Module is designed to get participants closer to "clients" and to inform an appreciation of the challenge of poverty reduction and of the importance of partnership in that venture. Wolfensohn is particularly keen on this component of the EDP.

The module has three components. First, there is a role-playing simulation which provides a safe environment where participants can learn more about listening to their World Bank "clients." Second is the opportunity to live and learn in a poor community and to experience life from the perspective of the poor villager or slum dweller. And, third, some time after returning to their desks, participants review their experience and search to integrate what they learned into their work. The objective is "to help us re-examine how we work and to explore other methods of achieving our mission of poverty reduction. The exposure is intended to provoke in us some doubts about the efficacy of our current approaches; to produce in us some respect for the capacity and resourcefulness of poor communities."

Impact of the Experience

Reflecting on the program experience as a whole, EDP director Tariq Husain noted, "It has been among the most educational experiences of my work life—the partnership with faculty is seamless and the outcomes are impressive, way beyond expectations. It feels like a family engaged in joint work with common goals. Such a partnership is what we are attempting to accomplish within the Bank." With regard to the program's impact on participants, Husain went on to say, "The content is relevant, the pedagogy is outstanding and the impact on participants is magical. We felt this on March 14 when Cohort 1 graduated and Jim

Wolfensohn visited. The learning experience produced a change in a dramatic way—it transformed a group into a team."

A program participant echoed Husain's reflections, noting, "The program is about poverty. It is about the clients. What we learned is not about what to say, it is about what to do." Expanding on that view, another participant summarized the impact of EDP by noting, "For me, the World Bank's EDP was the most outstanding executive education I have received and even far exceeded my initially high expectations. It is a watershed for the institution, an enormously far-sighted and effective investment in cultural change that will expand our capacity to carry out our vital mission."

The overall impact of the experience and the value of the consortium delivery model was summarized by another participant:

> I can already see the group cohesion that is building up among us. Working together for long hours has built a strong feeling of shared goals. We are starting to use the same language; we are, in fact, changing our corporate culture within the group as a result of what we learned. . . . Several elements of the program design contribute particularly to this: coming back together several times, with intervals in between, but not too far apart, is proving to have a great impact; having a wide range of faculty, brought together from the different training institutions gives a richness that would not be available with only one institution.

Jim Wolfensohn also believes the lessons of EDP are taking root:

> From the outset, I think everyone agreed that the enhanced education of the Bank Group's staff was fundamental to change the way we do business in today's challenging development environment. What we have witnessed, in less than two years, is a complete overhaul in our approach to seeking and achieving that education; one that is evolving with each intake to meet our institution's needs; and one that has sent a veritable breath of fresh dynamism and enthusiasm throughout the institution. Thanks to the EDP, we are now equipping more and more of our managers with a level of training that will not only improve their client-orientation, but will allow them to harness and develop the technical skills of their teams. This, to my mind, is crucial if the Bank is to be the responsive and effective development institution it was created to be. This has been a bold initiative that has paid off, and I know the end results will

bring in enormous dividends for the 4.7 billion clients served by our institution.

Summary

The World Bank EDP is a powerful example of a multimethod, experience-driven leadership development experience. As reflected in the participant reactions and evaluations, the mix of focused classroom instruction and relevant experiential activities can have an enormous impact on both individual learning and organizational development. And, as more and more organizations begin to focus, like the World Bank, on leadership development as a core tool to drive strategy and shape culture, they are expressing greater interest in the consortium-based design and delivery model so effectively utilized in EDP. The degree of expertise required of providers, as well as the degree of customization required to truly impact an organization in the manner of EDP, is likely to push providers even further toward larger-scale, collaborative initiatives that combine the best talent and expertise available to help an organization succeed in a changing world.

STRATEGIES FOR LEADERSHIP AND ORGANIZATIONAL DEVELOPMENT

Going beyond a programmatic focus, we now shift our discussion to strategies for leadership development. Here we have chosen to look at Johnson & Johnson (J&J). The key to understanding leadership development (and almost everything) at Johnson & Johnson lies in the commitment to its Credo and its philosophy of decentralization. In 1886, when Robert W. Johnson founded the firm, his aim was "to alleviate pain and disease."[8] Shortly after the turn of the century, he expanded this view into a business ideology rooted in the belief that service to customers and concern for employees should be ranked ahead of returns to shareholders. This philosophy was articulated in a number of ways throughout the history of the company until, in 1943, Robert W. Johnson, Jr., codified the ideology in a document entitled "Our Credo." The article has been periodically reviewed, challenged, and slightly revised, although the hierarchy of responsibility from customers to employees to shareholders along with the concept of *fair* return rather than maximum profitability has remained constant throughout the firm's history.[9] The

Harvard Business School dedicated one of its case studies to how J&J puts its Credo into action—including how the Credo impacts organizational structure, internal planning processes, leadership development, compensation systems, and strategic business decisions. The case also discussed how the Credo serves as a tangible guide for action in such critical times as the 1982 Tylenol crisis.[10]

J&J believes a total commitment to and universal familiarity with the Credo is the key to successful implementation of a decentralization philosophy that is also sacrosanct for the company. Its structure, with approximately 168 separate companies with their own presidents, management boards, financial statements, brand names, and corporate logos sends the signal "We want leaders to operate the autonomous, entrepreneurial business units with total commitment to our core values." Commitment to decentralization, allowing leading units tremendous autonomy beneath the umbrella of the Credo, explains why the J&J leadership development initiatives previously discussed in this book were not undertaken with more direction from top corporate management. J&J is constantly looking for ways to add value at the corporate level without diminishing the autonomy of managers throughout its family of companies.

In 1993, partially because of input from the "Creating Our Future Program" (Executive Conference II discussed in Chapter 6) and with direction from McKinsey & Company, the Johnson & Johnson Executive Committee began a process called "FrameworkS" to examine and clarify key issues facing the firm. FrameworkS initiatives were created that focused on matters such as U.S. health care reform, global consumer health care opportunities, and organizational changes, as well as specific opportunities in Europe and China. A 1995 FrameworkS initiative (FrameworkS VI) was specifically targeted to "Leadership, People and Team Work." As one might expect at Johnson & Johnson, a mix of executive committee members and senior managers from a range of J&J companies were involved as participants in this project. Through this initiative, in the midst of widespread recognition for its business successes in 1995, Johnson & Johnson began the process of "reinventing" its approach to leadership development both in response to feedback on its current initiatives and in anticipation of challenges expected to emerge over the coming decade.

FrameworkS VI began with a short but intensive research effort, which included an executive-level survey of needs and activities in the field, an analysis of information generated from the 360-degree feedback database, highlights of previous Credo Survey results, and a 1994 study, "Views on Leadership," which reported on interviews with 35 key J&J executives. An executive report based on this analysis revealed that the company saw education as a strategic lever to "increase the capability of leaders as well as a method to solve immediate organizational issues through action learning or combining classroom education with focus on business problems." The report further indicated that, although J&J viewed learning as a core competence, its career planning, evaluation, and succession planning systems could be improved. The FrameworkS group used this information to debate the challenge of developing leadership talent in a company expected to triple in size within a decade and committed itself to making continuous learning and knowledge creation a core competence.

Leadership development had always been viewed as an important contributor to Johnson & Johnson's ability to create a talent pool of leaders throughout the organization. Still, there was concern that anticipated levels of growth would strain its capacity to develop leaders who would be able to staff, energize, and manage a $50 billion organization by the year 2005. To help focus leadership development on this important challenge, and to align the overall HRD system, the firm began the process of auditing, coordinating, and revising its HRD efforts to practice the best tenants of "anticipatory learning."

If It's Not Broke, Fix It Anyway!

As previously suggested, leadership development at Johnson & Johnson would have been viewed by almost anyone as a tremendous success. The Executive Conference series was drawing rave reviews from participants and had been publicly recognized by the chairman as being instrumental in shifting the thinking of the executive team and in providing a stimulus for new business development. Successful "Advanced Management Programs" were being conducted for middle-level managers throughout the world at such prestigious academic institutions as IMD in Switzerland, Northwestern University, the University of California at Berkeley, and Duke University. Supervisory training was conducted on a decentralized basis, but built on a competency study conducted in the late 1980s to "identify specific characteristics that affect Johnson & Johnson supervisors and to develop a behavior model of the effective supervisor." The Key Attribute Model (KAM) which grew out of this effort was the foundation for very successful supervisory training that was offered by internal trainers as well as external providers. In order to gain some economies of "shared services" while maintaining the rights and initiatives associated with decentralization, a "Learning Services Consortium" had been created to pull together a catalog of courses offered by outside vendors who had been certified to meet J&J standards. A total of 82 courses in six major locations were available for a variety of skills and managerial training, ranging from "Active Listening" to "Writing for Impact."

In order to create the future rather than react to it, reexamination of the existing successful base began in 1995. Ongoing programs like the "Advanced Management Program" were put on hold, and a new concept of "core" educational strategy began to evolve. It was understood that the Credo along with its attendant J&J values would be the single greatest differentiator for the company and, along with leadership issues, should provide the foundation for the majority of any "core program." It was further recognized that some core programs would probably need to be designed specifically for individuals as they first became managers, as they became managers of managers, and as they became board members of operating companies and moved into their first executive-level responsibilities.

As a result of their debates, the FrameworkS group came up with a set of recommendations for a new approach to leadership development at J&J. For first-level managers, one module would focus on the Credo and what it means to individuals in basic management jobs. Because of the large numbers of people involved in this constituency, delivery would be by line executives and advanced technology, to minimize time away from the job. While content would be "suggested" for the regions, local autonomy would be preserved.

For middle-management programs, it was determined that line managers would deliver with assistance from appropriate technology such as CD-ROM or interactive video programs. These would gradually replace classroom education in the twenty-first century. For managers of managers, the program would focus on Credo issues and their impact on regional leadership challenges, in sessions delivered regionally around the world.

Because of the corporate-level responsibilities associated with executive roles, the core program for new board members would focus members on how the Credo of leadership values played out within the J&J organization. To provide direct contact with executives throughout the world and to provide exposure for high-potential individuals in this category, this level initiative would take place in New Brunswick, with some traditional classroom sessions involving global leadership issues and 360-degree feedback relative to the Credo and key leadership competencies.

By mid-1997, the impact of this reassessment and evaluation was being seen. A FrameworkS group involving 70 people had developed a set of "leadership standards" for the executive and midmanagement levels, which outside consultants had molded into a customized 360-degree feedback instrument. Succession Planning and Management Development had been combined into a single reporting unit. In addition, the "standards of leadership" became incorporated into the performance evaluation process. In the midst of these changes, CEO Ralph Larsen suggested that the theme for the next Executive Conference should be leadership. As had been true with the previous conference, after giving a sense of direction for the program, Larsen used the decentralized management style of Johnson & Johnson to empower other executives to work out the details of the initiative.

Program Process

The program, called "The Standards of Leadership," has three components. The first is "personal leadership." This includes a 360-degree feedback process utilizing the competencies that had been previously identified. The second component, "Credo leadership," involves one of J&J's senior executives facilitating discussions about the statement of values that has provided a moral anchor for the company over the past century. Finally, there is the third component, "organizational leadership," which is based on targeted action learning projects. After meetings with company group chairs and the group operating committees, the director of Executive Conferences and the lead consultant providers meet with high-level corporate sponsors for various initiatives to decide what business issues will be addressed and which executives should attend a session. Once attendees and issues have been identified, a team leader from within the company is identified, along with team consultants. The sessions are designed for an average of 55 people, divided into five teams, although there could be as many as 33 teams or as few as 3.

Approximately two months before a session is scheduled, each team's project sponsor meets with participants and makes presession work assignments. Participants distribute the feedback instruments and begin a series of team conference calls to determine what data will be needed in order to address their particular assignment. The actual sessions are conducted on a geographically decentralized basis, usually close to where the greatest concentration of participants works. The sessions begin on a Sunday evening and conclude on Friday. The first two days address the 360-degree feedback process and Credo leadership. Wednesday and Thursday are intensive days devoted to the action learning project, culminating on Fridays with reports on each team's proposed action steps for the next three months. Over the next 90 days, with limited involvement from the external consultants, the teams continue to work on their projects and plan for a formal "Business Review" with the session sponsor (senior line executive with responsibility for the sponsoring business). Although the results of action learning projects are important, the ultimate goal of the Executive Conference III is for participants to learn about leadership. According to one company group chairman, "Elegant solutions without learning is not as desirable as mediocre solutions with great learning about leadership."

The university-based programs for middle managers have not been restarted. A new program entitled "Advanced Management: The Leadership Challenge" has been created, with themes similar to the Executive Conference. These include "standards of leadership" (with 360-degree feedback) and Credo issues along with corporate executives leading modules on leadership.

A "Standards of Leadership" program for first-level managers is currently being developed along with plans for the HRD group to facilitate train-the-trainer sessions for internal delivery of the programs. After exploring the potential of utilizing CD-ROM and other high-tech delivery for this program, concerns about both cost and adaptability make this alternative less probable than had been originally thought.

Impact of the Experience

As this book goes to press, the third Executive Conference at Johnson & Johnson is still in its early stages. Yet the early assessments seem to agree that the process of applied action learning will yield great benefits, especially when there is a committed champion or top management supporter working with skilled facilitators on a challenge that is clearly seen as an urgent issue.[11]

One of the most successful experiences involved a senior executive in a very mature business who began the session by saying, "I am staking my career on you people and this process. You are my partners in saving this business." Because both the challenge and commitment were real, participants agreed to creative, stretch objectives that promise to revolutionize the business. Another company group chairman instructed his group, "I am more interested in crude plans that people will commit to than elegant analysis that is merely interesting."

Two major challenges have become obvious, even in the early stages of the rollout. First, a successful business may be slower to see the importance of the process. The successful business units seem to approach the process with an attitude of "why do we have to go through this kind of exercise again?" Second, coming up with truly significant projects is sometimes a challenge—especially for larger sessions where ten teams of ten executives are working on different questions around a central theme. "The first two or three projects that a sponsor develops are usually critical and exciting. After that, it's hard to find questions with the same level of significance and obvious urgency." While sponsors of the program will continue to refine and tune the approach, there appears to be wide agreement that Executive Conference III is meeting its objective of "providing new solutions to the challenge of leading with a new sense of leadership urgency."

Summary

Johnson & Johnson seems to recognize the importance of leadership development in a world where leaders, and therefore organizations, are

expected to be continuous learners. Its approach to leadership development has become an ongoing process which involves leaders from
throughout the highly decentralized company in the creation of initiatives that constantly reflect and address the firm's changing environment. In this manner, leadership development at Johnson & Johnson is
conducted in a manner consistent with the values and strategy of the
total organization. The current redesign of their leadership development
is based on a view of where the organization wishes to be in ten years.
Because of this, the company is committed to the utilization of emerging technologies and addressing evolving issues crucial to long-term
competitiveness. And, by involving line executives in various regions of
the world, Johnson & Johnson is creating a cadre of "partners" with
whom the challenge of leadership development will be shared. The company exemplifies the move toward creating processes that blend experience, training, education, and other forms of development into a knowledge creation cycle that is tied into an aligned and integrated HRD system.

UNIVERSITY APPROACHES TO CORPORATE PARTNERSHIPS

Throughout this book, we have commented on the challenge facing university business schools in the field of executive education/leadership
development. Although some institutions are struggling, others are
moving to provide a bridge between the creative thinking done in academic institutions and its application in the business world. The MIT
Center for Organizational Learning (OLC) provides a striking example of
how one university reaches out to various corporate partners to bridge
the gap between research and practice while enriching the competencies
of all participants.

For years, Peter Senge labored in relative obscurity as a research director of the "New Management Project" at MIT's Sloan School of Management. A protégé of Jay Forrester (the inventor of core memory and the
father of systems dynamics), Senge was attempting to bring some of the
rigor of systems dynamics to the softer areas of leadership and organizational behavior. The tremendous success of Senge's best-selling book
The Fifth Discipline[12] in 1990 moved him and his work into the forefront of American thought. As a result, the New Management Project

has evolved into the Center for Organizational Learning—one of the best examples of a partnership between talented researchers and leading business practitioners.

The center officially began in 1991 and grew rapidly to its self-imposed limit of 20 company sponsors. In January 1996, another 20 firms were on a waiting list to become members. Over 1,000 had attended the five-day Core Competencies program. The center was in the process of assessing its organization and mission. The statement of purpose was evolving but seemed to include the following:

> To encourage a global community of people and organizations working together to develop, test, disseminate, and implement theory and method for more effective systems of:
>
> - organizing work
> - organizational learning, and
> - leadership[13]

The Center for Organizational Learning describes itself as "a consortium of innovative organizations working with MIT researchers to advance the state-of-the-art in building learning organizations through collaborative research and practice." One major premise underlying the center's work is that individuals and organizations must fundamentally alter both thinking and management practices in order to thrive in an increasingly dynamic and interdependent world. A second premise is that these essential fundamental changes, because they *are* so fundamental, are difficult to achieve while working in isolation. Although individual companies have different purposes and businesses, the core processes and systems that define their work have a great deal in common. To explore and test the hypothesis, the OLC was formed as a research consortium focused on developing new learning tools. OLC's goal is to achieve a "significant impact on management practice and on management education."

According to Senge, "the center is designed to spread ideas, to create a few successful models of the learning organization that cannot be ignored."[14] Recently, the following organizations were involved in various aspects of the center: Amoco Production Company, AT&T, EDS, Federal Express, Ford Motor Company, GS Technologies, Harley-Davidson,

Herman Miller, Hewlett-Packard, Intel Corporation, Merck & Co., Motorola, National Semiconductor, Pacific Bell, Philips Display, Quality Management Network, Shell Oil Company, and US West.

The Structure of the OLC

The research agenda of the center is determined by representatives of sponsoring organizations, working with faculty and research staff at MIT. Together, they select and research areas of common interest. Most projects entail designing learning processes within an organization and studying their effectiveness. Typically, during their first year of involvement, sponsoring organizations participate and focus on a variety of core *foundation-building* activities. These activities establish a base of experience and understanding on which more specific learning capabilities can be developed. Essentially, year one of membership emphasizes gaining an understanding of center language, tools, and perspectives in order to build a foundation for creating a project specifically tailored to the sponsor's needs and interests. This involves sending a cadre of managers to various center programs and activities to gain an understanding of OLC's work and its philosophies. In addition, sponsoring organizations have opportunities to participate in a variety of capacity-building activities. These activities are designed to develop a core group of people inside the organization with the requisite skills, knowledge, and commitment required to support pilot projects and additional organizational change efforts.

Sponsoring organizations make a substantial annual contribution that enables them to participate in the foundation-building activities of the center. These include a five-day core course, semiannual meetings, seminars, advanced courses, dialogue courses, and opportunities for networking with researchers and other sponsors. Organizations may also participate in optional capacity-building activities which are research focused and involve additional costs depending on the level of MIT resources required. Although some potential members wince at the high membership fee, OLC provides three major benefits to sponsoring organizations:

1. Sponsors are guaranteed several places in center seminars and workshops. In many instances, the tuition for these programs would cost as much as the membership fee.

2. Membership provides an unparalleled opportunity to network with highly involved (and evolved) managers who are wrestling in innovative ways with some of the most significant issues of the day. Membership meetings provide detailed insight into the successes (and setbacks) of cutting-edge projects.
3. Project formulation and execution are often handled by MIT faculty and staff whose time is billed at a fraction of their usual consulting rates.

Research and Learning Agenda

OLC's current research agenda and member projects can be grouped into four major areas:

Learning Laboratory Projects. These efforts focus on particular areas where teams are attempting to build in-depth knowledge of generic management issues. The learning laboratories may help managers understand how to reduce the time of new product development, examine the effects of service quality and "value-added services," and streamline the supply.

In these projects, OLC staffers work in partnership with companies to develop, implement, and assess ongoing learning processes that can be integrated with how people actually do their work. For example, a learning laboratory for surfacing, testing, and improving mental models may become part of a company's product development process, or customers and salespeople may be combined to build a joint knowledge of complex global logistics issues. Current learning laboratory projects are under way at Ford, Federal Express, Harley-Davidson, and National Semiconductor. These projects are likely to utilize some of the tools and concepts associated with the discipline of systems dynamics, the original thrust of the center.

Dialogue Projects. These activities focus on enhancing the depth and generative nature of "conversation" in diverse "working teams." Teams are defined as groups of people who need one another to take action. First-generation dialogue projects have been conducted in different types of organizational settings and have been characterized by embedded sources of conflict. Examples of current dialogue projects include union-management relations at GS Technologies (formally ARMCO Steel);

health care organization stakeholders in the community of Grand Junction, Colorado; and urban leaders in Boston, Massachusetts.

A recent issue of *Organizational Dynamics* focused on the practice of "Dialogue."[15] The process appears to be a powerful way to break down some of the barriers that affect attempts at communication. Despite the praise of its advocates and of most participants in this process, the concept of openness and honesty is frightening to many. The Ford Project was viewed by everyone involved as a great success. A new-model Lincoln Continental was ahead of schedule with record lows in defects, yet the project manager was asked to take early retirement. He feels, and others agree, that this action may have been precipitated by the fact that many managers were uncomfortable with the new environment being created through the work with OLC.

GS Technologies (GST) makes steel for mining machinery and mattress coils. In 1990, when it joined OLC, markets were eroding, labor relations were hostile (almost 500 grievances were on file), and employment had been reduced from 5,000 to 1,000 in just a decade. Three years later, the firm had successfully skirted bankruptcy and had seen sales and profits increase dramatically. Unfortunately, workers who were not involved in the "dialogue" process grew suspicious and voted out the union leader who had championed learning-organization ideas at GST. The new union leadership passed a motion banning dialogue from the shop floor. In retrospect, management realizes that it made the mistake of not spreading the program fast and deep enough. Company CEO Robert Cushman remains committed to the ideas of the learning organization, but realizes that his vision will now take longer to achieve.[16]

As new dialogue sites are being initiated, the center expects to begin to distinguish between different types of dialogues, such as "generative dialogue," which is a sustained inquiry into the deepest assumptions and habits underlying everyday experience, and "strategic dialogue," which focuses on particular questions critical to the success and effectiveness of the organization.

CEO Leadership Project. This initiative involves an inquiry into the evolving nature of leadership required to build and sustain learning organizations and the particular issues that must be addressed by top management, such as the evolution of corporate governance and the moral foundation of senior managers. Current participants in the project include CEO- or president-level executives from Harley-Davidson, Herman Miller, GS Technologies, Philips Display Components, Shell Oil, and Analog Devices.

Learning Organization Curriculum. These projects currently involve implementing and assessing the effectiveness of a five-day learning organization core curriculum. This curriculum is intended to provide an experiential introduction to the core concepts and disciplines required to build learning organizations. Also, there is a pilot project under way at EDS aimed at developing, implementing, and assessing an extended learning experience involving classwork, business projects, and ongoing coaching. The target audience for this effort is a group of 40 EDS managers, all of whom are committing about half their time over the year to the project. Current plans include making a similar project available to other OLC sponsoring organizations.

In addition to the four major research areas, the Learning Center itself has been a conscious experiment in building a learning organization at MIT. Staff members at the center attempt to actively practice the principles associated with the "Five Disciplines." Regular staff meetings utilize the dialogue process. Support staff, as well as researchers, are highly conversant with the tools of systems dynamics and practice systems thinking. There is general agreement as to the vision of how the Learning Center could "make a difference in the world." This is not simply a grandiose statement. People at the Learning Center are committed to a better vision of organizational life than most of them have known in any other setting. Each person at the center seems committed to improving his or her own "personal mastery."

The Evolution of OLC into SoL

This desire to extend the impact of OLC led a group from MIT, consortium companies, and affiliated consultants to embark on an extended process of reflection and inquiry into OLC's underlying purpose. By 1997, the result was the creation of the Society for Organizational Learning, Inc. (SoL), a nonprofit member-governed organization, designed to maximize the potential for self-organizing and continuous evolution. To serve a wider audience, SoL was accepting both individual and organizational members, although as this book went to press, MIT was the only institutional research member.

SoL is designed as a membership organization involving corporate members, research members, and consultant members linked together as a network of colleagues, not employees. The intent is to bring together these three communities in an effort to invigorate and integrate the knowledge-creating process in the area of fundamental institutional change. SoL is also designed as a fractal organization to be part of a global network of similar "SoL"-like consortia at the local, national, and multinational levels (connected through an SoL international, which is expected to be established within one to two years).

The articulation of an integrated research agenda for SoL is a priority for SoL's new governing council. Nonetheless, many initiatives are already under way, led by SoL's corporate, research, and consultant members, illustrating the kinds of research that SoL will pursue. For example, an initiative currently under way at Shell Oil focuses senior executives, consultants, and researchers on understanding the transformation process required to produce a companywide learning environment. One component of the Shell project focuses on the profound shifts in the work of top management in a learning culture.

Another new initiative, "Creating Sustainable Learning Organizations," focuses on how present industrial organizations can meet their economic and social needs without compromising the ability of future generations to meet their own needs. The initiative derives its inspiration in part from a collaborative environmental movement started in Sweden, called "The Natural Step," which links business, scientists, government, and consumers. Several SoL companies have begun to work together to develop the conceptual framework and practical tools that would apply organizational learning principles to building healthy organizations for the long term.

Summary: A Win-Win Partnership

Both OLC and SoL are built on a model of partnership between academic researchers and business practitioners. Research is focused on areas that are of strategic importance to business, as well as interesting and relevant from an academic research perspective. Such a partnership will be viable only if it leads to mutual benefits that are both significant and unique.

Research sponsors can expect the following more specific benefits:

- Develop internal capacity in the form of individuals and groups with competence in basic learning disciplines, including systems thinking, work with mental models, dialogue, and personal mastery.
- Gain access to leading-edge learning tools under development at the center.
- Gather knowledge of what is being learned about building learning organizations—for example, new roles of leaders, innovations in organizational structures and processes, and dilemmas in moving from traditional authoritarian cultures.
- Work with and learn from other companies committed to developing new learning capabilities.
- Gain assistance from MIT staff with in-house learning projects.

In turn, MIT still benefits from the partnership through access to research funding that enables them to develop better theories of generic organizational systems and processes, new tools that embody these theories, and practical knowledge of the barriers to organizational learning and the capabilities needed to overcome these barriers. Specifically, the organizations participating in the Learning Center enrich the research process through:

- Focusing research on critical management issues
- Providing field research sites
- Bringing practical know-how of leading organizations
- Establishing credibility, based on field testing, for innovative tools and methods
- Creating internship opportunities for MIT students

Collaborative arrangements like OLC and SoL, in which researchers and sponsors work together to further the practice of leadership development, seem to create "win-win" situations. Sponsoring organizations do make a significant financial contribution. In return for this commitment, however, they gain access to some of the best minds in contemporary business thinking. Universities and research centers benefit when faculty get unique exposure to real-life business laboratories, graduate students receive internships that provide a wonderful blend of theory and practice, and new knowledge and learning tools are developed and refined to benefit the practice of management far beyond the base of sponsoring organizations.

10
Meeting the Challenge

IN OUR INTRODUCTION we discussed the analogy between the discovery of a "new world" in 1492 and the contemporary discovery of a new world for leadership development. In a new world, old maps are no longer appropriate. No matter how thoroughly he looked, Columbus could not find the Ganges River in his Caribbean new world. The maps showing that river were accurate in a totally different environment but irrelevant to his new surroundings. It was necessary for Columbus to create new maps of reality. These maps were quite primitive at the beginning. The mapmaker could see only what was in the immediate vicinity but had no idea what might be over the next horizon. Yet, despite being far from finished products, these crude maps made life easier for the next adventurers.

As we ponder today's changing business environment, and as we review the exemplars presented in Chapter 9, it appears that our old maps for leadership development no longer accurately reflect contemporary reality. At the same time, it appears that where we stand today is simply a temporary stage. Throughout this book, we have presented a perspective on the field of executive education/leadership development—where it was in the past, where it is at present, and where it appears the field is headed. The "map" in Table 10.1 illustrates what we call the "seven Ps"—the seven key elements of the leadership development process. The map follows the evolution of these key elements from the past, through today's transition state, to the future. In presenting this map, we are both summarizing the discussions in this book and proposing a prescription for enhancing future strategic leadership development initiatives.[1]

TABLE 10.1   The Evolution of Leadership Development

Key Elements	Past	Transition	Future
Participants	Listener	Student	Learner
Program design	Event	Curriculum	Ongoing process
Purpose	Knowledge	Wisdom	Action
Period focus	Past	Present	Future
Players	Specialists	Generalists	Partners
Presentation focus	Style	Content	Process/outcome
Place	University campus	Corporate facility	Anywhere

Source: Reprinted by permission of the publisher, R. Fulmer, "The Evolving Paradigm of Leadership Development," from *Organizational Dynamics*, Spring 1997, © 1997 American Management Association, New York. All rights reserved.

PARTICIPANTS

Participation in a leadership development program today is very different than it was a generation ago. Many of our readers will recall programs for which participants arrived with little understanding of the curriculum that lay before them. At check-in, they were usually given a series of books, a notebook, and an agenda that outlined how each hour was to be spent for the duration of the program. Huge amounts of blank paper were provided in the notebook, because the major role of each participant was to be a listener. He (only occasionally was it a she) was expected to take voluminous notes from the assembled presenters who would share their insights and knowledge, often in discrete 90-minute segments.

That model has evolved dramatically over the past few years. Today, participants expect not just to listen to information presented by experts, but also to put that information to work by engaging in case discussions, debating recommendations or alternatives, and sometimes making presentations based on their conclusions. During the transition period, these assignments frequently were related to a business case that had little direct relevance to participants' situations back at the office; however, it was hoped that participants would be able to make applications when and if similar situations presented themselves.

In the evolving new world of leadership development, participants will listen occasionally, interact frequently in situations simulated to test their skills or understanding, and devote a significant amount of time to demonstrating their ability to apply concepts to real challenges through some form of action learning, as described in Chapter 9. In that chapter's examples and others throughout this book, we discuss the value of hands-on, real-world leadership development initiatives. These efforts are paving the way toward a new world for leadership development, one that blends work experience, classroom instruction, and teamwork into a powerful process for change and development.

We now know that participants generally take learning to the level most relevant to their immediate needs or level of motivation. With action learning, some participants may make minimal effort and learn relatively little. However, our experience is that most individuals rise to demanding challenges, expand their knowledge base, and make significant contributions to organizational goals when learning takes place through a hands-on approach. Participants who take the experience seriously usually find themselves rewarded both personally and professionally. Organizations that take the experience seriously usually find that their investments in leadership development have a true payoff. By making learning actionable, interest and motivation tends to increase. What's more, as we saw in the examples in Chapter 9, the end results of participation in a program are more observable and measurable.

PROGRAM DESIGN

As we have noted, most organizations traditionally viewed participation in an executive or leadership development program as a once- or twice-in-a-lifetime event. A person viewed as having the potential to become a CEO might be sent to the one-year Sloan Program at MIT or the 13-week Harvard Advanced Management Program. Individuals who were viewed as having significant potential, but not a probable future as a CEO, might be sent to a four-week program at another leading business school. Attendance was always an important rite of passage, but often with little relationship to other developmental activities taking place in a career. As we reported earlier, current research suggests that participants in executive/leadership development programs no longer are specially targeted individuals who have been "anointed" by senior management for future promotion.[2] At General Electric, the "Work-Out" program has involved a total of 220,000 people, and on any given week,

20,000 GE employees will be participating in some stage of a Work-Out effort.

It appears that, during the transition period, leading companies evolved beyond the "programs as an isolated event" mentality toward a focus on preparing leaders for key career transitions by designing somewhat lockstep, career-long corporate curricula.[3] One successful corporate practitioner described his firm's approach as a "slalom course." Figure 10.1 diagrams the approach used by one of the leading corporate educational programs of the 1980s.

Every manager was expected to engage in at least 40 hours of management education each year. At each stage of an individual's career, he or she was expected to attend a program appropriate for that stage of development. Individuals promoted to a management job were expected to attend a "new manager program" within 30 days of receiving their new position. This would take place at a corporate facility where a carefully defined curriculum was presented to new managers from throughout the company. The next one or two development events were expected to take place in individual business units.

Once managers achieved the level of "midmanagement," they were expected to again make the pilgrimage to corporate headquarters, where they would receive training that was appropriate for their new responsibilities. After having satisfied this corporate requirement, future events would be scheduled on a regional or divisional basis until the rank of "executive" was achieved. At that point, they were invited to attend the top-level corporate program focused on general management issues. There they would probably have a chance to interact with the CEO or key members of the executive committee. This particular firm was often cited as an industry leader because it had evolved development to an organized set of events that were planned over a person's entire career. Table 10.2 reveals that most leading corporations were using this approach by the early 1990s.

This growing commitment to continuous learning as a source of competitive advantage has led to college-sized organizations being created to help their firms become "learning organizations."[4] Jeanne C. Meister identified 30 companies that share the common goal of seeing "training as a process of life-long learning rather than a place to get trained." As Meister pointed out in her 1993 book *Corporate Quality Universities,*[5]

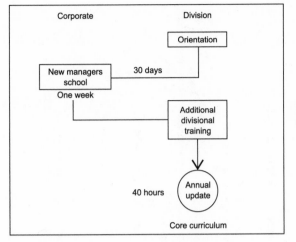

New Manager
Training Process

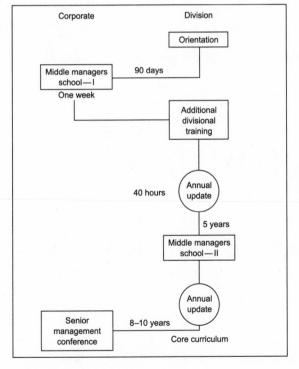

Middle Manager
Training Process

Figure 10.1 Training in the 1980s

Source: Robert M. Fulmer and Ken Graham, "A New Era of Management Education," *Journal of Management Development* 12, no. 3 (1993): 37. Reprinted by permission.

TABLE 10.2 Management Education Program Coverage

Company	Premanage-ment	Supervisory	Manager level	Director level	Officer level	Internal executive program senior executive
GE	Yes 6–12 months	Yes New appointment 90 days	Yes New appointment 90 days	Yes New appointment 90 days	Yes New appointment 90 days	
HP	None —	Yes New appointment 90 days	Yes New appointment 90 days	Yes New appointment 90 days	Yes New appointment 90 days	
IBM	Yes 6–12 months	Yes New appointment 90 days	Yes New appointment 90 days	Yes New appointment 90 days	Yes New appointment 90 days	Yes New appointment 90 days
Tenneco	None —	Yes Company selects	Yes Company selects	Yes Company selects	Yes Company selects	
UTC	Yes —	Yes New appointment 90 days	Yes Company selects	Yes Company selects	Yes Company selects	None —
Xerox	Yes 6–12 months	Yes New appointment 90 days	Yes New appointment 90 days	Yes New appointment 90 days	Yes New appointment 90 days	

AlliedSignal	None / —	Yes / Sector selects	Yes / Sector selects	Yes / —	In progress / —	Yes / —
Lockheed	Yes / 12–18 months	Yes / Branch selects	Yes / Branch selects	Yes / Company selects	Yes / Corporation selects	Yes / Corporation selects
Bell	Yes	Yes / New appointment 90 days	Yes / New appointment 6 months	Yes	Yes	None
Coca-Cola	None	Yes / Division selects (develops and conducts)	Yes / Division selects	Yes / Company division selects	Yes / Company division selects	None
Federated	None	Yes / New appointment	Yes / New appointment	Yes / Ongoing	Yes / Ongoing	Yes / Corporate

Source: Robert M. Fulmer and Ken Graham, "A New Era of Management Education," *Journal of Management Development* 12, 3 (1993): 35. Reprinted by permission.

successful firms—those who will be prominent players in the 21st century—must do more than commit to training their work force. Truly dominant players understand the need to organize themselves as learning systems, where every part of the system—hiring, training, and recognition of employees—promotes both individual and collective learning.

In March 1996, Meister updated her original research and indicated that almost 1,000 firms had or were actively investigating the formation of a corporate university. Although the average operating budgets for corporate universities had grown to $12.4 million, 60 percent of the groups reported budgets of $5 million or less. Of course, the budgets of giants like Motorola, GE, and Anderson significantly increased the "average" figure. Perhaps more significantly, organizations with corporate universities reported spending 2.5 percent of their payroll on learning—almost twice the national average.[6]

In a recent study, Bob Miles analyzed four leading corporate universities sponsored by Motorola, GE, Arthur Andersen, and Apple Computer. He observed that all four were part of organizations that shared similar strategic orientations: a focus on aggressive growth and continuous innovation. However, whereas some placed more emphasis on supporting employee career development through their corporate university, others tilted in the direction of addressing key business issues.[7] For example, Arthur Andersen has a carefully designed career ladder, with courses required at each stage in a person's career. The company is developing a career tracking system that includes every employee throughout the world. On the other hand, GE has organized its Crotonville facility around the concept that there are particular "moments of opportunity," when leadership development can have a major impact on individual and organizational performance. These "moments" are related to when an individual moves into a position of expanded scope or responsibility and is therefore struggling to transition to a new level of management thinking.

Although the corporate university movement has been viewed as a positive affirmation of an organization's commitment to lifelong learning, a slight danger looms on the horizon. Traditional universities typically are not viewed as the most flexible, progressive, or change-oriented of institutions. Practices that date back several centuries are still embraced because of tradition rather than for contemporary appropriateness.[8] Any strength, if carried to excess, will become a weakness. The commitment to learning that leads to an organization's establishment of a corporate university must be clearly monitored, kept flexible, and focused on the strategic imperatives of the sponsoring organization if maximum benefit is to be attained. To add real value, a corporate university must maintain its focus as a means to corporate success and avoid the pitfalls of becoming a storehouse of programs and courses.

As we look toward the future, the pace of change and competition has significantly increased the stakes for leadership and organizational development. This pace is so relentless that the need for lifelong education is now a given. Just as professionals in other disciplines must commit to a lifelong process of learning and updating their knowledge, so, too, must leaders and their respective organizations. In this environment, organizations are looking for approaches to development and learning that make a real difference. The following discussion describes one of the most dramatic current examples.

Work-Out at GE

As discussed briefly in Appendix A, GE's "Work-Out" is not a typical leadership development program. Rather,

> It is a process of concentrated decision making and empowerment to resolve issues. A team of experienced, knowledgeable people with a stake in the issue is charged to develop solutions and action plans. They are sanctioned by the key stake holder to proceed with implementation (or given clear reason why not to proceed, or specify direction for further study). There is follow-up to ensure completion of the action plans.[9]

The Work-Out initiative is part of General Electric's effort to create a culture of speed, simplicity, and self-confidence in a manner consistent with continuous improvement. Expected results of Work-Out activities include

- Boundaryless, cross-functional teamwork
- Empowered employees

- Building of trust
- Focus on customers
- Focus on greater use of process thinking
- Improvement of business process

Key Roles in Work-Out

Business leaders within a particular GE organization will define the issues to be addressed in Work-Out sessions, select team members, and approve recommendations made by the initiative. They also have responsibility for removing barriers to the implementation of an approved recommendation.

Although the program was originally facilitated by an elite team of university-based professors, GE now has several hundred trained Work-Out *facilitators* whose job it is to sense problems in the organization, facilitate team building and problem solving, and ensure that support for followup actions actually takes place.

The heart of Work-Out is a team of *employees* who are sometimes joined by customers or suppliers. They are asked to articulate problems, develop recommendations to address these problems, and then get whatever help is needed to implement the recommendations when they have been approved.

Typically, 60 to 100 people meet for an open agenda event aimed at *reducing work.* These are Phase I Town Meetings. Smaller groups (20 to 60 people) become involved in Phase II meetings which focus on *problem solving.* Phase III sessions typically involve *process mapping* and may involve subgroups of 10 to 20 people who focus on a process rather than a problem. In Phase IV, natural work teams facilitate the *implementation* of their own recommendations. Note the key factors in "Elements of an Effective Work-Out Process" on the next page. And what about Work-Out's effectiveness? Has it made a difference at GE? In the book *Control Your Own Destiny or Someone Else Will,* Noel Tichy noted:

> Work-Out has made believers of GE's top 1,000 or 2,000 executives. I've been inside scores of the world's best and biggest companies, and I can't think of another where intellectual freedom and like-mindedness coexist to an equal degree. . . . As a formal mechanism for sustaining a revolu-

tionary process—and for transferring real power to employees—Work-Out is unsurpassed so far.[10]

Elements of an Effective Work-Out Process

1) Issue: The issue or topic of the Work-Out session is selected by the Sponsor(s). The issue is linked to the key business initiatives.

2) Sponsor(s): The key stakeholder(s) who will benefit from the workout process charters a Champion to form a Work-Out team. Sponsors communicate the Work-Out plan and objectives.

3) Champions: A Champion frames the issue, clarifies the topics to address and selects participants for the Work-Out team. (A planning committee and support resources may be needed to plan and conduct the more complex Work-Out sessions.)

4) Participants: The participants are chosen to represent a broad cross-section of people who have the knowledge and skill to resolve the issue and (given that they are empowered) can implement action plans to permanently fix the issue.

5) Planning/ data: The Champion and/or planning committee plans the Work-Out session, assembles background information and makes expert help available to the Work-Out team so that action plans are data-based.

6) Facilitators: People experienced in building teams and capable of coaching groups through the process are made available to the Work-Out team.

7) Empower- ment/ Accountable: The Work-Out team is given time to resolve the issue, develop action plans, and present them to business leaders. It is empowered and held accountable for implementing the action plan.

8) Follow-up: The Champion is responsible for following up to ensure that the team has the resources and help to implement the action plan on a timely basis. A reunion is scheduled to ensure follow-up.

Source: "Work-Out Continuous Improvement," unpublished student presentation, College of William and Mary, Williamsburg, VA, 15 March 1995, 10.

PURPOSE

In a simpler era, it was assumed that, at discrete stages of a person's career, specific types of new knowledge were required. Consequently, it was possible to design programs that would provide this knowledge in advance of the time when it would be needed. This was particularly true as a person approached the stage of general management. As functional specialists began to be considered for additional promotion, or sometimes immediately before becoming "general managers," they would be sent to a "general management program" at a leading university. These programs often were referred to as a "mini-MBA." These programs provided fundamental knowledge of the tools and techniques of core functional disciplines. This knowledge was viewed as critical to broadening the arsenal of management tools and techniques in an executive's repertoire.

During the transition period, more sophisticated programs provided opportunities for executives-in-training to practice the use of those tools in complex simulations (often computerized business games). These sophisticated simulations were used to help participants apply the knowledge they had acquired to solving problems in a simulated world. Although simulations offer a good opportunity for "informal" practice, contemporary approaches to leadership development are addressing this issue by emphasizing the solution of actual business problems in a real-world setting through action learning typified by the ARAMARK, AT&T, World Bank, and LeaderLab examples from Chapter 9. Similarly, Peter Senge of the MIT Center for Organizational Learning (discussed in Chapter 9) has written eloquently about the importance of "practice fields" or "micro-worlds" in which managers have an opportunity to practice some of the concepts they are learning in real time.[11] Unlike professional athletes or symphony orchestra musicians, leaders seldom have an opportunity to practice their skills and receive feedback other than in the real world. The growing interest in action learning techniques, as well as anticipatory learning techniques such as those taught by SoL, are intended to address this critical problem.

At Motorola University, an Application Consulting Team (ACT) was created in the late 1980s to help facilitate workplace application of knowledge gained from Motorola courses. The ACT is staffed by managers with over 20 years of experience, who prefer to mentor, coach, and assist in the transfer of learning in their organizations rather than continue with traditional management responsibilities. Another approach to action learning at Motorola University involves corporate partnerships that focus on developing knowledge in a mutually important arena with a series of other leading firms. One illustration of this approach is the "Six Sigma Institute." In 1990 Motorola joined with ABB, Digital Equipment, Eastman Kodak, and IBM to accelerate the development of "Six Sigma Quality" and to transfer this knowledge in the most effective possible manner.

Another key illustration of action learning was a workshop sponsored by Bob Galvin, former chairman of Motorola, to help over 100 Motorola senior executives understand the market potential of selected Asian countries. Rather than bringing in experts to talk about the subject, participants were asked to analyze the existing competition and to determine how Motorola could compete in those markets. After "doing their homework," teams of executives traveled to Asia to analyze local market opportunities firsthand. They were then asked to teach what they had learned to the next 3,000 Motorola managers. They first studied the issue, then verified their impressions with firsthand observations, and finally solidified their learnings—and contributed to the company's knowledge base—by teaching what they had learned to others.[12] This approach is a good example of the knowledge creation cycle (Chapter 5) in action.

PERIOD FOCUS

Because of its real-world orientation, the case method has had tremendous impact on business education. Long associated with the Harvard Business School, it is utilized in a majority of executive development programs both within companies and in a variety of other business schools. Despite the many positive aspects of the case method, the system has an inherent drawback in that a case is almost always a historical document. It reflects what could have been done, given a particular set of circumstances that existed in the past.

Many readers will recall attending programs in which 10- to 20-year-old cases were used to illustrate "classic" concepts. The "Chain Saw Industry in 1974"[13] is still used in many business policy programs because it does such a superb job of illustrating the difficulty of forecasting demand because of various environmental constraints and the impact of interacting strategies that actually play out in the competitive marketplace. Although participant feedback has encouraged most instructors to utilize more contemporary cases, there is still an inherent problem of time frame.

The current focus on "best practices" has changed the time horizon of leadership development. Companies now seek to know who is doing the best job in a particular area even if that firm is not a direct competitor. Firms in a variety of industries may look to Wal-Mart to understand its excellence in logistics management or the extent to which ABB is able to manage the paradox of being a global company with 1,300 local operating business units in 140 countries.

As we move into the new world of the future, organizations are beginning to utilize techniques like "future-oriented cases" or scenario development as means of coping with this challenge. In perhaps the most comprehensive treatment of this subject to date, John Gutman concluded that future-oriented cases can bring projections and future issues to life by making it relevant for problem solvers to consider the issues they will be addressing.[14] In a future-oriented case, participants are asked to develop scenarios of what the business environment will be like some time in the future.

The "J&J 2002" case used in the Johnson & Johnson "Creating Our Future" program discussed in Appendix A is a good example. Using this technique, participants can challenge conventional wisdom about how their industry will evolve. Discussion, background research, and expert advice can dramatize the trends that are beginning to shape industry practices and forecast important ways that business might be different in the future. In addition, participants can focus on how actions in their own organization may help to create or mold the future. This helps them realize that it is within their power to influence the external environment. Finally, future-oriented cases can, under the tutelage of good case leaders, begin to explore the assumptions that undergird various participant views about the future. Awareness of common mental models that can impede creative thinking is the starting point for effectively creating a new future for an organization.

This level of sophistication appears to be part of a conscious attempt on the part of firms to anticipate where opportunity is going to be rather than where it is at the current moment. Gary Hamel and C. K. Prahalad have alerted large numbers of managers to the importance of "Competing for the Future."[15] They continually emphasize that the best way for an organization to deal with continuous change is for it to extend its "opportunity horizon." The Johnson & Johnson FrameworkS process for revitalizing leadership development strategy, discussed in Chapter 9, is a good example of this kind of thinking. We believe that a similar "future focus" will dominate all aspects of the field in the years ahead.

PLAYERS

In a more comfortable and predictable world, the major players in the field of leadership development were specialists who became proficient in their roles and management's expectations. Professors developed teaching modules that could be inserted in a variety of program contexts. Executive program administrators in universities were expected to know the various areas of expertise that existed among their faculty and how this expertise could be combined and packaged into a program. Corporate human resource specialists became adept at knowing which university programs seemed to offer the best fit for the needs of their managers. Going to professional meetings of groups such as UNICON (the International University Consortium for Executive Education) was a pleasant, predictable event because people stayed in their appropriate roles.

During the transition period, roles began to blur. Universities began to do customized programs. Open-enrollment programs offered by consulting firms proliferated. Companies began to conduct more and more programs themselves. Even individuals began to change roles, with corporate HRD managers moving to leadership positions within universities and university professors going to work in corporate HRD units. Interestingly, individuals who top today's lists of "leading practitioners" in leadership development often have experience across two or three of these sectors. Noel Tichy of the University of Michigan not only has served as a professor at several major business schools, but also has worked for several years at GE while on sabbatical, in addition to running his own successful consulting firm. Steve Kerr, currently chief learning officer at GE, was formerly dean of the University of Southern California Business School and a successful consultant in his own right. Todd Jick, managing partner at the Center for Executive Development in Cambridge, Massachusetts, a very successful consulting firm, is a former faculty member at both Harvard and INSEAD.

This cross-fertilization of perspectives has contributed to the professionalization of the field and set new standards of performance for leadership development professionals.[16] Senior practitioners across all sectors are expected to be generalists, capable of designing initiatives that contribute to the strategic development of the firm, but with the professional networks needed to bring these designs to a rapid reality. In effect, they are expected to be experts at establishing partnerships. University-based program experience provides an individual with exposure to cutting-edge thinking in a variety of disciplines. It promotes commitment to honest inquiry and a willingness to seek new answers. Corporate experience adds the dimension of relevance. In a corporate setting, ideas have little currency unless they can be applied and related to corporate performance. Because most corporate executive educators operate without line authority, their success depends on their ability to build relationships, engender trust, and demonstrate the added value of the function. These abilities are critical to the partnership-building process. Consultants must develop a broad set of analytical skills and must learn to listen more acutely than most other people. Because their own resources are often quite limited, they tend to become very good at networking and supplementing their own capabilities.

In the new world, leading practitioners build partnerships and networks that blend the above skills to enhance both organizational learning and personal/professional development. As mentioned in our earlier analysis of competitive forces, a number of firms are developing partnerships with key academics or consultants who become a semipermanent part of the organization. This may be seen as part of a "shadow pyramid," as discussed earlier, or part of what Charles Handy called the "shamrock organization."[17] Handy argued that, like the leaves of a shamrock, today's business organization is made up of three very different groups of people. Each group is managed, paid, and organized differently, and each has quite different expectations for work. The first leaf in the "shamrock organization" is made up of core employees. These are permanent employees who are viewed as essential for the ongoing business of the firm. They are expensive, and their number is shrinking. The next leaf of Handy's shamrock consists of part-time and temporary workers—the contingency workforce. The third shamrock leaf is made up of organizations and professionals to whom jobs are farmed out. These may be specialized subcontractors who can do certain jobs better and cheaper. Or, as in our illustration, they may be highly trained professionals who are too expensive and too opposed to constraints to work for a single organization. Yet, by spending a significant number of days per year with a single organization, those contract employees tend to invest both time and intellectual capital to become more productive partners with that organization and leverage their skills within and have a much more visible, often dramatic impact on its performance. When, for example, Philips asked a number of academics to invest 90 days per year in the Centurion Project, it was making a major commitment to these individuals in terms of learning and income. On the other hand, the individuals who were given this opportunity brought with them high-level experience with a variety of other organizations. The same is true of many of the major corporate initiatives mentioned throughout this book.

PRESENTATIONS

In traditional executive programs, the presenter's style and ability to entertain often seemed to count more than content. During today's transition period, although entertainment value is still important, the demand for content relevance has increased significantly. The message not only must be presented well, but it must also be an important message. There is little tolerance for sessions that might be described as "fluff," despite their ability to entertain. As we move through the nineties, the challenge for presenters is developing the ability to process as well as

present applicable, relevant information. The most noted executive educators are now those who are able to involve participants in application
processes that often result in the resolution of real business issues. This
kind of processing is at the heart of action learning.

There is a Chinese proverb that says, "A good leader is one whom the
people respect, the poor leader is the one who people hate, but the great
leader is one who, when the people have finished, they say, 'We did it
ourselves.'" This sentiment is very appropriate for future leadership development initiatives. In many ways, the future is calling for a difficult
adjustment by traditional presenters. No longer revered simply for what
they know, success for presenters is equally related to what they are able
to stimulate others to accomplish. This shift toward a more process-
oriented delivery mode requires new approaches to program design such
that, when a program is completed, participants say, "We have done it
ourselves." Again, the exemplars discussed in Chapter 9, as well as others mentioned throughout this book, reflect this new approach.

PLACE

As we have suggested, executive education traditionally was reserved
for a select handful of future senior leaders and delivered primarily by
business schools. As recently as 1988, a report prepared for the International Association for Management Education, formerly the American
Assembly of Collegiate Schools of Business (AACSB), reported that two
business schools, Harvard and Stanford, had one-third of the total market for executive education programs in general management.[18] Corporate HRD directors, university program managers, and participants
agreed with the importance of "getting away from traditional surroundings" in order to contemplate, listen, and learn. Location even played a
part in some people's decision making. Occasionally an executive would
report, "I prefer to go to Sea Island, Georgia, in February rather than to
Chicago." One British participant in our research commented, "Management development's greatest contribution in the UK has been to the
restoration of country houses." Clearly, he was joking about the recent
tendency for both users and providers to make massive investments in
training centers as evidence of their commitment to executive educa-
tion/leadership development. However, commitment to learning and
leadership development can be measured in many other ways.

University campuses are still important settings for leadership development. Participants often report that it is easier to change their own paradigms and see things from a different perspective when they are "on sabbatical" in the midst of a bustling academic environment. Nevertheless, more and more leaders are participating in leadership development programs that are conducted in their own facilities. Many companies now boast "campuses" that compete with those at major colleges and universities. Arthur Andersen purchased a former college campus outside Chicago and has satellite educational facilities in Europe and Asia. Andersen's worldwide investment in education exceeds $300 million, or more than 7 percent of the company's total revenues. The Andersen Center at St. Charles, Illinois, operates with a staff of 200 educational specialists. Over 60,000 trainees come to the St. Charles campus each year to study accounting practices, gain industry knowledge, and study fundamental business skills, such as business ethics, negotiation, and presentation effectiveness. Slightly more than half of them work for Andersen. The remaining trainees are clients or outside customers. Andersen has invested almost $150 million in the 645-acre St. Charles campus, which it purchased from Saint Dominic College in 1971. The facility can accommodate 1,700 overnight students. It boasts 130 classrooms, 6 auditoriums, 2 amphitheaters, 5 large conference centers, 1,000 computer workstations, a staff complex, several restaurants, a barber shop, a shoe repair shop, a bookstore, a discotheque, and a nine-hole golf course. In addition to the professional staff of 200, the center employs 200 support personnel and a comparable number of operations people.[19]

Organizations like Andersen, General Electric, and Motorola can justify their large commitment to such facilities because of their tremendous throughput of participants. Most companies, however, are finding it more efficient to make a commitment to what we might call "learning space" rather than to hotel operations or conference centers. For example, rather than making an investment in major conference and lodging facilities, Johnson & Johnson conducts its Executive Conference on approximately half a floor of a New Brunswick, New Jersey, office building. Participants stay at negotiated rates at a nearby Hyatt Hotel. Rather than a dedicated "case room," the Executive Conference series utilizes portable risers that create a tiered room and provide space to run wiring for individual computers that tie into the company's LAN system.

Breakout rooms for small group discussions are available on the same floor. Meals are served buffet style in a room adjacent to the company cafeteria on a different floor. Because the Executive Conference runs approximately ten times per year, the flexibility provided by this arrangement is a more cost-effective alternative than going off site to a specialized conference center or making the commitment to the fixed costs associated with a full-time corporate conference facility.

CSX Corporation, a $10 billion international transportation company offering a variety of transportation, intermodel logistics, and related services, announced in 1995 its commitment to create a "State of the Art CSX Learning Center" which would "provide a learning environment for present and future CSX leaders that fosters efficient individual growth and promotes effective inter-unit collaborative learning." The company's commitment included a plan for effective physical space and for the best use of technology as a learning tool. Although this was to be a "world-class" facility, it would be located in one of the division headquarters buildings. The center would include two large classrooms, an auditorium, breakout rooms, networking areas, and support services. Again, CSX concluded that this type of facility would be the most effective solution to its needs rather than the creation of a separate "campus" for learning. Regardless of which alternative an organization chooses, it is clear that the caliber of ideas discussed is more important than the quality of facilities dedicated to learning.

Despite this focus on facilities, learning in the future is far less likely to be associated with a particular place. As noted in the new Johnson & Johnson strategy discussed in Chapter 9, participants increasingly will log onto interactive learning experiences via networked computers. They will participate in videoconferencing involving colleagues from around the world, without extensive travel time. They also will go physically to a variety of places where people are brought together for some form of "distributed" learning, whether that be through simultaneous broadcast of presentations and discussions, some other form of electronic multimedia learning experience, or rather than bringing people to massive training centers with all the time and expense involved, through more traditional programs delivered at numerous sites around the world. These could include a hotel conference room in Singapore, a public conference center in Brussels, or a corporate meeting facility in

New Jersey. In fact, research sponsored by UNICON and Quality Dynamics, Inc., reported that respondents from corporate universities predicted that 50 percent of all their training would be delivered via technology by the year 2000.[20]

Federal Express provides a dramatic illustration of education that is not restricted by place. The company has spent almost $70 million to create an automated educational system. Annually, it spends almost 5 percent of its payroll to enhance learning among its 40,000 couriers and customer service agents through the use of interactive videodisks (IVD). Federal Express owns 1,225 IVD units in 700 locations. Each has a 20- to 25-video-disk (equivalent to 37,500 floppy disks) curriculum that is updated on a monthly basis. Each employee receives four hours of company-paid study and preparation in addition to two hours of self-administered tests semiannually.[21] Although the FedEx example involves more of a training focus, a better illustration of this movement might be MIT's effort to deliver distance learning to China by satellite. Given the size of China's managerial population and the travel distances and time commitments involved for U.S.-based faculty to go there for developmental programs, MIT has decided that the use of new telecommunications technology is essential if MIT really wishes to serve this expanding market.

An example of distributed learning on a face-to-face basis was the experience of Sterling Winthrop, which offered a series of senior and middle management programs on six continents during a three-year period. Put most simply, the company found that it was easier and far more cost-effective to transport three to five instructors/facilitators to distant locations than to bring people from every corner of the world to a central location.

ANY TIME, ANY PLACE, GRAY MATTER

Since the days of Albert Einstein, we have generally recognized that the basic building blocks of the universe are time, place, and matter. Yet perspectives on all three of these elements are being subjected to reexamination and redefinition within today's new paradigm of physics. Similarly, new paradigms for business development are causing HRD professionals to reexamine and redefine processes for leadership development. In his book *Future Perfect*, Stan Davis suggested that, in the evolving "age of information," the rules of competition will be "any-time, anyplace, no matter."[22] Davis made the point that customers will favor the organization that is able to provide goods or service whenever and wherever the consumer wants—any time, any place. Those demands pose a significant enough challenge, but the challenge of Davis's third rule, "no matter," is perhaps even more profound. The world of "matter" as has traditionally been defined in "products" is being more and more defined by information that is collected from or about the consumer or organization for whom a "value" is being provided. The most effective competitors feed this information back to customers along with their products and services, further enhancing the value of the product or service and enabling the customer to leverage their "investment." Clearly, this accurately describes the current trend in leadership development.

ASSESSING YOUR OWN SITUATION

There is little in the way of bricks or mortar (matter) that can compete with the caliber of good ideas. As organizations attempt to map their leadership and organizational development processes against the companies and programs discussed throughout this book, they may wish to ask themselves the following questions:

- Do you recognize leadership development as a competitive capability that can assist in the development, implementation, and revitalization of organizational strategy?

- Have you made continuous learning and knowledge creation a core competence?

- Do your leadership development efforts focus on building both the individual talents of leaders and the collective knowledge base of the organization?

- Do you view leadership development as a tool for creating a talent pool of leaders at all levels of the organization?

- Do you view leadership development as a system?

- Do you focus on the leadership development process and not on programs?

- Does your leadership development process blend experience, training, education, and other forms of development into a knowledge creation cycle?

- Do you utilize the real-time solving of real-life business problems as part of your leadership development process?

- Do you make leadership development part of a consistent HR strategy that blends the processes of recruitment, selection, development, and appraisal into an integrated system for talent pool management?

- Do you view leadership development as a process for the continuous revitalization of your organization?

When an organization can answer "yes" to all of these questions, it is well on its way to joining the ranks of those companies that are creating the future for strategic leadership development—companies that are mastering the challenge of creating leaders in a world of change.

Appendix A
The State of the Practice: Our Research Base

IN WHAT MIGHT BE called the "Age of the Learning Organization," the major challenge facing leadership development practitioners may well be coping with closed minds in a world of constant change.[1] Arie de Geus, former head of strategic planning at Royal Dutch/ Shell, summarized this challenge very well when he said, "Over the long term, the only sustainable competitive advantage may be a corporation's ability to learn faster than its competition."[2] He went on to add, "The purpose of planning (at least at Shell) is not to create plans, but to change the way managers see the world."

If de Geus and Shell are right, creating leaders who can build learning-oriented competitive advantage should be a big business. N. Nohria and J. D. Berkley estimated that corporate expenditures for employee education and training have grown from $10 billion to $45 billion during the past decade.[3] In 1996 Jeanne Meister of Quality Dynamics reported that the number had grown to over $50 billion.[4] *Business Week*[5] estimated that approximately $12 billion of this amount was devoted to executive education, the traditional vehicle for leadership development. This included corporate investment in university-based open-enrollment programs, executive MBA programs, company-designed and -delivered programs, and customized courses developed and taught by business schools and consultants.

The research effort on which this appendix is based was conducted in 1995 and was partially sponsored by the International Consortium for Executive Education (UNICON) and the Penn State Institute for the Study of Organizational Effectiveness. It involved a comprehensive review of the literature as well as the collection of interview and/or survey data from an international group of 78 executives from 47 companies, 48 consultants, and 52 university leaders representing 35 business schools throughout the world. The survey was updated in 1997.

Approximately one-fourth of the $12 billion investment in executive education is directed through business schools. University-based executive education at both degree and nondegree levels has become a major source of income for these institutions. In 1994 *Bricker's International Directory* listed 472 executive education programs offered by business schools throughout the world. The price range was from $695 for a three-day course at George Washington University to $50,500 for a nine-month program at Stanford University. A *Wall Street Journal/Bricker* survey in 1994 revealed that costs in general average more than $3,700 per week for each participant.[6] In 1997 a Penn State research effort found that annual corporate executive education expenditures had grown to a median of $1 million per year and that the pool of potential attendees within each firm had grown to over 2,400. These same firms projected even more dramatic growth in future executive education efforts.[7]

When asked by *Business Week* to rate the return on time and money invested in executive education programs, former program graduates estimated an average return of 81 percent on the cost of attending an executive education session.[8] Motorola reports even more dramatic results. From a forecasted budget of $35 million over a five-year period, a sum that Bill Wiggenhorn, president of Motorola University, reported that many people felt excessive, Motorola now spends over $60 million annually for programs, plus an additional $60 million in time spent away from the job.[9] Motorola's emphasis ranges from an intensive program designed to give 400 executives a four-week "MBA" to a $50 million annual commitment to address literacy problems. Perhaps the most dramatic lesson of the Motorola experience is their often quoted statistic that a dollar invested in education and training can yield a return of $33. The details are as follows:

> In those few plants where the work force absorbed the whole curriculum of quality tools and process skills and where senior managers reinforced the training we were getting a $33 return for every dollar spent, including the cost of wages paid while people sat in class.
>
> Plants that made use of either the quality tools or the process skills but not both, and then reinforced what they taught, broke even.
>
> Finally, plants that taught all or part of the curriculum but failed to reinforce with follow-up meetings and a new, genuine emphasis on quality had a negative return on investment.[10]

Executive education and leadership development can also be good business for organizations and individuals that provide high-quality executive programs. Although few institutions are willing to divulge their profit margins, several leading business schools report that executive education efforts generate from $1 million to $10 million a year in discretionary income for their schools. Professors who excel in executive education may double or triple their teaching income.

However, not everyone is impressed. Jim Baughman, a former Harvard professor, who headed the executive development function at General Electric before assuming responsibility for this function at Morgan Guaranty in 1994, believes that "[university] programs are too long. They're not flexible enough. They're too expensive, and they lack action learning [situations where executives work on real problems to come up with actual solutions which companies can implement]."[11] But, although Baughman may be opposed to university-based education as it is traditionally practiced, he nevertheless has utilized many leading faculty members from various business schools around the world in his programs, a fact not lost on today's resource-constrained business school deans. Business schools have unparalleled access to the basic raw materials for excellence in executive education. Their challenge seems to be managing these materials in a more innovative, flexible manner.

THE CURRENT STATE OF THE PRACTICE

A recent study documented the fact that total budgets for executive education are growing significantly (see Table A.1).[12] Most of this growth is for in-company programs aimed at a relatively large number of corporate executives. The size of corporate budgets and the number of people who are participating in executive education are indicators of its growing role in implementing strategic initiatives. Interestingly, the "numbers" reported in that study reflect a distribution that is bimodal. Firms that are typically viewed as being among the best managed, as well as those undergoing major change efforts, often report budgets that are two or three times higher than the median average. Conversely, a number of firms report relatively small budgets for formal executive education or leadership development.

Also reflected in Table A.1, over 75 percent of all executive education dollars now go to customized programs, rather than to traditional public

---

TABLE A.1   Analysis of Budget and Eligible Pool for Executive Education

---

Total Executive Education

Median Total Budget $1,000,000

In-Company Programs		*External Programs*	
Median in-company budget	$2,000,000	Median external budget	$200,000
Median in-company pool size	2,400	Median external pool size	860
Median number attending	700	Median number attending	90

Source: A. A. Vicere, "Changes in Practices, Changes in Perspectives: The 1997 International Study of Executive Development Trends" (University Park, PA: Institute for the Study of Organizational Effectiveness, 1997).

or open-enrollment courses offered by business schools or external consultants and marketed to individuals from a wide variety of companies and countries. Most companies indicate plans to focus even more on customized programs in the future. Firms such as Motorola, Xerox, and General Electric have set up the equivalent of corporate universities to develop and run internal educational programs on a huge scale. ADL (formerly Arthur D. Little Co.), based in Cambridge, Massachusetts, offers an MBA program that is regionally accredited and is a precandidate for accreditation by the International Association for Management Education (formerly the American Assembly of Collegiate Schools of Business)—the first corporate university to achieve this status. Coopers & Lybrand has indicated that learning capability is one of the core competencies it wants to develop for internal purposes as well as to deliver to its external clients. A number of other leading firms, including Coca-Cola, British Airways, Digital, and AT&T, either have established or are seriously exploring establishment of a corporate university.

The lines between the major players became even more blurred in 1997 when a former principal of Global Access Learning and associate dean for executive education at Emory University became executive vice president of EduTrek International, a for-profit firm that has purchased several financially troubled colleges and now operates accredited graduate and undergraduate business programs (along with other academic majors and management development programs) in Atlanta, Los Angeles, London, and Dubai.

Since 1982, Jim Bolt of Executive Development Associates (EDA) has conducted a biannual survey of the field of executive education. In 1997 he reported that respondents most frequently mentioned the following trends as core objectives for executive education/leadership development initiatives:[13]

Trend 1   The integration and interdependence of strategy and executive learning

Trend 2   The need for fully integrated executive leadership development systems

Trend 3   An increased focus on individual development

Trend 4   The endurance of leadership as the critical focus for development

Trend 5   The growing realization of the importance of innovation and entrepreneurship

Trend 6   The rapid ascent of action learning as the preferred learning paradigm

Trend 7   The increased importance and impact of technology

We concur with Bolt's findings and develop our view of how these trends are being translated into leadership development initiatives in the pages that follow.

Development and Delivery Costs

Table A.2 presents our analysis of reported budgets for development and delivery of one-week executive education/leadership development pro-

---

TABLE A.2   Program Development and Delivery Costs

	Development*	Delivery*
Corporations	$89,000 (75,000–242,000)	$32,880 (20,000–100,000+)
Consulting firms	$33,050 (3,000–129,000)	$34,000 (3,000–70,000+)
Universities	$19,000 (5,000–32,000)	$61,000 (18,000–120,000)

* Average costs followed by range of survey responses.

grams from the standpoint of corporate users as well as consulting firm and university providers. The average figures are somewhat distorted because of the inclusion of low-priced, packaged programs offered by some consulting firms. In general, for programs that are clearly executive in level and scope, numbers at the top end of the reported ranges are more typical.

The relatively low figures for development costs reported by consulting firms and universities are surprising but can be explained by the fact that many, perhaps most, organizations have standard programs that they offer as "open-enrollment" programs but that may be customized and offered to individual clients with minimum modification. Customized versions of existing courses can be developed less expensively than courses specifically designed to drive a corporate initiative. Truly custom programs frequently require a minimum of $100,000 for development, and may cost significantly more.

Myron Goff, director of Executive Conference at Johnson & Johnson, makes an important point when he states, "We [Johnson & Johnson] do not want *customized* programs; we want *custom* programs. That basically means we want the program consultant to start from scratch." To establish a custom program, consultants start with a series of interviews to collect information about the company and its needs. One recent Johnson & Johnson initiative involved interviews with over 100 executives in six countries. Based on that information, original cases and exercises were developed. In Johnson & Johnson's most recent Executive Conference, ten computerized exercises utilizing LotusNotes were developed, along with an extensive scenario called "J&J 2002" and a future-oriented, integrative exercise.

Our figures suggest that universities tend to be more expensive in delivering a one-week program. However, it is important to look behind the figures. If consulting firms utilize their own salaried people to deliver a packaged program on a regular basis, the daily rate for instruction tends to drop significantly. If consulting firms utilize presenters/ facilitators who are "world class" in reputation and ability, their costs are closer to those of business schools. High-visibility consultants or well-known business school professors tend to charge prices that are at least comparable to those charged by universities. In other words, professors may be paid $2,500 per day to deliver a program for their university, but charge $5,000 or more to do the same kind of program for a company-specific seminar—whether they are working directly for the company or for a consulting firm that has put the entire program together.

Principals of consulting firms suggest that their major competitive advantage is not cost but the ability to listen to and respond directly to client requests. Consultants see themselves as being more flexible in drawing resources from a variety of sources and even in their ability to motivate professors to be more adaptive to client requests. For example, corporations report offering a typical program twice as often as universities. Several university respondents talked about not wanting to repeat programs several times a year because it would "make undue demands" on their faculty. They also reported that faculty members tend to "get bored if they repeat the same program too many times." Our conclusion is that such boredom occurs only when a business school pays its faculty below-normal-market rates. Off campus, some professors are delivering the same or similar programs 10 to 50 times per year.

Even though custom and customized programs sound more expensive, it does not necessarily work out that way—especially if an organization plans to send a significant number of executives through a program. For example, the University of Pennsylvania's Wharton School reports that it charges companies an average development fee of $20,000 to $25,000 per one-week session. There is no development fee for public programs, but the weekly tuition may run $4,350 per person, as opposed to $2,500 a week per person for a customized program. Simple arithmetic shows that, if a company sends 30 executives to a public program, the total cost for this "off-the-shelf" initiative is $130,500 compared to a total of $100,000 for a customized program, even with the development costs. That may be why some 60 percent of the 4,500 to 5,000 professionals attending executive education courses at Wharton are enrolled in programs sponsored by specific clients.[14]

Similarly, Harvard, like many other leading business schools, was slow to embrace the idea of customizing programs for specific clients. In 1995, 3 percent of its revenues came from experimental custom offerings. In 1996 revenues from customized programs doubled, and by 1998, it is anticipated that 18 percent of total executive education revenues will be from customized programs. This is taking place against a backdrop of an overall increase of 50 percent in projected executive education revenues from 1996 to 1998.

Despite movement toward customization, Harvard has very strict criteria for the type of programs considered. These include

- Support from the CEO for the initiative aimed at the top echelon of management
- A maximum of 300 to 400 people over a two-year period
- Opportunity for the development of course materials and research
- Opportunity for junior faculty to be involved (in course materials or breakout session activities)
- Global scope
- A financial contribution to the business school

To offer a one-week customized program at Harvard, the cost would run approximately $250,000 for 50 participants, including lodging, meals, materials, and program delivery. The development of cases and other course materials is additional.

Some corporations attempt to reduce the cost of a program by contracting directly with individual faculty members rather than engaging a consulting firm or university to coordinate the details of program design and delivery. Of course, the actual savings may be distorted, because the figures reported may not include the corporate staff time that must be allocated to the various aspects of a program.

One final note regarding cost. Although it is possible to pay too much for the development and delivery of an executive-level program, our experience indicates that price is seldom the deciding factor in the decision-making process. More often, it is the perceived quality of the experience, which is often related to the perceived quality of the developers/presenters involved.

Who Delivers Strategic Leadership Development?

Table A.3 compares consulting firms' and universities' use of faculty/facilitators for executive programs. Surprisingly, the survey from which the data emerged indicated that there was little difference in the composition of program faculty. Both groups tended to emphasize the utilization of their own staff in the programs they delivered.

Although a relatively minor development at this point, there seems to be growth among consulting organizations that have a very small inter-

TABLE A.3 Who Delivers Strategic Leadership Development?

	Internal Staff/Faculty	Other University Professors	Nonuniversity Presenters
Consulting firms	81%	9%	11%
Universities	79%	12%	9%

nal staff but a large network of faculty from business schools around the globe who deliver their programs. Executive Development Associates (La Jolla, California) operates with a staff of two but utilizes faculty and independent consultants from a wide variety of sources. Global Access Learning, Inc. (Atlanta, Georgia), utilizes a cadre of current and former university professors to design a program, provide course management, and deliver some of the content. It reports having utilized 60 professors from 24 business schools along with 14 independent consultants in a variety of programs during the past decade. In its promotional literature, the firm describes itself as a "virtual business school." Such access to a wide variety of intellectual resources may emerge as one of the important sources of competitive advantage in the new environment.

How Revenues Are Allocated

Table A.4 compares how consulting firms and universities allocate revenues received from their executive education/leadership development activities. Perhaps the most important distinction is that 42 percent of revenues received by universities are allocated to internal activities (marketing and overhead), whereas only 25 percent of consulting firms' revenues are utilized for this purpose. This also means that 67 percent of revenues received by consulting firms go into program delivery, whereas only 55 percent of university revenues are allocated to program delivery.

TABLE A.4 Allocation of Revenues

	Marketing	Overhead	Delivery by Staff	Account Mgt.	Course Mgt.	Delivery by Outsiders	Other
Consultants	9%	16%	34%	10%	8%	15%	8%
Universities	14%	28%	29%	7%	12%	7%	3%

This may be because university executive program operations typically have extensive overhead commitments for residential facilities, classrooms, and related expenses. In addition, the open-enrollment programs that they frequently offer as part of their portfolio require an extensive marketing investment. On the other hand, because most consulting firms do not have such overhead, and because the principals of consulting firms are very likely to be involved in the delivery process, they can allocate a greater portion of total revenues to the delivery of the program. Often, this includes paying business school professors more than they receive from their home institution.

One leading corporate practitioner helped put the above comparison into perspective. He noted that the $67,000 consulting fee for a recent senior-level executive/leadership development initiative represented only 65 percent of out-of-pocket costs. That number dropped to 50 percent if classroom rental charges were included and dropped further, to 35 percent, if lodging costs for participants were included.

Industry Dynamics

If the emergence of executive education and leadership development as a lever for strategic change is one of the most significant trends in the field, then it seems appropriate to utilize industry analysis to look at ways the competitive environment is changing. As Michael Porter pointed out in his classic work on competitive forces, "The essence of strategy formulation is coping with competition."[15] He asserted that the state of competition in an industry depends on five basic forces. These include the degree of competition between existing participants in an industry, along with the power of customers, suppliers, potential entrants, and substitute products or services. Understanding these underlying sources of competitive pressure provides the foundation for any type of strategic plan or action agenda. Figure A.1 applies Porter's "forces of competitive analysis" to the field of executive education/leadership development.

Competitors. At the present time, the field is dominated by approximately 20 leading business schools and a handful of specialized consulting firms (discussed in the section "Potential Entrants"). These business schools comprise the traditional competitive cohort. Excellence in

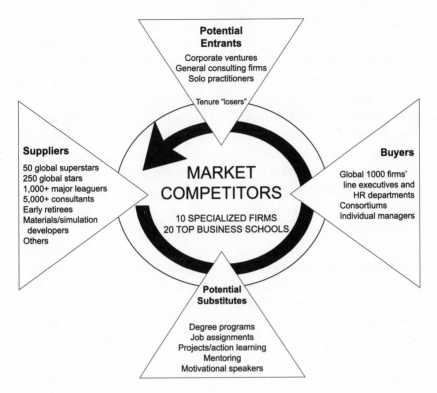

Figure A.1 Forces Driving Competition

executive education/leadership development often creates a virtuous cycle for business schools. Corporations typically look to the "best" business schools for assistance with their needs for leadership development. Business schools that are trying to build a reputation often find that a commitment to high-quality executive programs helps build the reputation of their MBA program and its graduates. Several surveys have attempted to establish which schools are the real leaders in the field. A list compiled by *Business Week* appears in Table A.5.

There is intense competition among the major players in this arena. Several less-renowned business schools have dropped programs or have suffered major setbacks in recent years. Emory University, for instance, has dropped its 25-year-old Advanced Management Program. MIT has taken a "hiatus" from general management programs. Most business school programs—even the venerable Harvard Advanced Management

Program (AMP)—have been shortened in length. As the field of leadership development changes, the university business school cohort is finding itself challenged by a new set of competitive dynamics.

Global dynamics also are playing a part in the emerging competitive environment. Although U.S. providers dominate Table A.5, five European institutions are already significant players. In addition, strong new competitors are emerging in Spain and the Scandinavian countries, and significant players are beginning to emerge in developing sections of the world. The Asian Institute of Management conducts programs throughout the Pacific Rim. INCAE (Costa Rica) offers courses and programs in seven Latin American countries and has executive education revenues of nearly $10 million per year.

The Harvard Example. The Harvard Business School occupies a unique position in the arena of business education. Without question the most heavily endowed business school in the world, HBS has been widely recognized for its leadership in advancing the professionalism of business education and practice. The mission of the school is "improving the practice of management." The major approach to this mission is the education of potential general managers in the venerated Harvard MBA program. Other traditional approaches include public programs in executive education materials (largely cases written by HBS professors and reprints from the *Harvard Business Review*). More recently, HBS Publishing has become a major source of business trade books.

In the 1990s, however, changing market conditions and new technologies forced the institution to reevaluate its approach to meeting the mission. The Business School recognized that its leadership position in executive education was being challenged. Some of the flagship programs, such as the AMP and the Program for Management Development (PMD), were operating at less than capacity for the first time in the school's history. Longtime corporate sponsors expressed frustration with the lack of responsiveness demonstrated by the leader in this field.

In 1996 McKinsey & Company was asked to analyze this market and make recommendations for the future directions of executive education and leadership development. The summary of its market analysis is provided as Appendix B. As a result of this market analysis, Associate Dean Earl Sasser continued a process for restructuring executive educa-

TABLE A.5 Corporate America's Global Top 20 for Nondegree Study

Ranking/University	1996–97 Revenue	5-Yr. Growth (%)	Programs Offered	Customized Programs (%)*
1. **HARVARD** Cambridge, Mass.	49.0**	65**	56	15
2. **MICHIGAN** Ann Arbor, Mich.	. 26.4	40.4	62	15
3. **NORTHWESTERN** (Kellogg) Evanston, Ill.	33.0	73	60	41
4. **PENNSYLVANIA** (Wharton) Philadelphia	29.0	141.7	110	35
5. **STANFORD** Stanford, Calif.	8.3**	88**	15	3
6. **VIRGINIA** (Darden) Charlottesville	14.5	81.3	59	47
7. **COLUMBIA** New York	12.7	61.8	41	48
8. **INSEAD** Fontainebleau, France	40.0	73.9	128	40
9. **DUKE** (Fuqua) Durham, N.C.	10.4	44.4	25	70
10. **MIT** (Sloan) Cambridge, Mass.	11.8	31.1	57	21
11. **CHICAGO***** Chicago	1.3	—	10	37
12. **IMD** Lausanne, Switzerland	23.4	17.2	67	44
13. **NORTH CAROLINA** (Kenan-Flagler) Chapel Hill	5.8	114.8	47	65
14. **DARTMOUTH** (Tuck) Hanover, N.H.	3.7	131.3	12	25
15. **INDIANA** Bloomington, Ind.	4.2	281.8	46	70
16. **LONDON BUSINESS SCHOOL**† London	9.4	61.5	50	50
17. **BABSON** Babson Park, Mass.	6.4	120.7	29	85
18. **SOUTHERN CALIFORNIA** (Marshall) Los Angeles	5.4	61.6	39	52
19. **PENN STATE** (Smeal) University Park, Penn.	4.5	40.6	72	45
20. **CORNELL** (Johnson) Ithaca, N.Y.	2.2	126.8	13	48

* Percent of revenues from programs designed specifically for client companies

** *Business Week* estimates

*** Launched exec-ed program in 1996

† Latest available data

Source: Reprinted from the October 20, 1997 *Business Week* by special permission. © 1997 by the McGraw-Hill Companies, Inc.

tion that had been launched by his predecessor, Jay Lorsch. The AMP and the International Senior Management Program (ISMP) were combined into the General Manager Program and reduced to nine weeks plus an optional course at the beginning which covers basic finance and accounting. It was also decided to offer PMD only once a year, rather than the traditional two offerings per year.

Although competitors have reduced their general management program to four weeks or less, Harvard believes it is impossible to do a good job of general management in less than six weeks. At the present time, however, it is exploring programs that can be offered in three-week modules, separated over a block of time.

The same is true for a new offering aimed at general managers, which would involve two three-week modules. One of the creative aspects of the General Manager Program is the focus in the initial segment on tools for diagnosis, with expectations that each participant will apply those tools during the interval away from the program and return for Module II with an action plan for how they are going to make improvements within their own areas of responsibility. No staff executives are admitted to this program. Only division presidents or country managers need apply.

A new program for functional managers in global firms, the Program for Global Leadership, will be launched in 1998. To deal with capacity restraints on campus, Module I (in 1998) will be offered in Singapore, with the second three-week module offered on the HBS campus. Associate Dean Sasser believes that students should spend some time on campus but that, by dividing the time in this manner, the school is able to double the capacity of on-campus facilities and bring together smaller groups of "decentralized" module participants for a large, integrated exercise with a variety of Harvard Business School professors.

One of the issues that Harvard faces is capacity constraints. These operate in two ways. First is the limitation of physical facilities on the Boston campus. Currently, 150 of the total 315 bedrooms could best be described as adequate dormitory space. These rooms are currently being replaced with 165 hotel-quality rooms, with plans within three to four years to add 80 rooms. HBS is also expanding capacity by offering portions of some courses off campus.

The second challenge is the limited availability of key faculty members. Without being specific about numbers, Sasser reports that he is attempting to induce faculty members to spend some of their outside consulting days developing materials or doing customized programs. This means it will be necessary to pay "market" rates. Although HBS staff has not been supplemented with outside faculty members, this policy will no doubt be reexamined on a regular basis. The World Bank programs described in Chapter 9 offer one approach to this dilemma by partnering with other leading schools around the world.

Suppliers. From our standpoint, the major suppliers of executive education/leadership development are the individuals who deliver programs for corporate customers, whether they be university professors or consultants. Table A.6 summarizes our analysis of this key group.

Although exact figures are difficult to develop, our best estimate is that there are about 50 people in the world who are "global superstars." Many are riding the crest of a very successful book and are able to charge prices that range from $20,000 to $50,000 per session for over 100 teaching and/or consulting days per year, working throughout the world. Tom Peters, Ken Blanchard, Steve Covey, and Mike Hammer probably fall into this category. Others, such as Ram Charan or Maurice Saias, bill an incredible number of days each year. A few, including John Kotter of the Harvard Business School and Peter Senge of MIT, charge extremely high rates in order to limit the number of days they spend on the road. Most academic institutions limit the amount of time that professors are able

---

TABLE A.6 Individual Suppliers of Executive Education/Leadership Development

Classification	World Total	Daily Rates	Days per Year
Global superstars	50	$10,000+	100+
Global stars	250	$5,000–10,000	75+
Major leaguers	1,000–1,500	$2,500–5,000	50+
Professionals	2,500–5,000	$1,000–2,500	50
Semipro	5,000–25,000	Under $1,000	10+

to spend away from campus. High demand and limited availability can result in daily billing rates of $20,000 or more for the *crème de la crème* of individual faculty suppliers.

There are probably another 250 "global stars" who charge $5,000 or more per day and bill at least 75 days per year for a variety of companies around the world. These individuals tend to be as effective as the "superstars" in terms of dealing with clients, but they frequently have done less visible research or lack the popular book that can catapult an author into superstardom.

It appears that $2,500 per day or more is the mark of a "major leaguer," especially if the individual is able to generate 50 or more days per year. We believe there are 1,000 of these individuals around the world. Often they will work a significant number of days for a limited number of clients. In return for guaranteeing a "major leaguer" 20 to 50 days per year, a client gets the services of the individual on a retainer arrangement. These individuals may become a semipermanent part of their client's staff and have genuine understanding of the corporate strategy, culture, and challenges.

There are probably another 2,500 to 5,000 "professionals" who charge between $1,000 and $2,500 per day and generate $50,000 per year or more as a full-time occupation, to supplement their university incomes, or to supplement early retirement pensions. Often these are former professors who have decided to become independent consultants or individuals who have taken early retirement but maintain a working relationship with their former employer.

Finally, there is a large number of individuals, perhaps 25,000 in total, who tend to work at relatively low rates either to supplement faculty employment or to provide a career that offers a degree of flexibility and independence. These "semipros" typically are platform presenters who utilize materials developed by others, but are quite capable in delivering material to specific audiences. Tighter academic and corporate markets and corporate downsizing are significantly increasing the bottom portion of this talent pool. When EduTrek International advertised in 1997 for prospective faculty members to teach in its Los Angeles campus (American College of Los Angeles), it had over 250 responses to an ad that described an opportunity to teach ten four-hour sessions for $1,100.

One of the key challenges to providers of executive education/leadership development is the ability to identify facilitators/educators who have not yet become "stars" but have the potential to develop this capability. Motorola has done an exceptional job of identifying individuals who have not hit the "big time" but are very effective teachers and facilitators.

A major new source of potential suppliers is being created by early retirees from leading business firms. As corporations encourage early retirement to reduce headcount and streamline operations, talented, experienced executives are leaving organizations and beginning second careers as independent consultants. To ease the transition into actual retirement, many are able to negotiate consulting contracts with their former employers, to provide a few days per month consulting, often in the area of management development or executive education. Hoechst Celanese and General Electric have been quite successful with this concept. As these individuals begin to network more efficiently, they may become significant players in the field.

Another category of suppliers to the executive education/leadership development market are firms that develop, package, and market materials utilized in programs, including questionnaires that provide insight into managerial style, organizational culture, or competitive orientation. These materials often are used by consultants and professors as part of standard programs, or by corporate trainers or other managers as an alternative to more traditional programs. Firms that design these materials, such as Harbridge House (Boston), Zenger-Miller (San Jose), and Forum (Boston), also may put together entire programs on themes such as team effectiveness, quality, customer service, and diversity. These programs may be delivered by consultants associated with the firm that developed the package, or may be sold or licensed to corporations for use in internal programs delivered by company-selected personnel. Frequently, a large-scale, corporatewide initiative may start with senior-level consultants delivering programs to top executives. As the program cascades throughout the organization, "graduates" of the program may be trained to deliver many of the modules in order to reduce the cost and to increase the cadre of qualified instructors.

Computerized and noncomputerized simulations can be powerful components of a corporate learning experience. Generic simulations often are utilized to illustrate various aspects of competitive strategy, financial analysis, or leadership styles. Customized simulations can give managers low-risk experience in making decisions that reflect current organizational challenges in the operating environment. In fact, skillfully customized simulations actually can reflect the industry in which a participant may be operating. These kinds of vicarious learning experiences are called "Managerial Practice Fields" by Peter Senge.[16] Senge and the Center for Organizational Learning at MIT are perhaps the best-known academic source of managerial practice fields. The Center for Managerial Leaning and Business Simulation at Georgia Southern University also has gained international recognition through the contributions of Bernard Keys, who also leads the Association for Business Simulation and Experiential Learning (ABSEL). INSEAD, a leading business school in France, also has done an excellent job developing and using simulations for executive education/leadership development. The Strategic Management Group in Philadelphia, Executive Perspectives in Boston, Interpretive Software in Charlottesville, Virginia, and the Burgundy Group in Colorado Springs are other corporate leaders in the creation of computerized business and management simulations.

Potential Entrants. Although relatively few firms actually specialize in customized, high-level executive education/leadership development programs, this is clearly a significant growth area. A list of the non-university providers that we studied, and their specialties, appears in Table A.7. Revenue assumptions are based on the authors' estimates and have not been verified by every firm. These data were gathered in 1995 and updated in 1997.

Recent entrants may illustrate how other nonuniversity competitors may emerge. One of the most successful ventures of this sort, the Center for Executive Development (CED), based in Cambridge, Massachusetts, is a firm whose partners are exclusively former Harvard Business School professors whose teaching excellence was not rewarded with tenure. During the past five years, CED has become a leader in the development and delivery of top-level executive education/leadership development programs. Another emerging player, Global Access Learning, Inc., an Atlanta-based firm, has among its principals former professors who gave up tenure, others who decided that academia had become "more and

TABLE A.7 Key Nonuniversity Providers of Executive Education/
Leadership Development

Firm	Location	Specialty	Estimated Revenue[a]
Blanchard Training and Development	San Diego, CA	Leadership	15.0
Blessing/White, Inc.	Princeton, NJ	Individual & group alignment	20.5
Center for Creative Leadership	Greensboro, NC	Leadership, 360° feedback	30.0[b]
Center for Executive Development	Cambridge, MA	Strategy, leadership, & change	25.0
Covey Leadership Institute	Provo, UT	Leadership/values	90.0
Executive Development Associates	La Jolla, CA	Global strategy	1.5
Executrain Corporation	Alpharetta, GA	Computer training	164.0
Forum Corporation	Boston, MA	Customer service teams	39.5
Global Access Learning, Inc.	Atlanta, GA	Strategic leadership	2.5
Institute for Management Studies (IMS)	Reno, NV	One-day seminars	6.5
Keilty Goldsmith & Company	San Diego, CA	360° feedback	13.0
Pecos River Learning Center	Santa Fe, NM	Outdoor action learning	25.0
Personnel Decisions, Inc., International	Minneapolis, MN	Skill development; leadership development; 360° feedback	50.0
Strategic Management Group, Inc.	Philadelphia, PA	Performance development; simulations	16.0
Westcott Communications	Carrollton, TX	Distance learning	95.0
Wilson Learning Corporation	Minneapolis, MN	Training	40.0

[a] In millions of dollars.
[b] Approximately one-third of CCL's revenue is from customized programs.

more about less and less" and resigned from the tenure race, and other professors who continue to maintain academic affiliations.

In conducting interviews throughout the world, we were amazed at how many universities had stories about the "best teacher award curse." Significant numbers of "best teachers" wind up failing to generate the publication record required for tenure. Consequently, universities sometimes launch talented competitors by denying tenure to their best executive educators. Hence, they retain excellent researchers but have relatively few individuals who are able to meet the special challenges of the executive-level classroom.

Traditional views on research and tenure seem to be shifting, however, as leading business schools, such as Northwestern, Michigan, Duke, Cornell, and the University of Southern California, experiment with a category of faculty members often called *clinical* appointments. Sometimes these individuals have been given five-year contracts without tenure. They may have regular academic teaching assignments, but more typically have a specific level of responsibility for executive education and occasional MBA teaching. They may have little other involvement with the university other than participating in executive education. For example, before joining GE full time in 1994, Steve Kerr lived in Los Angeles, had a contract to spend ten weeks each year at the University of Michigan doing executive education, and still did a number of consulting days with GE through his private practice. Kerr exemplifies a new breed of practitioner-academic who partners with a university and with a series of clients to extend the capabilities of each.

In the United Kingdom, several schools, such as Manchester and Ashridge, employ a core faculty that is widely supplemented with a variety of associate faculty or visiting professors who may teach in several executive programs or merely serve as occasional guest lecturers. With the advent of the virtual corporation, consultants and professors are in the process of creating "virtual business schools." Without bricks, mortar, or significant capital investment, some firms are able to call on exceptionally talented resources throughout the world. Keilty, Goldsmith & Company describes itself as a firm of 17 principals and approximately 50 associates with absolutely no overhead. Whereas various partners and associates have overhead expenses with their individual practices, the firm itself operates with zero commitment to support staff and other administrative overhead. As mentioned previously, one firm uses the term *virtual business school* in its promotional literature.

General consulting firms seem to be busy enough dealing with strategic management issues and have yet to make a major move into the executive education/leadership development field.[17] As the lines between consulting and education continue to blur, this could change. JMW Consultants (Stamford, Connecticut) has identified leadership development as a means of enhancing relationships developed through consulting, and plans to leverage educational activities to expand its consulting practice. In 1997 this firm was conducting a study to explore the feasibility of offering a Master of Business Leadership (MBL) certificate to participants in client companies who were identified as technical specialists with the potential to move to higher levels of management. The program design called for the essence of each course in the core MBA curriculum to be covered in four six- to twelve-day sessions spread over an eighteen-month period. The participants were expected to gain the tools of the typical MBA, and participate with three to five colleagues from the sponsoring company in a project that would demonstrate a return to the sponsor of twice the cost of the program. Although the program graduate would not have a degree, this was seen as a potential benefit to the sponsor. One potential corporate sponsor observed, "We don't want to create an 'MBA Doll' which we wind up and then they go off to work for a competitor."

Other firms, such as Arthur Andersen and McKinsey, have the resources to become significant players in executive education and leadership development. To date, however, they have not judged these activities to be as profitable as their traditional consulting practice. That may be due to the fact that it is nearly impossible to hire freshly minted MBAs who can manage the demands of the corporate learning laboratory. As discussed previously, individuals who are skilled in this area command much higher levels of compensation than do new MBAs. As a result, many general consulting firms do not see the potential margins they seek in the field. Nevertheless, firms that specialize in the executive education/leadership development arena often talk, off the record, of margins that exceed 40 percent.

Some corporations have become so proficient at their own internal education programs that they have begun to market them to suppliers and to the public. After receiving favorable press from *In Search of Excellence,*[18] Walt Disney University has opened its doors to firms of all types, and Disney is actively investigating further opportunities in the field. IBM's Skill Dynamics planned to utilize experienced IBM educators in a separate business unit providing educational services to other corporations. Lack of initial success, however, led to the project's being canceled.

Potential Substitutes. The advent of the executive MBA program—wherein a midcareer individual, usually with ten years of experience, is able to complete a regular MBA curriculum while holding down a full-time job—is another rapidly growing area of the field which is supplanting more traditional methods. Pioneered by the University of Chicago and Wharton, these programs are now offered in most schools accredited by the International Association for Management Education (formerly the American Assembly of Collegiate Schools of Business). The concept of executive MBA programs is now spreading throughout Europe and Latin America.

In April 1996, one U.S. consulting firm was conducting a feasibility study to determine the potential of creating an independent business school which offered, for profit, an executive MBA program. The firm was considering the use of an international faculty from a variety of institutions, interactive technology, and action learning components. Whether or not this project is successful, the future will probably hold an increasing number of "business schools" that are not affiliated with any traditional university. Already such major players as IMD, INSEAD, INCAE, Ashridge, and Thunderbird operate without university ties. Some U.K. schools, such as London Business School and Manchester, operated with considerably more independence than their U.S. counterparts. As business schools are asked to enter into more "partnership" arrangements with their corporate clients, the lines between business schools will continue to become more blurred.

Another area in which business schools are offering competition to their own traditional executive education programs is through the creation of university research centers. The Center for Effective Organization (CEO) at the University of Southern California, led by Ed Lawler, a recognized leader in the area of participative management, conducts courses and programs for its members that could just as well be offered by the executive education arm of the university. MIT's official Office of Executive Education does not offer customized programs. Yet the Organizational Learning Center at MIT offers a series of courses on the "Core Competencies of the Learning Organization" for its members. It also designs comprehensive programs in systems thinking, dialogue, mental models, and other aspects of the five disciplines articulated by Peter Senge in his landmark book *The Fifth Discipline*.[19] Reportedly, Electronic Data Systems (EDS) recently invested $740,000 in a seven-month program for 35 people who are pioneers in changing the company's culture. The extent of these types of activities is such that one university-based executive program director commented, "Our dean would be amazed at how much executive education is being done on this campus that he is not receiving his percentage on."

Executive education itself is a relatively small part of the leadership development process. Most organizations recognize that only 10 to 20 percent of a person's preparation for top management will come through educational activities. The overall objective of the varied activities associated with leadership development is to "grow" individuals who have the experience, wisdom, and insight to move their organizations successfully into the future. Consequently, job assignments and mentoring are key elements of the process but are seldom discussed in an analysis of the subject. Formal budgets are seldom directed to these activities. Yet they are probably the most significant part of the overall development process. As the emphasis on real-time, hands-on leadership development initiatives continues to grow, these areas may well receive more attention within the corporate community.

As firms look for more efficient ways to achieve objectives, action learning projects can be used to replace consulting assignments traditionally given to outside individuals and firms. Naturally, it is not in consulting firms' short-term interest to emphasize this trend. However, when this practice becomes more widespread and more widely recognized, we believe that corporations will question the decision to spend several million dollars for outsiders to do work that could be performed by high-potential executives from within the organization who have been given appropriate coaching and direction. At that point, the impact on both the executive/leadership development and traditional consulting markets will be significant.

Customers. Most of the corporate buyers for custom or customized executive/leadership development programs are among the Global 1000 firms. The costs of developing and delivering a custom program make the ticket for admission too high-priced for many smaller firms. At the same time, executives from medium-sized firms and from emerging companies and countries are rapidly becoming a core source of enrollment for the public programs offered by university business schools.

In many instances, a strategic initiative championed by a corporate executive is the impetus for a customized program. In fact, consultants and university executive education directors agree that the chances for significant impact are much greater if they are able to have an initiative sponsored by the CEO or by senior line executives within a firm. On the other hand, provider selection is typically handled by human resource executives. As one consultant described it, "I want to get to the top person in the organization, but I don't want to upset the HR executive in that process. The HR person may not be able to make a major initiative happen, but he or she has the ability to 'shoot me out of the saddle' if I haven't played the game appropriately."

A new approach to the buying process, pioneered by Babson College, is the "consortium." This new model typically features a team of consultants, usually university-based faculty, who link together with several noncompeting corporations. These corporate "members" have agreed to work over an extended period of time to create executive/leadership development initiatives that specifically address the collective objectives of the corporate membership. Although universities have been slow to embrace this concept, a few schools have been successful with consortia. The University of Indiana, for example, has focused its efforts on this distinctive niche. According to Cam Danielson, director of the Indiana program, most of those projects have led to more detailed involvement in consulting or ongoing coaching for the faculty members who participated in the on-campus sessions. Atlanta's Emory University has just inaugurated a consortium program which was put together through the initiative of Ed Adison, CEO of the Southern Company, but involving several other leading Atlanta firms.

The Strategic Transnational Executive Programme (STEP), coordinated by Olle Bovin of International Leadership (Switzerland) and Maurice Saias, Institut d'Administration des Enterprises, Aix-en-Provence (France), is perhaps the most successful consortium program for senior executives in Europe. It has been running since 1983 and has included such members as Volvo/Renault, Wartsila, Midland Bank, Alcatel, Hewlett-Packard, Shell, ABB, and Tetra-Laval. Each initiative is viewed as a joint venture of five or six noncompeting member firms. Each firm nominates four or five participants per year, appoints a senior executive to serve as sponsor, and identifies "challenge work" projects for their participants to address during the program. The programs consist of three modules of five days each conducted over a full year. Historically, the three modules have been offered in Europe; however, plans call for expanding the programs to include at least one module in North America.

The corporate community also seems to be embracing the idea of collaboration among executive development providers. In planning an initiative for 800 middle-level managers at Hoechst Celanese, one of the key requirements for identifying contractors was a "willingness to partner." One of the potential suppliers being interviewed mentioned that the project's scope was beyond its capacity and recommended partnering with another firm based in a different city. The term *partnering* excited the evaluation committee, as most of the universities and firms with whom they had talked seemed to be focused only on pushing their own ideas and resources. The willingness of two potential competitors to collaborate became the key to the selection decision.

Open-enrollment programs will continue to serve the specific career development needs of individual managers. Although public programs offered by universities are the largest source for these individual initiatives, organizations such as the American Management Association (AMA), the Young Presidents' Organization (YPO), and Management Centre Europe provide many programs for their members. Additionally, the Institute for Management Studies (IMS), headquartered in Reno, Nevada, offers programs in 25 North American and European cities for managers who work for any of their 454 corporate members. A number of the leading individual suppliers of executive education/leadership development offer one-day programs on a variety of subjects through IMS. Trade and professional associations also tend to provide various forms of executive education/leadership development. Because of their involvement with an industry or profession, they often are able to effectively focus on the special needs of their members.

The American Society of Association Executives (ASAE) offers a wide range of programs to increase the proficiency and professionalism of the professional staff that manages trade, professional, and individual membership organizations. The management development programs offered by the Atlanta-based Life Office Management Association (LOMA) are highlighted elsewhere in this book.

WHAT'S AHEAD?

Throughout the remainder of this appendix, we describe trends we observed in our research and make a number of predictions about the immediate future of executive and leadership development. One of the early reviewers of this manuscript reminded us of the Chinese proverb "It is very difficult to make predictions . . . especially about the future." In reality, it is very easy to make predictions about the future. It is just difficult to be *right* with any degree of consistency. We look forward to the challenge of reviewing these predictions when the twentieth century comes to a close—in just a few short years.

Trend 1: More Customized, Strategic Programs

As executive leadership development comes of age, it is increasingly viewed as a key lever for strategic change rather than a series of disconnected programs and initiatives. As such, generic programs are becoming less and less appropriate. Consequently, corporations are demanding programs that support their specific strategic objectives, reflect their vision or values, and involve a critical mass of key players.

As previously stated, over 75 percent of all executive education dollars go toward custom or customized programs rather than to "public" or open-enrollment courses. In order to provide examples of the scale and scope of custom/customized initiatives, two mammoth projects and two significant, but smaller, initiatives are summarized in the following paragraphs.

Work-Out at GE. In their "Handbook for Corporate Revolutionaries," Tichy and Sherman suggested that, in a country or company, revolution requires control of the police, the schools, and the media.[20] The key to "organizational revolution" is not simply structural change, but *cultural* change as well. In order to successfully complete a revolution in a corporate setting, "revolutionaries" must shrewdly use rewards and punishment (the police) to shape behavior. Instigators of change also need to maintain control over the educational system (the schools) and the media (corporate communications), in order to drive and institutionalize strategic change. In an increasingly competitive global environment, contemporary corporations are using all three levers to make their organizations faster, leaner, smarter, and more innovative.

At General Electric (GE), Tichy's leadership of the Crotonville Executive Education operation was critical to CEO Jack Welch's corporate revitalization effort. Welch, upon taking the reins at GE, recognized that, despite its being one of the world's most successful organizations, GE had to make dramatic changes if it was to remain competitive in the global marketplace. He recruited approximately 20 business school professors and top-flight consultants to initiate the highly lauded "Work-Out" effort. Work-Out is a forum in which "participants get a mental workout. They take unnecessary work out of their jobs, and they work out problems together."[21]

One report on how the Work-Out name was generated suggests that Professor Kirby Warren of Columbia University jokingly asked Welch after a breakfast meeting, "Now that you have gotten so many people out of the organization [at this point, over 100,000 of the workforce had been cut], when are you going to get some of the work out?" The creative Welch picked up on the phrase because it suggested not only the possibility of eliminating work but also the imagery of a physical workout whereby a flabby organization might become more fit. Work-Out became a transformational initiative at GE and the concept has been widely emulated elsewhere.

First announced in early 1989, the program involved town meetings of 40 to 100 employees picked by management from all ranks and functions. As a first step in the three-day sessions, a member of the management team set up the agenda, which could be summarized as "the challenge of eliminating unnecessary work." In the next step, after the "boss" disappeared, the participants worked in smaller groups to tackle different parts of the agenda. For a day and a half, the groups discussed complaints, debated solutions, and eventually prepared presentations. On the third day, they presented their proposals to management, who were held accountable for responding to and acting on the participants' recommendations.[22]

The Work-Out process has been very successful. Not only has it contributed to GE's competitiveness, but more important, it has fostered a sense of trust between the rank-and-file and management by providing all employees with an avenue to raise their concerns and voice their suggestions on improving the company's performance.

Philips's Centurion Project. Executive and leadership development were also recognized as powerful levers for change by another corporate giant. At troubled Philips International N.V., former CEO Jan Timmer recognized the potential of using the function as a catalyst for a massive turnaround effort called "Operation Centurion."

In early 1990, after several years of losing money and market share, Philips went through its greatest crisis. Its share price dropped to an all-time low, and within several months Timmer had been named the company's new chief executive officer.[23] By this time, external and internal factors had led to such deterioration of the company's financial and competitive positions that a detailed investigation concluded that the organization's future was "hopeless." Confronted with Philips's dire situation, the newly appointed CEO developed a dramatic plan, Operation Centurion, to engage the organization in a drastic change process including both cost cutting and building internal capabilities. The key threads of the effort were restructuring and revitalization through cascading initiatives that generated consensus and commitment to an urgently felt agenda for change.[24]

The Operation Centurion communication process involved top-down Centurion Sessions and bottom-up Town Meetings. The former consisted of three-day meetings of 30 to 70 individuals from the top levels of the company. The first step was to familiarize the group with the real state of the business. Subsequently, participants were encouraged to list the most important issues facing the company. The next phase was to present the group with approaches for "building a winning organization." This was designed to help them formulate and build commitment to "stretch targets" for improving the business. The last step involved project formulation and action planning.

In the first top-level sessions, a decision and commitment to cut the workforce by some 45,000 people was reached collectively by 120 people, rather than being dictated by the board. This communication process was then "cascaded downward" in similar three-day sessions with large groups at lower levels, where specific targets were discussed to help generate "buy-in" throughout the organization. The three-day sessions were followed up by meetings four to six months later to review the implementation of change projects and to plan the next stages.

Town Meetings, the second part of the communication process, involved much larger groups of up to 400 employees—from operator level to senior management. These meetings provided a forum for discussions on how to improve business performance and led to a significant number of practical suggestions for positive organizational change.

Timmer's Centurion project was quite successful in its early stages. Philips's financial performance improved steadily and significantly despite a recession-plagued industry. As Sumantra Ghoshal and Christopher Bartlett pointed out in *Linking Organizational Context and Managerial Action*,[25] the specific decisions to dramatically cut employee headcount and working capital were key. However, these business actions worked in conjunction with "deeper, less visible" changes in the internal environment. Many of the people involved in the turnaround effort emphasized that the cultural changes were at least as important. As a junior employee explained, "What matters most is that the smell of the place has changed. I now enjoy coming to work. It's not one thing, but overall it's become a very different company."[26]

Unfortunately, the pace of change slowed down over time at Philips, and new CEO, Cor Boonstra, is now launching a new developmental initiative. Yet the early success of Centurion, coupled with the success of GE's Work-Out process and the success of other companies, such as British Airways which has used a series of cascaded initiatives to evolve itself from "Bloody Awful" in 1984 to the "World's Favourite Airline" in 1997, provide testimony to the value of large-scale, cascaded efforts.[27]

Smaller Projects with Impact. Although not as dramatic as in the two cases mentioned above, a significant cultural shift was precipitated at Bertlesmann Music Group, a privately owned division of the German media powerhouse, when it acquired RCA and Arista Records from GE in 1986. A clash of cultures seemed unavoidable. To prevent this from materializing, CEO Michael Dornemann, International President Rudi Gasner, and Joe Isenstein, senior vice president of human resources, created a one-week leadership development program for key executives. The program reinforced Bertlesmann's corporate philosophy of team-work and partnership. It combined the efforts of four senior corporate executive speakers and business school professors from Columbia, William & Mary, UCLA, Emory, and Aix-en-Provence. Over the past ten years, program offerings have alternated between Europe and the United States, and now are part of the corporate enculturation process as new executives are brought into the growing concern.

At Johnson & Johnson, Chairman Ralph Larsen became concerned that the world's largest and most diverse health care products company might become complacent because of its past successes. Previously, the company had conducted "Executive Conference," a very successful, three-year executive education initiative focused on competitive analysis. To build on this success, Larsen created a high-level working committee to create a new Executive Conference program designed to challenge complacency and stretch the thinking horizons of his top 700 executives. The consulting team responsible for this project interviewed over 100 executives in six countries. Eventually the Corporate Working Committee identified the theme as "Creating Our Future." Part of this program involved groups of executives from around the world working together for one week under the guidance of outside consultants to create or invent a future to which they could feel committed. The program concluded with presentations to a member of the Executive Committee, outlining the team's recommendations. These presentations were transcribed and circulated, along with the presentation overheads, to all the members of the corporate Executive Committee on a regular basis. Within the first year, company executives could identify multiple business initiatives that had begun as a result of suggestions made during the program and from a top-level effort that paralleled the program.

Although Executive Conference is viewed as the flagship of Johnson & Johnson's executive programs, the firm also utilizes a number of customized programs offered by leading business schools. For example, during the early 1990s middle managers throughout the world attend advanced management programs offered at institutions like the International Institute for Management Development (IMD), Northwestern University, Duke University, and the University of California at Berkeley. Functional finance and marketing courses are also offered in collaboration with the University of North Carolina.

Trend 2: Shorter, More Focused, Large-Scale, Cascaded Programs

With almost universal corporate pressure to do more with less, executive education/leadership development initiatives are being designed to reduce their major cost; that is, managers' time away from their jobs. This is essential as larger numbers of people are involved in programs in order to have companywide impact in shifting strategic directions or changing corporate cultures. There appears to be widespread recognition that many vertical slices rather than one thin horizontal slice of the organization must be involved in executive/leadership development efforts to have significant impact.

A leader in developing shorter, more focused programs is Keilty, Goldsmith & Company (KGC). Since 1981, KGC has served a variety of companies by specializing in helping "organizations achieve their vision and live their values by developing leaders in a manner that meets their organizations' unique needs."[28] KGC clients include BellSouth, General Electric, McKinsey & Company, and Texaco. At BellSouth, they were responsible for developing the "Leadership Inventory Process," a mechanism for leaders to receive feedback on their perceived effectiveness in living BellSouth's vision and values. The program was delivered to the top 1,500 executives in the organization. At General Electric, KGC was responsible for a part of four different leadership programs at Crotonville. The firm has developed leadership inventories for General Electric and trained 2,000 of GE's leaders throughout the United States. At the premier management consulting firm, McKinsey & Company, KGC developed a feedback process that is currently being used on an ongoing basis by McKinsey partners and directors around the world.[29]

A typical format for KGC is to begin an initiative with a two-day orientation and a customized 360-degree feedback exercise. Six months after the initial two-day program, the group reassembles for another one-day session designed to reinforce action plans that participants developed based on their initial feedback. One year after the initial session, participants return for a second dose of 360-degree feedback, hoping to have made progress in at least two or three of the major variables identified during the initial session as areas for improvement.

The Center for Creative Leadership in Greensboro, North Carolina, is probably the world leader in the utilization of 360-degree feedback for executives, and their "Benchmarks" may be the most widely used profile. Their strength is the tremendous database gathered from managers around the world. The converse of this strength is the fact that programs built around this profile are not as customized as those from some other providers, such as KGC.

An even more dramatic example of scope is offered by the Pecos River Learning Center (PRLC), founded by Larry Wilson, the dynamic entrepreneur who recently sold his Wilson Learning Corporation. Although the Pecos River group can bring its unique business enhancement programs to almost any city in North America, Europe, or Asia, PRLC encourages clients to visit the "largest permanent training site in the enchanting state of New Mexico," some 30 miles north of Santa Fe. The land surrounding this site often served as a gathering place for Native American tribes to meet to make agreements. PRLC attempts to carry this tradition forward by "helping companies to reach agreements, take action, and move into a successful future."

A typical Pecos River Learning Center program is three days long and has the following objectives:

1. Team building and strategic planning for small companies or individual departments
2. Experiential outdoor adventure program for individuals and teams who want to discover their potential
3. A taste of the PRLC curriculum and teaching techniques which can be customized to meet specific corporate needs

During the startup phase of Saturn, General Motors believed that success depended on retraining tradition-bound GM employees to work as teams, solve problems creatively, master quality principles, and bridge the traditional chasm between union and management. As part of the effort to achieve this transformation, Saturn partnered with Pecos River Learning Center to build a training facility near its Tennessee complex and design a curriculum for all employees. Over 2,500 manufacturing team members attended the three-day "Playing to Win" course. Additionally, a two-day program was designed for marketing and retail managers, and a five-day introduction was created for Saturn's 500 dealers. Many business schools and other consulting firms utilize similar "adventure learning programs," but no one seems to approach the same level of volume as the Pecos River Learning Center.

Trend 3: More Action Learning Projects with Measurable Results

The ultimate test of relevance is the ability to observe and measure significant change. As mentioned previously, Motorola has led the way with its research indicating that targeted educational efforts can generate better than a 30:1 return within three years.[30] Moreover, the previously discussed Work-Out program at General Electric and the Centurion Project at Philips are examples of efforts that were designed to apply concepts introduced in the corporate classroom to real-life situations in measurable ways.

Obviously, this trend calls for a totally new outlook on executive education/leadership development. Professors are less able to rely on notes developed several years ago. The analysis of cases originally written in the 1970s, even though classic, becomes much less relevant than the application of concepts to contemporary issues. History is not likely to hold the interest of today's executive-level audiences, who are much more interested in thinking about how to shape the future. These executives are more driven by action, which is why action learning approaches are gaining such widespread interest.[31]

Corporate, university, and consultant respondents to our survey agreed that the majority of their new initiatives were relying less on classroom time led by a professor and more on facilitated, small group, action learning applications. This is not just a question of how time is divided among lecture, discussion, and case analysis. Rather, classroom time increasingly is being seen as a way of illustrating a concept or developing tools which then must be applied to a current challenge or issue on a real-time basis as part of the developmental experience. In fact, several firms, such as the Swedish MiL Institute, view the action learning approach as their specialty.

In this arena, corporations such as General Electric and Philip Morris have emerged as leaders in making executive education and leadership development a "hands-on" process. British business schools have been much more innovative than their American counterparts in designing programs that take the learner out of the classroom and into the real world—often with projects suggested by the program sponsor. In fact, MBA programs in several British institutions have strong action learning components. Manchester, Oxford, Cambridge, Ashridge, and Henley programs all utilize classroom sessions interspersed with application projects. This means that an executive-level student will spend more time learning on the job than on the university campus.

Conclusions

Based on the above analysis, we have concluded that executive education and leadership development are evolving toward a systems perspective—a recognition that training or education alone cannot develop a leader, nor can assignments without adequate coaching and career plans, nor can experiences that are unrelated to corporate strategic objectives. Having the right people ready to assume new responsibilities at the right time requires the integration of all the above activities into a leadership development system that provides momentum for the overall growth and development of the entire organization. Corporations are recognizing the power of executive education and leadership development initiatives as part of a system that can help align managers, workers, and organizational processes in pursuit of strategic objectives.

This means the field is changing. As opposed to the traditional objectives of "improving the knowledge and broadening the perspectives of participants," contemporary leadership development initiatives are more likely to focus on "improving customer satisfaction ratings by 20 percent" and "opening up new markets among emerging economies." Measurement has long been the most difficult and challenging aspect of the field since traditional programs were primarily knowledge based. Contemporary programs tend to be more activity- or challenge-oriented. As a result, outcomes are easier to measure. As a further result, future initiatives are likely to be even more focused on real-world, hands-on learning and measurable output.

Appendix B
Executive Education Market Overview

The nondegree executive education market generated approximately $3.3 billion in 1995 and is growing at roughly 10 to 12 percent annually. Business schools represent about one-quarter of this market, with internal corporate training units, private firms, and individual consultants accounting for the remaining three-quarters. In recent years, changing customer objectives have led to the emergence of distinct executive education segments, each with its own economics and operating requirements. To retain their historical leadership position in executive education, business schools must now choose which segments to focus on and then adopt best practices for developing, delivering, and managing their programs.

CHANGING MARKET REQUIREMENTS

Executive education has traditionally been viewed as a rite of passage for high-potential managers. For all types of programs, the overall reputation of a business school was often the most important buying factor. Most customers who participated in our study agreed that the reputation of a university's executive education program is closely linked to the quality and stature of the school's MBA program and to the perceived strength and depth of its faculty. But, although provider reputation continues to be a critical factor in the selection of programs, the ability to demonstrate tangible impact on the sponsoring organization has become an equally important customer buying factor in executive education.

This information was circulated by Kim Clark, dean of the Harvard Business School, in July 1996. It summarized an in-depth market assessment in which HBS was assisted by McKinsey & Company.

Rather than a perquisite, executive development is now seen as a necessary, even routine investment, for which companies demand a concrete return. Consequently, executive education is used not only for individual development, but also for implementing organizational charge, for developing solutions to company-specific issues, and for achieving bottom-line results.

As corporate objectives for executive education have grown broader, most companies have started to use more providers, both external and internal, to meet their needs. To ensure that the education they pay for is truly relevant, corporations are taking an increasingly active role in developing and delivering their own programs. Consider, for example, the growth of highly visible corporate universities (such as Motorola and Walt Disney), as well as the flurry of dedicated, in-house corporate training and development professionals and facilities at many large companies (IBM, AT&T, UN-LJM, ARAMARK, British Airways, Bell Atlantic). Clearly, the heyday of the traditional business school as the sole domain of executive education is over.

In response to this challenge, many business schools have begun to manage executive education more professionally. Although treating executive education like a business represents a cultural departure for more traditional academic institutions, it also creates new opportunities for business schools to retain credibility in today's rapidly shifting business environment. Academic providers must respond to the atmosphere of intensified competition by focusing on impact, becoming more responsive to customer needs, modifying sales and marketing approaches, and providing greater value for the tuition dollar. Success will be realized not only financially, but in our continued influence on the practice and theory of management.

EMERGING SEGMENTATION

Both changing customer objectives and the deliberate provider responses to them have contributed to the emergence of distinct market segments over the past five years. We have chosen to define market segments by both the content and the beneficiary of the program (see Figure B.1). Content may be either broad (general management) or focused (functional or specific cross-functional topics). The primary customer may be either an individual (open-enrollment programs) or an organization

		Individuals (open enrollment)	Organization (closed enrollment)

Program content

Focused

Traditional focused programs

Build specific skills or knowledge of individuals

Organizational problem-solving projects

Achieve measurable company objective via action learning

Broad

Traditional general management programs

Broaden perspectives and capabilities of high-potential managers

Custom programs

Transform capabilities or culture of an entire organization through management education

Individuals (open enrollment)   **Organization** (closed enrollment)

Program customers

Figure B.1 Evolving Segmentation

(closed-enrollment programs). The four resultant segments can thus be defined as: (1) traditional general management programs; (2) traditional focused programs; (3) custom programs; and (4) organizational problem-solving projects. Each segment poses unique challenges and opportunities for business school providers, with widely disparate economic and competitive dynamics (see Figure B.2). We will briefly consider each of these segments to frame the strategic choices facing business schools in executive education.

Traditional General Management Programs

Traditional general management programs—the foundation of many business schools' executive education portfolios—seek to broaden the perspectives and capabilities of high-potential managers by introducing them to new management concepts. Equally important, these programs expose individuals to an impressive network of managers from outside their companies, industries, and countries. The traditional general management program segment is relatively small, however, and because of difficulty demonstrating that these programs produce tangible results, it

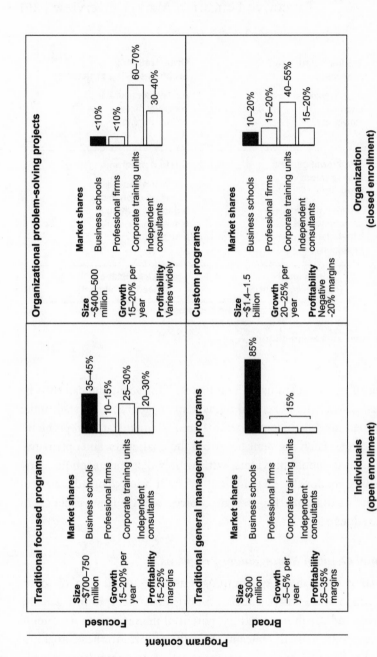

Figure B.2 Segment Characteristics (estimates)

has been most adversely affected by the increased emphasis on maximizing the return on investments in executive education. As a result, the segment has flat to negative growth, particularly in longer programs (greater than four weeks), where many business schools have either discontinued or curtailed their offerings.

Traditional Focused Programs

Traditional focused programs develop an individual's specific skills or knowledge. This segment is significantly larger than the general management segment and is growing more rapidly. Within this segment, programs based on cross-functional topics, such as leadership and globalization, have been growing at slightly faster rates than the functional courses. Growth in both types of programs, however, has been driven largely by the more measurable impact that they can have on building participants' capabilities in specific subject areas (in contrast to broad general management programs).

Custom Programs

Custom programs are designed to help transform the capabilities or culture of an entire organization through management (re)education. The degree of customization ranges from repackaged off-the-shelf materials to organization-specific curricula developed from scratch. Custom programs represent by far the largest and fastest-growing segment of executive education. To date, internal corporate training units, independent consultants, and training firms have been the segment's dominant providers, but business schools are becoming increasingly influential as they adopt more collaborative approaches to developing and delivering programs.

Organizational Problem-Solving Projects

Organizational problem-solving projects develop managerial capabilities by using action learning to address a specific company issue or objective. The line between this segment and consulting assignments has become somewhat blurred; the key difference lies in the management development and education objective. The problem-solving segment is growing rapidly, driven by the clear link between facilitated action learning projects and specific organizational impact. Individual faculty members and consultants are best positioned to serve this segment largely because high cost overhead relative to independent or good internal providers tends to rule out major university participation in such projects.

UNIVERSITY PROVIDERS MUST ADOPT BEST PRACTICES

Business schools must become more responsive, more quickly, to the needs of customers—both individuals and organizations—than many academic institutions are accustomed to being. Overcoming this competitive disadvantage implies managing executive education more like a business than like an academic endeavor. This will require an ever-greater emphasis on understanding and implementing best practices. The business system provides a useful framework for evaluating what "best practices" means in executive education (see Figure B.3). The following best practices within each segment were identified through interviews with leading business schools and other executive education experts.

General Management Programs: Classroom Experience

World-class faculty and world-class participants (in other words, the classroom experience) are critical in general management programs. In particular, faculty must be excellent facilitators of classroom discussion and be able to integrate cross-functional topics to provide useful general management perspectives. Beyond using their own professors, some providers include leading practitioners, with roles ranging from lecturer to "living case" to full member of the academic team. Wherever they come from, the best faculty incorporate a wide variety of teaching methods and utilize multiple classroom learning tools (including case studies, simulation exercises, and electronic media) to provide realistic and dynamic learning experiences to what is ideally a highly selective mix of experienced executives.

Success in the general management segment also requires innovative program design. In particular, it is critical for business schools to offer multiple options for program length, including the increasingly popular split program format that allows executives to limit continuous time spent away from the job and to apply what they learn during breaks in

	Research	Program design	Marketing	Program delivery
General management programs	• Balance between theory and application • Multidisciplinary approach	• Flexible curricula • Multiple options for length of programs	• Direct sales relationships with core customers • Highly selective admissions	• Strong facilitation skills among faculty • Multiple classroom learning tools (e.g., cases, simulations)
Focused programs	• Distinctive reputation in 2–3 subject areas • Agenda shaped by corporate learning priorities	• Rapid development cycle time • Continuously updated program content	• Targeted direct marketing • Understanding of and selling that appeals to latest customer learning priorities • Competitive pricing	• Leading practitioners as guest faculty • Alternative venues to campus-based programs
Custom programs	• Program clients as research "laboratories" • Expertise in organizational change	• Integrates series of programs • Support from nonfaculty design specialists	• Deep, multifaceted relationships with clients • Client needs linked to faculty research	• Faculty knowledgeable in and sensitive to client issues • Emphasis on implementation across client organization • Mix of on-campus and on-site delivery
Organizational problem-solving projects	• "Consulting" approach	• Focused on clear, tangible objectives • Highly interactive process	• Individual faculty relationships	• Action learning as dominant paradigm • Predominantly on-site delivery

Figure B.3 Executive Education Best Practices

the curriculum. A number of providers also increasingly utilize pre- and postprogram assessment tools to help participants define their objectives and measure the program's impact.

Focused Programs: Topic Choice and Marketing

The increasingly short life cycle of business ideas provides an excellent opportunity for providers who can develop focused programs quickly and update them continuously to meet the specialized needs of corporate customers. Because focused programs are frequently very specific, topics range anywhere from "flavor-of-the-month" concerns to more fundamental issues (such as globalization) which will shape the practice of business over time. Successful university providers of focused programs work closely with customers to understand their pivotal management issues and to develop programs that best address these issues, often leveraging areas of distinctive faculty research. Business schools that possess a strong reputation and faculty in one or more topic areas—such as finance, marketing, or leadership—have an obvious base to support focused programs in these disciplines as customers seek to differentiate among providers to meet specific needs.

Aggressive, targeted marketing to reach individual customers is critical not only to fill program seats, but to keep prices down in this relatively price-sensitive focused program segment. Implicit in this finding is the reality that business schools have to be very good at managing their program portfolio, and at carefully tracking each program and eliminating those that do not meet performance targets. One leading business school, for example, has adopted a brand management approach to its focused programs. Each program is assigned to one of several associate directors, who plays a "product manager" role that includes P&L responsibility. Program-specific marketing plans are developed jointly by the associate director, faculty director, and marketing director, using market research to verify the level of interest before a potential program is developed. The small committee of faculty and administrators that drives the program development process has reduced the time to market for new programs to less than six months. This type of flexibility in responding to emerging topics of interest to a specialized group of customers exemplifies best practice for focused program providers.

Custom Programs: Collaborative Customer Relationships

Corporations justifiably expect custom program providers to work collaboratively to help the organization achieve its management development objectives. Largely because of their academic, as opposed to customer-oriented, perspective, universities have traditionally not been well suited to compete against independent providers in this area. Furthermore, competitive market pricing has made it difficult for many universities to cover costs. Yet several business schools have become quite creative at developing new models to succeed in custom programs. In program development, for example, several business schools employ a cadre of nonfaculty professionals to act as liaisons between the client and the university faculty. These development specialists interview senior management to identify the client's education objectives; they then design programs based on a more detailed assessment of the organization and work with faculty to develop client-specific course materials. Some pioneers have responded to corporations' desire to form education partnerships by creating an integrated series of programs that reach multiple levels within the client organization. These partnership relationships often go beyond executive education to include MBA recruiting, faculty consulting assignments, fund raising, and research.

Developing and managing multifaceted customer relationships obviously presents a very different marketing challenge than filling seats in open-enrollment programs. One business school has taken a uniquely proactive approach to custom program marketing. In addition to responding to unsolicited custom program inquiries, this provider targets desirable corporations based on geography, industry, and fit with faculty research interests, then devotes significant resources to cultivating relationships.

Organizational Problem-Solving Projects: Facilitated Action Learning

The distinction between executive education and consulting becomes increasingly blurred in the organizational problem-solving segment. Successful providers can design and implement programs that achieve clear, tangible objectives and facilitate a process in which participants learn by doing. Program design in this segment is a fluid, interactive

Segment	Size ($ millions)	Growth	Profitability	Market shares
General management programs	~$300	**Flat** (–5–5% per year) • Programs not responsive to increasingly important buying factors	**High** (25–35% margins) • Fixed marketing and administrative costs amortized over many more weeks • Very limited incremental program development • Sustainable, given flat growth?	Universities 85% Professional firms Corporate training units } 15% Independent consultants
Focused programs	~$700–750	**Moderate–high** (15–20%) • Easier to demonstrate payback with focused topics • Shorter length has broad appeal	**Moderate** (15–25%) • Influenced heavily by volume	Universities 35–45% Professional firms 10–15% Corporate training units 25–30% Independent consultants 20–30%
Custom programs	~$1,400–1,500	**High** (20–25%) • Meet very specific needs (by definition) • Can drive real organizational change • Can involve client in delivery	**Varies widely** (~25%) • Influenced heavily by pricing and program development costs	Universities 10–20% Professional firms 15–20% Corporate training units 40–55% Independent consultants 15–20%
Organizational problem-solving projects	~$400–500	**Moderate–high** (15–20%) • Driven by internal action learning projects	**Varies widely**	Universities <10% Professional firms <10% Corporate training units 60–70% Independent consultants 30–40%

Figure B.4 Segment Characteristics (estimates)

Universities' traditional strength has been general management programs—historically the most profitable segment, but one that is relatively small and no longer growing.

Source: *Bricker's Directory*; *Business Week*; HBS; team analysis.

process, driven more by the client organization's strategic priorities than by the provider's faculty research strength or agenda. Although university faculty members will continue to serve this market as independent providers, it is unlikely that business schools will play a significant role.

Executive education has come to encompass a broad range of programs, many bearing little resemblance to traditional university offerings. Indeed, new customer demands are contributing to the development of distinct market segments, each with its own economics and requirements (see Figure B.4). This means that all providers of executive education will have to focus on one or two segments for which they can best meet customer needs. Many business schools, in particular, will be challenged to reconcile their more conventional academic culture with corporations' desire to find educational partners that are responsive to their specific needs. Both our study and recent market trends suggest, moreover, that custom programs will play an ever-increasing role in executive education. Universities that can partner successfully will find that executive education provides a unique opportunity to develop and deliver programs that truly complement their research and faculty development objectives.

Notes

PREFACE

1. A. A. Vicere, "Changes in Practices, Changes in Perspectives: The 1997 International Study of Executive Development Trends" (University Park, Pa.: Institute for the Study of Organizational Effectiveness, 1997).

2. R. Fulmer and A. A. Vicere, "Executive Education and Leadership Development: The State of the Practice" (University Park, Pa.: Institute for the Study of Organizational Effectiveness, March 1995, updated 1997).

3. A. A. Vicere, "The Market for University-based Executive Education Programs," *Executive Directions* 2, no. 1 (January–February 1995).

INTRODUCTION

1. Attributed to Fray Hernando de Talevera, head of the Talevera Commission, in 1486.

2. See P. Senge, *The Fifth Discipline* (New York: Doubleday, 1994); also C. Wick and L. Leon, *The Learning Edge* (New York: Doubleday, 1993) and M. McGill and J. Slocum, *The Smarter Organization* (New York: Wiley, 1994).

3. This section is adapted from R. M. Fulmer, "A Model for Changing the Way Organizations Learn," *Planning Review* 22, no. 3 (May–June 1994).

4. C. Argyris and D. Schon, *Organizational Learning: A Theory-Action Perspective* (Reading, Mass.: Addison-Wesley, 1978).

5. See J. Botkin et al., *No Limits to Learning*, Club of Rome, 1979. For more details, see R. M. Fulmer, "Anticipatory Learning for the 21st Century," *Journal of Management Development* (special edition), 12, no. 6 (1993).

6. R. M. Fulmer and M. Sashkin, "How Do Organizations Really Learn?" manuscript draft, AMA Briefing, 1996.

7. S. E. Sullivan and R. S. Bhagat, "Organization Stress, Job Satisfaction and Job Performance," *Journal of Management* 18 (1992): 353–374, and S. J. Motawdlo et al., "Occupational Consequences for Job Performance," *Journal of Applied Psychology* 71 (1986): 618–629. See also Judith Bardwick, *Danger in the Comfort Zone* (New York: American Management Association, 1991).

8. See R. Kanter, *Change Masters* (New York: Simon & Schuster, 1985).

9. This section is based on A. A. Vicere, "The Changing Paradigm for Executive Development," *Journal of Management Development* 10, no. 3 (1991): 44–47.

10. See G. Hamel and C. K. Prahalad, *Competing for the Future* (Boston: Harvard Business School Press, 1994).

CHAPTER 1

1. P. Senge and R. M. Fulmer, "Simulations, Systems Thinking and Anticipatory Learning," *Journal of Management Development* 12, no. 6 (1993): 21.

2. This section is drawn from A. A. Vicere and K. R. Graham, "Crafting Competitiveness: Toward a New Paradigm for Executive Development," *Human Resource Planning* 13, no. 4 (1990): 281–295.

3. See A. A. Vicere, "University-Based Executive Education: Impacts and Implications," *Journal of Management Development* 7, no. 4 (1988): 5–13.

4. L. Porter and L. McKibbin, *Management Development: Drift or Thrust into the 21st Century?* (New York: McGraw-Hill, 1988).

5. L. E. Korn, R. M. Ferry, D. C. Hambrick, and J. W. Fredrickson, *Reinventing the CEO* (New York: Korn Ferry International, 1989), 85.

6. See C. Handy, *The Age of Paradox* (Boston: Harvard Business School Press, 1994).

7. T. Stewart, "Planning a Career in a World Without Managers," *Fortune,* 20 March 1995, 72–80.

8. J. R. Katzenbach and D. K. Smith, *The Wisdom of Teams* (Boston: Harvard Business School Press, 1993).

9. Ibid.

10. Ibid.; Stewart, "Planning a Career," 1995; Handy, *Age of Paradox;* C. Savage, *5th Generation Management* (Bedford, Mass.: Digital Press, 1990).

11. A. K. Naj, "GE's Latest Innovation: A Way to Move Ideas from Lab to Market," *Wall Street Journal,* 14 June 1990, 1.

12. J. P. Kotter, *The New Rules* (New York: Free Press, 1995), 5.

13. Stewart, "Planning a Career."

14. S. Davis and J. Botkin, *The Monster Under the Bed* (New York: Simon & Schuster, 1994), 110.

15. N. Tichy and S. Sherman, *Control Your Own Destiny or Someone Else Will* (New York: Doubleday, 1993).

16. Ulrich, "Executive Development for Competitiveness," in *Executive Education: Process, Practice and Evaluation,* ed. A. A. Vicere (Princeton, N.J.: Peterson's, 1989).

17. K. Labich, "Making over Middle Managers," *Fortune,* 8 May 1989, 58–64.

18. N. Tichy and R. Charan, "Speed, Simplicity and Self Confidence: An Interview with Jack Welch," *Harvard Business Review,* September–October 1989, 112–120.

19. See A. de Geus, "Planning as Learning," *Harvard Business Review,* March–April 1988, 70–74; R. Stata, "Organizational Learning—The Key to Management Innovation," *Sloan Management Review,* Spring 1989, 59–77; W. Keichell III, "The Organization That Learns," *Fortune,* 12 March 1990, 133–136; C. Wick and L. S. Leon, *The Learning Edge: How Smart Managers and Smart Companies Stay Ahead* (New York: McGraw-Hill, 1993).

20. See I. Nonaka, "Toward Middle-Up-Down Management: Accelerating Information Creation," *Sloan Management Review,* Spring 1988, 9–18.

21. R. Miles, "Adapting to Technology and Competition: A New Industrial Relations System for the 21st Century," *California Management Review,* Winter 1989, 9–28; Tichy and Sherman, *Control Your Own Destiny.*

22. R. Fulmer and A. A. Vicere, "Executive Education and Leadership Development: The State of the Practice" (University Park, Pa.: Institute for the Study of Organizational Effectiveness, 1995).

23. See A. A. Vicere, "Executive Education and Strategic Imperatives: A Formula for Crafting Competitiveness," *American Journal of Management Development* 1, no. 2 (1995).

24. R. Miles and C. Snow, *Fit, Failure and the Hall of Fame* (New York: Free Press, 1994).

CHAPTER 2

1. This section is adapted from A. A. Vicere, "The Strategic Leadership Imperative for Executive Education," *Human Resource Planning* 15, no. 1 (1992): 16–31.

2. See the work of L. Griener, "Evolution and Revolution as Organizations Grow," *Harvard Business Review*, July–August 1972, 37–46; I. Adizes, *Corporate Lifecycles* (Englewood Cliffs, N.J.: Prentice Hall, 1989); L. Miller, *Barbarians to Bureaucrats: Corporate Life Cycle Strategies* (New York: Fawcett Columbine, 1989).

3. M. Kirton, "Adapters and Innovators: A Description and Measure," *Journal of Applied Psychology* 61, no. 5 (1976): 622–629.

4. Ibid.; also see M. Kirton, *Kirton Adaption-Innovation Inventory Manual*, 2d ed. (Hatfield, UK: Occupational Research Centre, 1987).

5. Adizes, *Corporate Lifecycles*.

6. Ibid.

7. See I. Ansoff, *The New Corporate Strategy* (New York: Wiley, 1988); D. Ulrich and D. Lake, *Organizational Capability* (New York: Wiley, 1990).

8. The "labels" given to each stage are adapted from Miller, *Barbarians*, and Vicere, "Strategic Leadership Imperative."

9. S. David and W. Davidson, *20/20 Vision* (New York: Simon & Schuster, 1991).

10. C. K. Prahalad and G. Hamel, "The Core Competence of the Corporation," *Harvard Business Review*, May–June 1990, 79–91.

11. J. Spychalski, "Consolidated Rail Corporation (Case Study)," Penn State Executive Programs, 1991.

12. J. Kotter and J. Heskett, *Corporate Culture and Performance* (New York: Free Press, 1992).

13. Adizes, *Corporate Lifecycles*.

14. See J. Kotter, *A Force for Change* (New York: Free Press, 1990).

15. See N. Tichy and S. Sherman, *Control Your Own Destiny or Someone Else Will* (New York: Currency Doubleday, 1993); also N. Tichy, "GE's Crotonville: A Staging Ground for Corporate Revolution," *Academy of Management Executive* 3, no. 2 (1989): 99–106.

16. J. Noel and R. Charan, "Leadership Development at GE's Crotonville," *Human Resource Management* 27, no. 4 (1988): 443–447.

17. S. Butler, "Cutting Down and Reshaping the Core," *Financial Times* (London), 20 March 1990.

18. Ibid.; also see C. Lorenz, "A Drama Behind Closed Doors That Paved the Way for a Corporate Metamorphosis," *Financial Times* (London), 23 March 1990.

19. T. Mack, "Eager Liars and Reluctant Liars," *Forbes*, 17 February 1992, 98–101.

20. Spychalski, "Consolidated Rail."

21. R. Charan, "How Networks Shape Organizations for Results," *Harvard Business Review*, September–October 1991, 104–114.

22. C. MacQueen and A. A. Vicere, "Conrail's Management Program: On Track Toward Company Vision," *Personnel*, 10–14 December 1987; A. A. Vicere, "Universities as Providers of Executive Development," *Journal of Management Development* 9, no. 4 (1990): 23–31.

23. G. Hamel and C. K. Prahalad, "Stragetic Intent," *Harvard Business Review*, May–June 1989, 63–76.

24. G. Hamel and C. K. Prahalad, *Competing for the Future* (Boston: Harvard Business School Press, 1994).

25. See A. A. Vicere, "Executive Education and Strategic Imperatives: A Formula for Crafting Competitiveness," *American Journal of Management Development* 1, no. 2 (1995): 31–36.

26. Miller, *Barbarians*.

27. Charan, "How Networks Shape."

28. Tichy and Sherman, *Control Your Own Destiny*.

CHAPTER 3

1. A number of books and articles have described these emerging models of organizational structure, including C. Handy, *The Age of Unreason* (Boston: Harvard Business School Press, 1990); D. Q. Mills, *Rebirth of the Corporation* (New York: Wiley, 1991); J. B. Quinn, *Intelligent Enterprise* (New York: Free Press, 1992); T. Stewart, "The Search of the Organization of Tomorrow," *Fortune*, 18 May 1992, 91–98; R. Miles and C. Snow, *Fit, Failure and the Hall of Fame* (New York: Free Press, 1994); J. Byrne, "The Virtual Organization," *Business Week*, 8 February 1993, 98–102; S. Tully, "The Modular Corporation," *Fortune*, 8 February 1993, 106–114.

2. See Chapter 1 in M. Hammer and J. Champy, *Reengineering the Corporation* (New York: Harper Business, 1993).

3. See Chapters 1 and 2 in D. Nadler et al., *Organizational Architecture* (San Francisco: Jossey-Bass, 1992).

4. C. Loomis, "Dinosaurs?" *Fortune*, 3 May 1993, 36–42.

5. See P. Drucker, *Managing for the Future* (New York: Truman Talley Books/Dutton, 1992).

6. For discussions of the changing competitive environment and its impact on organizational design, see Nadler, *Organizational Architecture*; T. Stewart, "The Search for the Organization of Tomorrow," *Fortune* 18 May 1992, 91–98; P. Drucker, "The New Society of Organizations," *Harvard Business Review*, September–October 1992, 95–104; C. Handy, "Balancing Corporate Power: A New Federalist Paper," *Harvard Business Review*, November–December 1992, 59–72; Handy, *Age of Unreason*.

7. S. Davis and B. Davidson, *20/20 Vision* (New York: Simon & Schuster, 1991); G. Hamel and C. K. Prahalad, "Corporate Imagination and Expeditionary Marketing," *Harvard Business Review*, July–August 1991, 81–92.

8. R. Henkoff, "Getting Beyond Downsizing," *Fortune*, 10 January 1994, 58–64.

9. R. Jacob, "TQM: More Than a Dying Fad?" *Fortune*, 18 October 1993, 66–72.

10. Hammer and Champy, *Reengineering*; W. Cascio, "Downsizing: What Have We

Learned?" *Academy of Management Executive* 7, no. 1 (1993): 95–104; also *Best Practices in Corporate Restructuring* (Chicago: The Wyatt Company, 1993).

11. *Best Practices in Corporate Restructuring;* Henkoff, "Getting Beyond." Also Hamel and Prahalad, *Competing for the Future* (Boston: Harvard Business School Press, 1994).

12. D. Ulrich and D. Lake, *Organizational Capability* (New York: Wiley, 1994). Also Hamel and Prahalad, *Competing for the Future.*

13. Hamel and Prahalad, "Corporate Imagination."

14. M. Treacy and F. Wiersema, *The Discipline of Market Leaders* (Reading, Mass.: Addison-Wesley, 1995).

15. T. Goss, R. Pascale, and A. Athos, "The Reinvention Rollercoaster: Risking the Present for a Powerful Future," *Harvard Business Review,* November–December 1993, 97–108.

16. See D. Ready, *Champions of Change,* International Consortium for Executive Development Research and Gemini Consulting, 1994.

17. For the purposes of this book, the implications of the shadow pyramid are discussed from the standpoint of broad-based leadership and organizational development issues. We have elected not to discuss operational issues related to changes in the "base" of the new model, many of which are reflected in ideas like that of the "virtual organization."

18. For a discussion of this shift, see Handy, *Age of Unreason;* for a discussion of outsourcing, see Tully, "Modular Corporation"; for a discussion of challenges in outsourcing, see R. Bettis, S. Bradley, and G. Hamel, "Outsourcing and Industrial Decline," *Academy of Management Executive* 6, no. 1 (1992): 7–21.

19. Hamel and Prahalad, *Competing for the Future;* G. Hamel and C. K. Prahalad, "Strategic Intent," *Harvard Business Review,* May–June 1989, 63–76; C. K. Prahalad and G. Hamel, "The Core Competence of the Corporation," *Harvard Business Review,* May–June 1990, 79–91; G. Stalk, P. Evans, and E. Shulman, "Competing on Capabilities: The New Rules of Corporate Strategy," *Harvard Business Review,* March–April 1992, 57–69.

20. Hamel and Prahalad, *Competing for the Future.*

21. For a discussion of current developments at Daimler-Benz, see P. Gumbel and A. Choi, "Corporate Germany Revamps Operations—and Boosts Economy," *Wall Street Journal,* 7 April 1995, 1.

22. Handy, *Age of Unreason;* Handy, "Balancing Corporate Power"; T. Stewart, "How to Manage in the New Era," *Fortune,* 15 January 1990, 58–72; J. Huey, "Managing in the Midst of Chaos," *Fortune,* 5 April 1993, 38–48; W. Kiechell, "How We Will Work in the Year 2000," *Fortune,* 17 May 1993, 38–52.

23. See L. Hirschorn and T. Gilmore, "The New Boundaries of the 'Boundaryless' Corporation," *Harvard Business Review,* May–June 1992, 104–115.

24. See R. Kanter, "Collaborative Advantage," *Harvard Business Review,* July–August 1994, 96–108; M. Magnet, "The New Golden Rule of Business," *Fortune,* 21 February 1994, 60–64.

25. For a useful discussion of the changing role of logistics management, see R. Henkoff, "Delivering the Goods," *Fortune,* 28 November 1994, 64–78. For additional discussion of supply chain management issues, see notes on Chrysler in Tully,

"Modular Corporation." Also see D. Woodruff, "Chrysler's Neon," *Business Week*, 3 May 1993, 116–126.

26. Quinn, *Intelligent Enterprise*; Davis and Davidson, *20/20*; S. Bleecker, "The Virtual Organization," *The Futurist*, March–April 1994, 9–14.

27. C. Savage, *5th Generation Management* (Bedford, Mass.: Digital Press, 1990).

28. G. Hamel and C. K. Prahalad, "Strategy as Stretch and Leverage," *Harvard Business Review*, March–April 1993, 75–84.

29. For a discussion of IBM's revitalization efforts, see D. Kirkpatrick, "Gerstner's IBM," *Fortune*, 15 November 1993, 119–126.

30. See Goss, Pascale, and Athos, "Reinvention."

31. P. Evans, "Management Development as Glue Technology," *Human Resource Planning* 15, no. 1 (1992): 85–106.

32. See T. Stewart, "Planning a Career in a World without Managers," *Fortune*, 20 March 1995, 72–80; C. Handy, *The Age of Paradox* (Boston: Harvard Business School Press, 1994); also Mills, *Rebirth*; Savage, *5th Generation*.

33. See B. Dumaine, "The New Non-Manager Managers," *Fortune*, 22 February 1993, 80–84; Stewart, "Planning."

34. See B. O'Reilly, "The New Deal," *Fortune*, 13 June 1994, 44–52.

35. Ibid.; Handy, *Age of Unreason and Age of Paradox*; J. Fierman, "The Contingency Workforce," *Fortune*, 24 January 1994, 30–36; W. Bridges, "The End of the Job," *Fortune*, 19 September 1994, 62–74; Stewart, "Planning."

36. O'Reilly, "The New Deal."

37. See A. A. Vicere and K. Graham, "Crafting Competitiveness: Toward a New Paradigm for Executive Development," in *Shared Wisdom*, ed. R. Levit and C. Ghikakis (New York: Human Resource Planning Society, 1994), 181–201.

38. See C. Wick and L. Leon, *The Learning Edge* (New York: McGraw-Hill, 1993); also R. M. Fulmer and A. A. Vicere, "Executive Education and Leadership Development: The State of the Practice" (University Park, Pa.: Institute for the Study of Organizational Effectiveness, 1995).

39. This challenge is discussed in B. O'Reilly, "How Execs Learn Now," *Fortune*, 5 April 1993, 52–58; Wick and Leon, *The Learning Edge*.

40. See K. Kelly, "Motorola: Training for the Millennium," *Fortune*, 28 March 1994, 158–162.

41. See J. Fierman, "The Perilous New World of Fair Pay," *Fortune*, 14 June 1994, 57–64.

CHAPTER 4

1. Much of this section is based on J. Goodwin and R. M. Fulmer, "The Systems Dynamics of Executive Education," *Executive Development* 8, no. 4 (1995).

2. See L. Bertalanffy, *Perspectives on General Systems Theory* (New York: Braziller, 1975), for a review of the earliest work in systems theory.

3. We use the term *systems* to refer to a collection of parts that interact with each other to function as a whole.

4. P. Senge, *The Fifth Discipline: The Art and Practice of the Learning Organization* (New York: Doubleday, 1990).

5. Much of this section is adapted from D. Ready, A. Vicere, and A. White, *The Role of Executive Education in Executive Resource Planning* (Lexington, Mass.: Inter-

national Consortium for Executive Development Research, 1992), working paper, 92/3.

6. Appreciation is expressed to George Shaffer, SPHR, Leadership Development Director; Dick Sethi, Executive District Manager Corporate Human Resources; and Jane L. Rifkin, Corporate Human Resources, for providing information about AT&T's Approach to Leadership Development. Shaffer graciously reviewed this material to clarify our understanding of the AT&T approach.

7. These recommendations are drawn from Ready et al., *Role of Executive Education.*

CHAPTER 5

1. D. Ready, A. Vicere, and A. White, *The Role of Executive Education in Executive Resource Planning* (Lexington, Mass.: International Consortium for Executive Development Research, 1992), working paper, 92/3, 4.

2. A. Vicere, "Changes in Practices, Changes in Perspectives: The 1997 International Study of Executive Development Trends" (University Park, Pa.: Institute for the Study of Organizational Effectiveness, 1997).

3. I. Nonaka, "The Knowledge Creating Company," *Harvard Business Review,* November–December 1991, 96–104.

4. M. McCall, M. Lombardo, and A. Morrison, *The Lessons of Experience* (Lexington, Mass.: Lexington Books, 1988).

5. J. Conger, *Learning to Lead* (San Francisco: Jossey-Bass, 1992).

6. Ibid., 179–180.

7. Ibid., 170.

8. See A. Vicere, "University-based Executive Education: Impacts and Implications," *Journal of Management Development* 7, no. 4 (1988): 5–13.

9. A. Vicere, M. Taylor, and V. Freeman, "Executive Education in Major Corporations" (University Park, Pa.: Institute for the Study of Organizational Effectiveness, 1993).

10. Ibid. (Note that respondents could indicate more than one benefit.)

11. Personal correspondence from Cam Danielson, Indiana University.

12. Received via personal correspondence from Bric Wheeler, Miami University, Ohio.

13. Conger, *Learning to Lead,* xv.

14. See B. O'Reilly, "360° Feedback Can Change Your Life," *Fortune,* 17 October 1994, 93–100; also R. Hoffman, "Ten Reasons You Should Be Using 360-Degree Feedback," *Fortune,* April 1995, 82–85.

15. Conger, *Learning to Lead,* 170–171.

16. Ibid., 156.

17. R. Wagner, T. Baldwin, and C. Roland, "Outdoor Training: Revolution or Fad," *Training and Development Journal,* March 1991, 51–56.

18. Conger, *Learning to Lead,* 168.

19. J. Coyle, "Technology and Executive Development: The Promise and the Practice," *American Journal of Management Development* 1, no. 2 (1995): 37–46.

20. G. Rifkin, "A Skeptic's Guide to Groupware," *Forbes ASAP,* 5 June 1995, 76–97.

21. See D. Kirkpatrick, "Groupware Goes Boom," *Fortune*, 27 December 1993, 99–106.

22. Joann S. Lublin, "Schools Boot Up to Offer On-Line M.B.A.'s," *Wall Street Journal*, 24 September 1996, B1, col. 3.

23. S. Davis and J. Botkin, *The Monster Under the Bed* (New York: Simon & Schuster, 1994).

24. Ibid.

25. For a good overview of current perspectives on mentoring, see S. Applebaum, S. Ritchie, and B. Shapiro, "Mentoring Revisited: An Organizational Behaviour Construct," *Journal of Management Development* 13, no. 4 (1994): 62–72.

26. McCall et al., *Lessons of Experience*, 12.

27. See C. Smith, "The Executive's New Coach," *Fortune*, 27 December 1993, 126–134; also A. K. Naj, "The Latest Addition to the Executive Suite Is the Psychologist's Couch," *Wall Street Journal*, 29 August 1994, 1.

28. R. Shaw and D. Perkins, "Teaching Organizations to Learn: The Power of Productive Failures," in *Organizational Architecture*, ed. D. Nadler et al. (San Francisco: Jossey-Bass, 1992), 175.

29. Nonaka, "Knowledge Creating Company," 96.

30. C. Longnecker and D. Gioia, "The Executive's Appraisal Paradox," *Academy of Management Executive* 6, no. 2 (1992): 27.

31. Vicere et al., *Executive Education*.

32. Longnecker and Gioia, "Executive's Appraisal Paradox," 27.

33. Ibid., 25.

34. Ibid., also see M. McGill and J. Slocum, *The Smarter Organization* (New York: Wiley, 1994); and C. Wick and L. Leon, *The Learning Edge* (New York: McGraw-Hill, 1993).

35. R. Miles, *Corporate Universities: Some Design Choices and Leading Practices* (Atlanta: Emory University, 1993).

36. McCall et al., *Lessons of Experience*, 32.

37. Ibid.

38. Wick and Leon, *The Learning Edge*.

39. V. Marsick, L. Cederholm, E. Turner, and T. Pearson, "Action-Reflection Learning," *Training and Development*, August 1992, 63–66.

40. L. Keys, "Action Learning: Executive Development Choice for the 1990s," *Journal of Management Development* 13, no. 8 (1994): 50–56.

41. Nonaka, "Knowledge Creating Company," 98.

42. Davis and Botkin, *The Monster*.

43. See McGill and Slocum, *The Smarter Organization*; also Wick and Leon, *The Learning Edge*.

44. McCall et al., *Lessons of Experience*.

45. T. Esque and T. Gilbert, "Making Competencies Pay Off," *Training*, January 1995, 44.

46. Ibid.

47. D. Ready, "Building a Competitive Capabilities Infrastructure: A New Look at Leadership Competencies," Lexington, Mass., International Consortium for Executive Development Working Paper, May 1993, 1.

48. D. Ready, "Champions of Change," Lexington, Mass., Gemini Consulting and the International Consortium for Executive Development Research, 1994.

49. Personal correspondence with Mary Eckenrod of Allen Bradley; also see Ready, 1994, 9.

50. T. Bernard Wetzel, "The Role of Executive Education in Corporate Transformation," UNICON 1996 Conference, 19 March 1996.

CHAPTER 6

1. The EMP analysis was adapted and updated from A. Vicere, "Universities as Providers of Executive Education," *Journal of Management Development* 9, no. 4 (1990): 23–31.

2. *Bricker's International Directory of University-Based Executive Education Programs* (Princeton, N.J.: Peterson's, 1996).

3. See J. Conger, *Learning to Lead* (San Francisco: Jossey-Bass, 1992).

4. Ibid.

5. The "piper" is an element of the EMP program orientation given to participants on the opening day of a session.

6. Conger, *Learning to Lead*, 170.

7. A. A. Vicere, M. Taylor, and V. Freeman, "Executive Education in Major Corporations" (University Park, Pa.: Institute for the Study of Organizational Effectiveness, 1993).

8. Conger, *Learning to Lead*, 180.

9. Vicere et al., *Executive Education*.

10. See sections 3 and 5 of A. Vicere, ed., *Executive Education: Process, Practice and Evaluation* (Princeton, N.J.: Peterson's, 1989).

11. Vicere et al., *Executive Education*.

12. A. Vicere, "Foreword," *Bricker's International Directory of University-Based Executive Education Programs* (Princeton, N.J.: Peterson's, 1990).

13. Vicere et al., *Executive Education*.

14. See R. M. Fulmer, "A Model for Changing the Way Organizations Learn," *Planning Review* 22, no. 3 (May–June 1994).

15. See Brian O'Reilly, "Johnson & Johnson Is on a Role," *Fortune*, 26 December 1994; Michael Treacy and Fred Wiersema, "How Market Leaders Keep Their Edge," *Fortune*, 6 February 1995, 88–89; and "Dusting the Opposition," *Economist*, 29 April 1995, 71–72.

CHAPTER 7

1. R. Fulmer and A. Vicere, "Executive Education and Leadership Development: The State of the Practice" (University Park, Pa.: Institute for the Study of Organizational Effectiveness, 1995).

2. Ibid.

3. Reference quoted in Lori Bongiorno, "Corporate America's New Lesson Plan," *Business Week*, 25 October 1993, 102.

4. B. O'Reilly, "How Execs Learn Now," *Fortune*, 5 April 1993.

5. D. Ready, A. Vicere, and A. White, "Executive Education: Can Universities Deliver?" *Human Resource Planning* 16, no. 4 (1993): 1–11.

6. Ibid.

7. A. Vicere, "Changes in Practices, Changes in Perspectives: The 1997 Interna-

tional Study of Executive Development Trends" (University Park, Pa.: Institute for the Study of Organizational Effectiveness, 1997).

8. See D. Ready, A. Vicere, and A. White, *The Role of Executive Education in Executive Resource Planning* (Lexington, Mass.: International Consortium for Executive Development Research, 1992), working paper, 92/3.

9. Ibid.

10. *Wall Street Journal* special supplement on executive education, 10 September 1993.

11. D. Ready, "Executive Education: Is It Making the Grade?" *Fortune*, 14 December 1992, 39–48; Vicere, "Changes in Practices."

12. Vicere, "Changes in Practices."

13. Ready et al., "Executive Education"; Ready et al., *The Role of Executive Education.*

14. *Wall Street Journal*, 1993.

15. *Bricker's International Directory: University-Based Executive Education Programs 1996* (Princeton, N.J.: Peterson's, 1996); *Bricker's International Directory: University-Based Executive Education Programs 1993* (Princeton, N.J.: Peterson's, 1993).

16. Ready et al., "Executive Education"; Vicere, "Changes in Practice."

17. Ready et al., "Executive Education."

18. This section was developed from personal correspondence with Don Kuhn, former Employee Development Director with AT&T, and now Executive Secretary with UNICON, the International University Consortium for Executive Education.

19. D. McGinn, "Business by Best Seller," *Newsweek*, 3 April 1995, 47.

CHAPTER 8

1. W. J. Rothwell and H. C. Kazanas, *The Complete AMA Guide to Management Development* (New York: AMACOM, 1993), 265.

2. Cited in Donald L. Kirkpatrick, *Evaluating Training Programs: The Four Levels* (San Francisco: Berrett-Koehler Publishers, 1994), 17.

3. Adapted from S. Yelon, "Classroom Instruction," in *Handbook for Human Performance Technology*, ed. H. Stolovitch and E. Keeps (Washington, D.C.: National Society for Performance and Instruction, 1992), 385.

4. J. Fitz-Enz, *Benchmarking Staff Performance* (San Francisco: Jossey-Bass, 1993).

5. See J. Murphy, "Westinghouse Benchmarking Study," *efmd Forum* 3 (1994): 17.

6. Ibid.

7. See Donald L. Kirkpatrick, *A Practical Guide for Supervisory Training and Development*, 2d ed. (Reading, Mass.: Addison-Wesley, 1983 and 1994). See also Dana Gaines Robinson and James C. Robinson, *Training for Impact* (San Francisco: Jossey-Bass, 1989), 164–279; Donald Kirkpatrick, *Evaluating Training Programs: The Four Levels* (San Francisco: Berrett-Koehler, 1994).

8. Kirkpatrick, *A Practical Guide*, preface.

9. L. Rae, *How to Measure Training Effectiveness* (Brookfield, Vt.: Gower, 1991).

10. Kirkpatrick, *A Practical Guide*, 42.

11. Personal correspondence dated 2 May 1995.

12. Dana Gains Robinson and James C. Robinson, *Training for Impact* (San Francisco: Jossey-Bass, 1989), 196.

13. Brian O'Reilly, *Fortune*, 17 October 1994, 93.

14. Marshall Goldsmith, *The Impact of Feedback and Follow-up on Leadership Development* (San Diego: Keilty, Goldsmith & Company, 1994), 1–6.

15. Ibid.

16. Michael O'Bannon, *Topology of Top Management Skill Profiles,* unpublished, 17 January 1995.

17. Rothwell and Kazanas, *The Complete AMA Guide,* 273.

18. Jack J. Phillips, "Measuring Training's ROI: It Can Be Done," *William & Mary Business Review,* Summer 1995, 6.

19. Rothwell and Kazanas, *The Complete AMA Guide,* 273.

20. William Wiggenhorn, "Motorola University: When Training Becomes an Education," *Harvard Business Review,* July–August 1994, 72. On August 6, 1995, during an Academy of Management meeting presentation in Vancouver, Wiggenhorn indicated that this return on investment information had been so widely quoted that Motorola was trying to downplay the standard. He pointed out, however, that the company remains committed to measurement and expects leadership development and training initiatives to be profitable.

21. Reported in Kirkpatrick, *A Practical Guide,* 182–187.

CHAPTER 9

1. This description was based on personal correspondence with Victoria Guthrie and Bob Burnside of CCL. Also see R. Burnside and V. Guthrie, *Training for Action: A New Approach to Executive Development* (Report No. 153) (Greensboro, N.C.: Center for Creative Leadership, 1992); also J. Conger, *Learning to Lead* (San Francisco: Jossey-Bass, 1992), 192–198. Also see A. A. Vicere, "Executive Education: The Leading Edge," *Organizational Dynamics* 25, no. 2 (Autumn, 1996): 67.

2. Cheryl De Ciantis, *Using an Art Technique to Facilitate Leadership Development* (Report No. 166) (Greensboro, N.C.: Center for Creative Leadership, 1995), 7.

3. See D. A. Young and N. M. Dixon, *Getting Results from an Action Based Leadership Development Program,* unpublished manuscript.

4. This description was based on personal correspondence with Deepak (Dick) Sethi, LDP program director. Also see "AT&T Grooms Middle Managers with New-Look Leadership Program," *Training Director's Forum,* 11, no. 6 (1995); M. T. Moore, "AT&T Prepares Managers for Change," *USA Today,* 14 August 1995, 7B; H. Lancaster, "The Right Training Helps Even Dinosaurs Adapt to Change," *Wall Street Journal,* 28 March 1995, B1; D. Gatewood, "AT&T Managers Play a New Game," *New York Newsday,* 23 October 1994, 7. Also see A. A. Vicere, "Executive Education."

5. This information was taken from an unpublished presentation prepared by the AT&T School of Business, entitled "Beyond the Smiles Test."

6. This description is based on personal correspondence with Chris Giangrasso, director of ELI, as well as on firsthand experience with the institute.

7. The ELI Action Project process and roles were developed by Maria Taylor, Virginia Freeman Tucker, and Albert A. Vicere at Penn State. Also see A. A. Vicere, "Executive Education."

8. Lawrence G. Foster, *A Company That Cares* (New Brunswick, N.J.: Johnson & Johnson, 1986), 17.

9. Francis J. Aguilar and Arvin D. Bhambri, "Johnson & Johnson (A)," Harvard Business School Case No. 384-053, 3.

10. James C. Collins and Jerry I. Porras, *Built to Last: Success Habits of Visionary Companies* (New York: Harper Business, 1994), 80.

11. Interviews conducted by authors during field research at the third Executive Conference at Johnson & Johnson, October 3–12, 1997.

12. Peter M. Senge, *The Fifth Discipline* (New York: Doubleday, 1990).

13. Jeff Clanon and Peter Senge, correspondence dated 5 January 1996, 1.

14. Brian Dumaine, "Mister Learning Organization," *Fortune,* 17 October 1994, 148.

15. *Organizational Dynamics* 19, no. 2 (Autumn 1993).

16. Dumaine, "Mister Learning Organization."

CHAPTER 10

1. Much of this chapter is adapted from R. M. Fulmer, "The Evolving Paradigm for Leadership Development." *Organizational Dynamics* 25, no. 4 (Spring, 1997).

2. Albert Vicere, "Changes in Practices, Changes in Perspectives: The 1997 International Study of Executive Development Trends" (University Park, Pa: Penn State Institute for the Study of Organizational Effectiveness, 1997).

3. See Robert M. Fulmer and Ken Graham, "A New Era of Management Education," *Journal of Management Development* 12, no. 3 (1993); also Albert A. Vicere and Kenneth R. Graham, "Crafting Competitiveness: Toward a New Paradigm for Executive Development," *Human Resource Planning* 13, no. 4 (1990): 281–295.

4. See Robert M. Fulmer, "Executive Learning as a Strategic Weapon," *Executive Development* 3, no. 3 (1990).

5. Jeanne C. Meister, *Corporate Quality Universities* (New York: Richard D. Irwin, 1994).

6. Jeanne C. Meister, "Future Directions of Corporate Universities," UNICON Conference, 17 March 1996, 2–5.

7. Robert H. Miles, *Corporate Universities: Some Design Choices and Leading Practices* (Atlanta: Emory Business School, 1993).

8. A. Vicere, "A Little Something to Think About," *Journal of Continuing Higher Education* (Fall 1992): 52–57.

9. "Work-Out Continuous Improvement," unpublished student presentation, College of William and Mary, Williamsburg, VA, 15 March 1995.

10. N. Tichy and S. Sherman, *Control Your Own Destiny or Someone Else Will* (New York: Currency Doubleday, 1993), 212–213.

11. Peter Senge et al., *The Fifth Discipline Fieldbook* (New York: Doubleday, 1994), 30–37. See also Peter M. Senge and Robert M. Fulmer, "Simulations, Systems Thinking and Anticipatory Learning," *Journal of Management Development* 12, no. 6 (1993); also J. Bernard Keys, Robert M. Fulmer, and Stephen A. Stumpf, "Microworlds and Simuworlds: Practice Fields for the Learning Organization," *Organizational Dynamics* 24, no. 4 (Spring 1996): 36–49.

12. Based on Miles, *Corporate Universities,* 19–22.

13. Harvard Business School Case No. 379–157.

14. John A. Gutman, "Developing Cases and Scenarios for Anticipatory Learning," *Journal of Management Development* 12, no. 6 (1993): 52–59. See also John A. Gutman, "Creating Scenarios and Cases for Global Anticipatory Learning," *American Journal of Management Development* 3 (1995).

15. G. Hamel and C. K. Prahalad, *Competing for the Future* (Boston: Harvard Business School Press, 1994).

16. See D. Ready, A. Vicere, and A. White, "Executive Education: Can Universities Deliver?" *Human Resource Planning* 16, no. 4 (1994) 1–11.

17. See Charles Handy, *The Age of Unreason* (Boston: Harvard Business School Press, 1990).

18. Lyman Porter and Larry McKibbin, *Management Development: Drift or Thrust into the 21st Century?* (New York: McGraw-Hill, 1988).

19. Miles, *Corporate Universities*, 37–41.

20. Meister, *Corporate Quality Universities*, 7.

21. Stan Davis and Jim Botkin, *The Monster Under the Bed* (New York: Simon & Schuster, 1994) 96.

22. S. Davis, *Future Perfect* (Reading, Mass.: Addison-Wesley, 1987).

APPENDIX A

1. R. M. Fulmer, "Executive Learning as a Strategic Weapon," *Executive Development* 3, no. 3 (1990): 23. See also P. Senge and R. M. Fulmer, "Simulations, Systems Thinking, and Anticipatory Learning," *Journal of Management Development* 12, no. 6 (1993): 21.

2. A. de Geus, "Planning as Learning," *Harvard Business Review*, March–April 1988, 70–74.

3. Nitin Nohria and J. D. Berkley, "Whatever Happened to the Take-Charge Manager?" *Harvard Business Review*, January–February 1994, 130.

4. Jeanne Meister, "Future Directions of Corporate Universities," presentation to the International University Consortium for Executive Education, 17 March 1996.

5. Lori Bongiorno, "Corporate America's New Lesson Plan," *Business Week*, 25 October 1993, R4.

6. G. Fuchsberg, "Taking Control," *Wall Street Journal*, 10 September 1993, R4.

7. A. A. Vicere, "Changes in Practices, Changes in Perspectives: The 1997 International Study of Executive Development Trends" (University Park, Pa.: Institute for the Study of Organizational Effectiveness, 1997).

8. Bongiorno, "Corporate America's."

9. W. Wiggenhorn, "Motorola University: When Training Becomes an Education," *Harvard Business Review*, July–August 1994, 72.

10. Ibid., 75–76.

11. Quoted in Bongiorno, "Corporate America's."

12. Vicere, "Changes in Practices."

13. J. Bolt, *1993 Survey of Executive Education Trends* (LaJolla, Calif.: Executive Development Associates, 1993), 7–8.

14. N. M. Tichy and S. Sherman, *Control Your Destiny or Someone Else Will* (New York: Doubleday, 1993).

15. M. Porter, "How Competitive Forces Shape Strategy," *Harvard Business Review*, March–April 1979, 137–145.

16. P. Senge, *The Fifth Discipline* (New York: Doubleday, 1990).

17. See J. Byrne, "The Craze for Consultants," *Business Week*, 25 July 1994, 60–66.

18. T. Peters and R. Waterman, *In Search of Excellence* (New York: Harper & Row, 1982), 167–168.

19. Senge, *The Fifth Discipline*, 40–45.

20. Tichy and Sherman, *Control Your Destiny*.

21. T. A. Stewart, "GE Keeps Those Ideas Coming," *Fortune*, December 1991, 42.

22. Ibid., 42–43.

23. The following section is based largely on N. J. Freedman, "The Transformation of Philips: What Have We Learned About Learning," unpublished manuscript, Philips International N.V., 1994, 3.

24. Ibid., 4.

25. S. Ghoshal and C. Bartlett, *Linking Organizational Context and Managerial Action* (Fountainbleau, France: INSEAD Working Paper, 1994), 6.

26. Ibid.

27. Tracy Goss, R. Pascale, and A. Athos, "The Reinvention Roller Coaster: Risking the Present for a Powerful Future," *Harvard Business Review*, November–December 1993, 97–108.

28. *Keilty, Goldsmith & Company and the Leadership Excellence Process* (San Diego, Calif.: Keilty, Goldsmith & Company, 1994).

29. Ibid.

30. *Business Week*, 28 March 1994, 158.

31. See *The Journal of Management Development* 12, no. 2 (1993), a special issue focused on action learning techniques.

Index

About the Authors

Albert A. Vicere is a professor of business administration at the Smeal College of Business Administration, Pennsylvania State University, and director of the school's Institute for the Study of Organizational Effectiveness. As the president of the consulting firm Vicere Associates, Inc., he deals with executive and organizational development programs and strategies for major corporations worldwide. He holds a bachelor's, master's, and doctoral degree from the Pennsylvania State University. In addition, he is the editor of *Executive Education: Process, Practice and Evaluation*.

Robert M. Fulmer is the W. Brooks George Professor of Business Administration at the College of William and Mary. He holds a bachelor's degree from David Lipscomb College, a master of business administration from the University of Florida, and a doctorate from UCLA. He has been responsible for worldwide management development at AlliedSignal, executive education at Emory University, and has directed or delivered leadership development programs in twenty-two countries on six continents. He has taught organization and management at the Columbia University Graduate School of Business and served as a visiting scholar at the MIT Center for Organizational Learning. His previous books include *Executive Development and Organizational Learning for the Global Organization*, with Bernard Keys (forthcoming), *The New Management*, four editions, and *A Practical Introduction to Business*, five editions.